ETHNIC PATTERNS IN AMERICAN CITIES

STANLEY LIEBERSON

cNew York⌐
The Free Press of Glencoe
c1963⌐

ETHNIC
PATTERNS
IN AMERICAN
CITIES

Foreword

Ethnic Patterns in American Cities is an addition to the long series of studies on metropolitan problems issuing from the University of Chicago under the successive sponsorship of the Local Community Research Committee, the Social Science Research Committee, the Chicago Community Inventory, and the Population Research and Training Center. Monographs published as contributions of the Chicago Community Inventory include The Daytime Population of the Central Business District of Chicago, by Gerald William Breese (1949); Recent Migration to Chicago, by Ronald Freedman (1950); The Negro Population of Chicago, by Otis Dudley Duncan and Beverly Duncan (1957); and Housing a Metropolis--Chicago, by Beverly Duncan and Philip M. Hauser (1960).

Dr. Lieberson's work follows the tradition of these and earlier studies in applying rigorous methods of sociological research in the investigation of a salient urban social problem. His monograph, however, represents a significant departure from the pattern of inquiry of these earlier volumes, in that the analysis is made within a systematic comparative framework. While the single city or metropolitan area of Chicago is the focus of the studies enumerated above--the last two of which were actually commissioned by agencies of the City of Chicago-- in Lieberson's research Chicago is but one of ten cities examined comparatively.

The opportunity to go beyond the case study of a particular city was provided by a grant of funds specifically earmarked by the donor, The Ford Foundation, for a program of Comparative Urban Research. This program, intended to run for an initial period of five years, got under way in the fall of 1958. The study at hand is one of a number of reports on research employing a comparative design. Several such reports already have appeared in the periodical literature, and it is anticipated that additional book-length studies will be published.

Lieberson's study exemplifies in several ways the strong points of this approach to urban analysis, while suggesting some of the obstacles to the achievement of a fully satisfactory comparative design of research, foremost among which is the difficulty of assembling the requisite data in sufficiently standardized form. In future, it will doubtless remain true that much of what passes for knowledge of cities in general will, in fact, be based on intensive scrutiny of individual communities in particular. Studies like the present one, nevertheless, point the way to a strategy for broadening the basis of scientific inference.

The monograph will commend itself to its readers on its own merits, but it is appropriate to mention that the dissertation on which this book is based was awarded the Susan Colver-Rosenberger Educational Prize as an outstanding dissertation in the Department of Sociology during the period 1957-60.

PHILIP M. HAUSER, Director
Chicago Community Inventory and
Population Research and Training Center
University of Chicago

Acknowledgments

The author is indebted to the following persons for making available unpublished 1930 census-tract data for their cities: Mr. Joseph V. Dundon, Associate Executive and Research Director, Community Welfare Council of Buffalo, Buffalo, New York; Mr. Harlin G. Loomer, Chief, Planning Analysis Section, City Planning Commission, Philadelphia, Pennsylvania; Miss Dorothy W. Myers, Research Director, United Community Services of Metropolitan Boston, Boston, Massachusetts; Mrs. Moira Steiner, American Jewish Periodical Center, Hebrew Union College, Cincinnati, Ohio; Dr. C. V. Willie, Department of Preventive Medicine, Upstate Medical Center, Syracuse, New York.

Mr. John F. Grundy provided excellent clerical assistance, as did Rose Stamler, R. William Hodge, Erwin Stein, Sultan Hashmi, and Michael Ringer.

This monograph is a revised version of a doctoral dissertation in sociology, and the author is greatly indebted to the members of his dissertation committee, Otis Dudley Duncan and Philip M. Hauser. In particular, the advice and criticism of the writer's teacher, Professor Duncan, have been of considerable value.

STANLEY LIEBERSON

Contents

Centralization
Centralization and Suburbanization
White Ethnic Groups and Negroes

x

List of Tables

xiii

ETHNIC
PATTERNS
IN AMERICAN
CITIES

Chapter I

Human Ecology and Ethnic Relations

Immigrant assimilation was a major national issue during the hey-day of European migration to the United States. While some Americans found promise of new vigor and growth in a country composed of di-verse ethnic populations, others saw threats to the very core of the na-tion's heritage in the presence of these strange people. Yet for many, whatever their view of the long-term effect, the forces created by large-scale immigration required immediate action. Ward politicians and educators, welfare workers and realtors, union organizers and em-ployers all faced the opportunities and challenges presented by the new-comers.

Finding the immigrants a fascinating subject, sociologists early in this century set out to record their plight and progress in America's urban centers. Ethnic colonies produce a striking effect in the midst of our cities, and the clustering of immigrants into the poorer sections is documented for numerous groups and places. Ghettoes within Chi-cago and other metropolises offered a broad spectrum of cultural dif-ferences at one's doorstep, and sociologists investigated such facets of assimilation as intermarriage, language, residence, dress, recreation, and even food habits. The paradox of the second generation, estranged and yet at home with the ways of both their European parents and the American society at large, was explored under the dramatic rubric of the "marginal man." Immigrants and their children proved most intri-guing.

1

After the decline of immigration and with the inevitable mortality among the foreign born, concern with the processes and conditions of assimilation waned. To be sure, threads of old interests are found in current considerations of later generations, in the analogies drawn between European and Negro migrations to our northern cities, and the McCarran-Walter Act reminds us of the anxieties in past decades lest the eastern and southern Europeans overrun the nation. Through the years, however, historians have begun to replace sociologists as students of the great immigrant epoch.

By contrast, the development and diffusion of statistical techniques during the years since World War I provide contemporary investigators with more precise measurements and elaborate techniques than those employed by earlier sociologists in their studies of ethnic assimilation. These statistical developments, coupled with improvements in the processing of large quantities of data, offer us an opportunity not simply to re-examine the findings of earlier sociologists or document them, but to apply a somewhat different approach to the entire question of immigrant assimilation in our cities. By using a barely explored mine of past and present data about immigrants and their children, we can now gain a more comprehensive understanding of the status and process of ethnic assimilation than was possible in the earlier case studies of individual ethnic groups or particular cities.

It is hardly surprising that sociologists, dealing with the assimilation of but one or two groups in a limited time and place, were inclined to look to rather unique interpretations of the differences between ethnic groups. Since immigrant groups are generally viewed as population aggregates varying in a plethora of such attributes as religion, childhood training practices, attitudes towards education, and family structure, it is difficult to single out and apply thoroughly a given sociological perspective to their differential assimilation without investigating a number of groups and cities over a reasonably long period of time. Consideration of our central problem, the conditions influencing the assimilation of ethnic groups in American cities, is therefore enhanced, as we shall see, by the examination of roughly ten ethnic groups in each of ten cities between 1910 and 1950. In this study of a number of groups in different urban settings through a fairly broad span of time, attention is shifted away from the anecdotal and ad hoc interpretations frequently utilized in case studies and toward the general processes involved in assimilation irrespective of the particular group or city. In endeavoring to close the gap between earlier interests in ethnic assimilation and more recent sociological methods, our goal is a fuller understanding of one of the most significant and distinctive dimensions of American history.

Immigrant Assimilation as a Problem in Human Ecology

From the point of view of human ecology, the institutions, stores, factories, and population of a city compete between and among themselves for space and social position. That is, all individuals are rivals and compete--whether intentionally or not--for the occupational and general socio-economic positions of the city. In cases where supply and demand are unequal for a given position, choices must be made. These choices can have a variety of bases. In housing, rents and home costs are higher than all those wanting a given quality and location of residence can afford. Job applicants can be screened on the basis of their education, scores on tests, or physical dexterity. On the other hand, persons with skills in demand can select their jobs on the basis of the pay offered, the opportunities for advancement, or working conditions. Thus all kinds of factors, alone or in combination, enter into the competition between persons and work to raise or lower their competitive positions.

The significance of racial and ethnic groups lies in the fact that these groups are often factors in delimiting the rivalries and competition that can take place (Hawley, 1944; Lieberson, 1958b). The existence of racial and ethnic groups and the differentials in status attributed to these groups modify the purely individual or familial rivalry that would take place under any circumstances. Consequently ethnic or racial membership may lower or raise an individual's competitive position. To illustrate, consider Negro housing. Regardless of the occupation, education, or cultural level of a given Negro, his status is lowered with respect to whites because of his race. The Negro's ability to obtain housing or to locate in many residential areas is hindered by the introduction of the racial factor as a status variable. Thus Negroes must pay more than whites for housing of a given quality.

An important consequence of the differences between racial and ethnic segments in their abilities to compete is the propensity for the human populations of a city to locate unevenly, that is, to concentrate in some parts of the city and avoid other parts. In so far as the ensuing patterns of location are a function of the differences between racial and ethnic groups in their social position, these patterns tell us something about the nature of the populations or organizations involved. Park (1952, p. 177), in fact, concluded, "It is because social relations are so frequently and so inevitably correlated with spatial relations" and "physical distances so frequently are, or seem to be, the indexes of social distances," that social facts are susceptible of measurement.

If ethnic groups differ in status, then their presence or absence in a given residential area affects the desirability of the area for other segments of the population. For example, if Italian immigrants are relatively less desirable for neighbors than members of some other population merely because they are Italians, then the presence of Italian immigrants in a given area reduces the neighborhood's attractiveness for all but Italians. If, in addition, the Italian immigrants speak only Italian or if there are certain institutions, services, and organizations requiring a minimum number of Italians within a narrow radius, then the presence of such immigrants would serve actually to increase the area's desirability as a residential location for Italians but not for other segments of the city's population. Moreover, if members of an immigrant group migrate to a city in large numbers during a relatively short period of time, then their increase may be in excess of the expansion of the housing supply. Under such circumstances we would expect a greater degree of option on the part of owners and landlords and thus a greater relevance of the ethnic status of potential renters or buyers. (See, for example, Ball and Yamamura, 1960.)

In short, aside from economic differences between ethnic groups, we would expect residential segregation under two sets of circumstances:

first, if the ethnic group was of undesirable status, then the group would
be involuntarily segregated; secondly, if proximity to members of the
same group facilitated adjustment to the conditions of settlement in a
new country or if members of an ethnic group simply viewed the residential proximity of members from the same group as desirable, there
would be voluntary segregation. In either case, a generally similar
model of the residential settlement of immigrants in a city would follow. Namely, the location of members of a group in an area decreases
the desirability of the area for members of other groups but not for
later arrivals from the same country. The areas of "first settlement"
are often the older areas of the city because they are the areas for
which there is least residential competition. This model of segregation involves several components, for the location of an ethnic group
in small numbers in a given area is assumed to have the following
effects:

1. Increases the propensity of other members of the group
   to locate in the area.

2. Decreases or at least does not raise the propensity of
   other ethnic populations to move into the area.

3. Increases or at least does not lower the propensity of
   members of other ethnic groups presently in the area
   to move away.

This viewpoint leads to the position that ethnic segregation is not
largely a function of simple economic factors such as the differential
incomes of ethnic groups combined with variations between areas of the
city in housing costs; nor is it a view that gives unlimited weight to the
cultural differences between groups in their propensity to prefer living
near each other. It does seek to view ethnic segregation in terms of
the situation faced by immigrants upon their arrival and in the context
of the conditions of their settlement. That is, the cities were in existence with their patterns of housing and commercial establishments before each wave of immigrants arrived during the great era of foreign
migration to our cities. Into this pattern or structure of the city came
each group of immigrants and, whatever else they might do in the city,
they had to adapt to its structure and order. As such, their segregation
may be viewed as a form of adaptation.

The topic of segregation becomes central to this study inasmuch as segregation influences other aspects of ethnic assimilation. Not only can the residential patterns of ethnic groups be viewed as a significant element in the study of their assimilation but, further, residential segregation has an effect on other aspects of ethnic assimilation. Hawley, in a stimulating if nevertheless provisional statement, has formulated the following hypothesis:

> Redistribution of a minority group in the same territorial pattern as that of the majority group results in a dissipation of subordinate status and an assimilation of the subjugated group into the social structure. (Hawley, 1944, p. 674.)

Hawley's reasoning is based on the dual effect of residential segregation. It accentuates the differences between a group and the remainder of the population by heightening the visibility of the group, and it enables the population to keep its peculiar traits and group structure. Or, to put it another way, residential segregation maintains visibility and awareness of the status of the ethnic group both for its own members and for other segments of a city's population.

As the reader can readily surmise, we shall consider immigrant assimilation by focusing on the residential patterns of ethnic groups in ten United States cities. Our first concern involves determining the conditions accounting for the differences among immigrant groups in their degree of residential segregation and in the changes taking place through the years. Initially, residential segregation is viewed as an important dimension of assimilation in itself. Our second problem revolves about the impact of residential segregation on other aspects of ethnic behavior, that is, the influence of residential segregation on other dimensions of assimilation.

Not only is the existence of immigrant ghettoes documented in case studies of numerous groups and cities (Park, 1952, p. 223; Cressey, 1938; Ford, 1950; Duncan and Lieberson, 1959; Younge, 1944; Zubryzcki, 1959), but there is reason to believe that the residential patterns of ethnic groups are at least associated with such indicators of assimilation as ability to speak English, citizenship, and segregation from other immigrant groups. A study of ten immigrant groups in Chicago between 1930 and 1950 (Duncan and Lieberson, 1959) found high

correlations between immigrant variations in residential segregation
and the aforementioned attributes of assimilation. In addition, variation between ethnic groups in their socio-economic status was shown
to be associated with variation in their degree of residential segregation; and an orderly decline was noted in the residential segregation of
the immigrant groups between 1930 and 1950. Despite the fact that in
a number of respects the present study employs a somewhat different
approach, particularly in regard to certain indicators of assimilation,
in many ways this entire investigation of ethnic segregation and assimilation may be considered as a test of the general hypotheses about the
segregation and assimilation processes developed in the Chicago study.

Ethnic Assimilation

The term "assimilation" has been used by sociologists for a long
time, particularly with reference to immigrant groups in the United
States. Crowell (1898), writing at the end of the nineteenth century,
used assimilation with reference to immigrants in his treatise, The
Logical Process of Social Development; and there is no reason to think
that this was the first such usage of the term. Assimilation is, nonetheless, one of the most elusive concepts employed in the study of race
and ethnic relations. Recently, an international conference on the cultural assimilation of immigrants failed to agree on the meaning of the
term or its measurement (International Union for the Scientific Study
of Population, 1950). Given the variety of ways in which sociologists
conceive of ethnic groups, that is, as population aggregates with distinctive psychological, cultural, institutional, and biological attributes,
it should not surprise us to find that the assimilation of these groups
also is approached from numerous directions. Furthermore, studies
of race and ethnic relations have been largely applications of the theories and methods of a number of social science disciplines rather than
efforts to develop a theory of race and ethnic relations (Blumer, 1958,
p. 406).

Although no effort is made here to offer the final definition or to
abstract the "essence" of assimilation from the various approaches, it

appears safe to say that the term assimilation is applied to a wide
range of ethnic changes and generally with implied direction towards
greater "homogeneity." As far as can be determined, its sociological
use is based on an analogy with a physiological process referring to
nutrition (Barron, 1957, p. 429). Park, who was by no means consistent in his use of the term, did however invoke such an analogy in describing assimilation:

> Assimilation, as the word is here used, brings with it a
> certain borrowed significance which it carried over from
> physiology where it is employed to describe the process of
> nutrition. By a process of nutrition, somewhat similar to
> the physiological one, we may conceive alien peoples to be
> incorporated with, and made part of, the community or state.
> Ordinarily assimilation goes on silently and unconsciously,
> and only forces itself into popular conscience when there is
> some interruption or disturbance of the process. (Park,
> 1950, p. 209.)

Since models of assimilation have sometimes been formed with reference to individual differences based on race or ethnic origin and
sometimes with respect to differences between aggregates, we shall examine the matter a bit more closely before plunging into our study

Individual and Aggregate Assimilation

Certain ethnic attributes can be considered indicators of an individual's assimilation For example, an immigrant able to speak English is
viewed as more assimilated than an immigrant in the United States who
has not learned English Similarly, one is inclined to attribute a relatively higher degree of assimilation to a naturalized immigrant than to
one who has retained allegiance to his country of birth. Bunle's working
definition neatly illustrates this view:

> Thus an immigrant appears to be assimilated when the bonds
> of his native country have lost all hold on him, when he feels
> himself a whole-hearted citizen of his new community, when he
> speaks its language, adopts its ways of life and thought, and
> when a practised foreign eye no longer detects any difference
> between his outlook, habits and behaviour and those of his new
> fellow-citizens. (Bunle, 1950, pp. 6-7.)

To be sure, there is an aggregate counterpart to this approach, that
is, one can consider an immigrant group as being more or less assimi-

lated by examining the proportion of its members able to speak English or the proportion naturalized. However, there are additional aspects of ethnic behavior that are essentially meaningful only on an aggregate basis. In the existence of ethnic colonies, for example, the behavior of an aggregate is relevant, but not that of a particular individual. The location of any member of an ethnic group in a particular section of the city is not itself symptomatic of assimilation. It is only when unusually high proportions of a group are located in specific areas that we become concerned with what we call segregation. Thus, if one wishes to consider an individual's residence as a criterion of assimilation, it can only be done after the existence and location of ethnic colonies are determined.

Similarly, an immigrant's occupation tells us nothing about his assimilation. For example, knowledge that an Italian immigrant is a barber, by itself, is insufficient to classify him as assimilated or not. By contrast, it is possible to determine the degree of similarity between the occupational distribution of all Italian immigrants and the native population's distribution in a city and then use the results as an indicator of an immigrant group's assimilation (Duncan and Lieberson, 1959, p. 374). Under these circumstances, that is with respect to residential and occupational behavior, one can also investigate the interplay between individual and group assimilation. It would be interesting to learn, for example, whether individuals living in ethnic colonies are less assimilated in other respects than those residing outside of their ethnic colonies.

Finally, since members may pass out of their group into the larger society while the group remains a distinct entity, it is worth noting that individual and group assimilation are sometimes in different directions. Within limits, a sizable proportion of an ethnic population can assimilate and yet the group maintain itself or even grow in size. Such would be the case with continued in-migration or, even without migration, if the fertility rate of non-assimilating ethnic group members is higher than that of the remaining population. Although biological amalgamation is an important factor affecting assimilation, it does not automatically mean assimilation in either an aggregative or individual sense. For example, the children of mixed ethnic or racial marriages may become members of one of the original ethnic groups. Such is the case for mulattoes in the United States or the children of Chinese men and Malayan women in Malaya who, according to Freedman (1955, p. 411), are brought up as Chinese.

Indeed, there are aspects of assimilation that may be identified solely in terms of the persisting ethnic group as such, rather than the particular cohorts of immigrants and their descendents of which it is composed at any given time. Changes in the position of the Irish in the United States through the centuries involve more than the specific persons or generations who at one time or another bear the Irish status. Simmel (1921, p. 349) neatly expressed this attribute of the group in dealing with the problem of continuity, "The persistence of the group presents itself in the fact that, in spite of the departure and the change of members, the group remains identical." In dealing with ethnic assimilation, we are perhaps hindered in examining this question by the fact that the children of immigrants certainly do acquire many characteristics indicative of what we choose to call "assimilation." However, concern solely with the changes taking place among immigrants themselves after their arrival in the United States is not necessarily the same as investigating the position of the group itself through the years.

The Operational Definition of Group Assimilation

Assimilation is used in this study with a predictive connotation to the term. An assimilated ethnic population is defined operationally as a group of persons with similar foreign origins, knowledge of which in no way gives a better prediction or estimate of their relevant social characteristics than does knowledge of the behavior of the total population of the community or nation involved. Thus we should not call an ethnic group assimilated if they are highly segregated residentially from the remainder of the total population of a given city. That is, to the extent that we can make a better prediction of the residential location of persons of Italian origin by knowing their origin than if we simply predicted on the basis of the distribution of the total city population, then to that extent we should say that the Italians are not assimilated.

Such an approach to assimilation is easier said than done. In a complex, poly-ethnic society such as the United States, selection of a standard population for determining the assimilation of a given ethnic group is somewhat arbitrary. If we select the remaining population as a standard for comparing the residential or occupational distribution of an immigrant group, then we are including Negroes, Orientals, and other European immigrants. Since these populations are themselves faced with difficulties and obstacles to open access of the community's facilities and opportunities, consideration of the position of a given foreign-born population would be only complicated by the inclusion of these groups in our analysis. Consequently, most of the comparisons will be made between specific foreign-born groups or their children and the native-white population of the city.

An additional problem raised by the earlier operational definition of assimilation stems from the fact that differences between an immigrant population and the city's native-white component are not necessarily due to deviations of the foreign born from the general social patterns in the city. Suppose, for example, that parents' residence influences the location of children's residence after the latter reach adulthood and establish their own independent family households. If Polish immigrants are highly segregated in a city then, under these circumstances, their children would be segregated after reaching adulthood if they followed the general tendency for people to reside near the area where they are raised. Thus if the children of Polish immigrants merely followed the residential mobility patterns for other groups, they might continue to have a highly distinct residential pattern.

Conceivably, the entire differentiation of an ethnic population could be due to non-ethnic factors without making the group less distinctive or less visible to the community's populace. The point is that social forces outside of ethnic control or influence can and do operate to accelerate or retard assimilation. A society in which there was little inter-generational occupational mobility could be expected to keep ethnic distinctions, at least in terms of differential working patterns, for a longer period than a more open society in which immigrants and their descendents were able to move out of their low initial positions. It is, in short, the structure of society and the changes through the years which play critical roles in the assimilation of ethnic groups. In examining and demonstrating differences between immigrant populations and the native-white segment of a city, it is of importance then to consider the societal factors influencing groups to differ in their degree of assimilation.

There is one additional complication. The definition of assimilation used here has, at least for the author, a somewhat awkward implication if carried to its logical conclusion. To wit, all differences between ethnic populations and the native-white population indicate lack of assimilation. If the Polish immigrant group, for example, has a greater proportion of its members following the Roman Catholic religion than does the native-white population of the city, this would suggest that Polish immigrants are less assimilated in this respect than members of an immigrant group whose religious distribution is more similar to that of the native-white population. There is, of course, no ready answer without dipping into the philosophies and polemics of the melting pot, cultural pluralism, and nativism. Readers with diverse perspectives on these issues will perhaps find less controversial the concerns of this study with such ramifications of assimilation as residential segregation, occupational distribution, intermarriage, ability to speak English, and citizenship.

In summary, the problem of this investigation is the assimilation of European immigrant groups in American cities, a subject that can be re-examined in a more systematic and quantitative fashion than was possible in earlier studies. Drawing upon a large body of hitherto unanalyzed census data about immigrants and their children, the study focuses upon the differential residential segregation of approximately ten immigrant groups in each of ten United States cities in the census years between 1910 and 1950. From an ecological standpoint, the existence of residential colonies and ghettos is viewed as both a significant dimension of assimilation and as a factor influencing other aspects of assimilation. The study explores the conditions accounting for the differential segregation of ethnic groups in each city as well as the impact of residential segregation on these other aspects of assimilation. The following paragraphs provide a brief conspectus of the research design and the major findings.

Overview of the Study

This study covers ten groups in ten cities through a forty year span. The most significant feature of methodology, then, is the possibility of controlling or holding constant factors frequently suggested as accounting for the differential assimilation of ethnic populations. This is particularly important in studying ethnic groups since they are aggregates that vary in a great range of attributes. In addition, inferences unavoidably based on crude and gross data are facilitated at times, since the study does not rely solely on the existence of statistically significant correlations in a single community. If in the study of a single community, a correlation is obtained that is in the hypothesized direction but lower than that required for a specified test of significance, it is difficult to decide whether to reject the hypothesis or to interpret the low correlation as due to large error variance in the data used. By contrast, the comparative method enables the investigator to test a hypothesis on the basis of the existence of a persistent pattern for a number of different ethnic groups in each of ten cities. Thus, in this sense, the comparative method used in this study aids the investigator in his use of crude data when necessary and in avoiding errors of the first kind, i.e., rejecting a hypothesis when it is correct.

Because census tract data are available for only a limited number of cities in 1930, the ten cities under investigation are not selected randomly. The cities studied are Boston, Buffalo, Chicago, Cincinnati, Cleveland, Columbus (Ohio), Philadelphia, Pittsburgh, St. Louis, and Syracuse. Since the 1930 census gives an unusually extensive array of data on characteristics of immigrant and second generation groups, it was all the more necessary to include cities for which segregation indexes could be computed for that year. The larger immigrant and second generation groups were studied in each city, although European

boundary changes (particularly around the time of World War I) made
it necessary to splice the investigation through the forty year period.
Residential segregation was computed by using indexes of dissimilarity
in a manner similar to that utilized in several recent studies (Duncan
and Duncan, 1955a; Duncan and Lieberson, 1959). With the exception
of Chicago, segregation between groups was determined on the basis of
their degree of similarity in distribution by wards during 1910 and 1920
and by census tracts during 1930 and 1950. Measures of association
most commonly used were Spearman's and Kendall's rank correlations.
The latter correlation proved to be of considerable value since it per-
mits first order partial correlations. In addition, where the data justified the procedures, product-moment correlation, linear regression,
and indirect standardization were utilized. Although the study is not
primarily a methodological one, an equation was discovered which aids
in interpreting the quantitative interrelations of segregation indexes.
Problems of method are discussed in some detail in Chapter 2.

The segregation of foreign-born groups from each other and from
native whites declined through the forty year period. In 1930, the only
year for which such data are available, the second-generation members
of the groups under consideration were found on the average to be less
segregated from each other and from native whites in their cities who
did not have foreign parents. Although the degree of residential segregation declined, the pattern of segregation remained highly stable, i.e.,
the relative positions of ethnic groups with respect to segregation from
native whites and from each other were very similar in the years measured.

Against this backdrop of declining residential segregation of foreign-born groups, a number of aggregate characteristics were considered to account for the wide differences between immigrant groups in
the magnitude of their residential segregation from the native white
population. In 1930, length of residence in the United States of the immigrant groups and their differences in socio-economic level (measured by inability to read or write in any language) were both found to be
independently influencing the magnitude of the immigrant groups' segregation. In 1950, using years of schooling as a measure of socio-

economic level, associations were also found between segregation and socio-economic position of the immigrant groups.

Because of the lack of information about the ethnic origins of native whites of native parentage in these cities, crude measures were used. However, the results indicate that members of a given immigrant group tend to be less segregated from native whites when earlier settlements in the city contained larger percentages of the group. Defining "old" and "new" immigrant groups in geographical terms, differences between them in their segregation from a segment of the native white population suggests that the ethnic composition of the native population operates to lower the segregation positions of the old immigrant groups.

Several economic factors, such as differentials in housing expenditures, were considered as alternate interpretations of the patterns of residential segregation observed earlier. Although relatively high correlations were obtained in several instances, use of indirect standardization led the investigator to reject these economic approaches as major factors since they accounted for a small proportion of the magnitudes of the segregation indexes found. An alternative view, that both segregation and housing expenditures reflect the differential status positions of the ethnic groups, is suggested. Cultural differences between immigrant groups in their propensity to own homes were considered as possibly influencing the degree of spatial mobility of the groups and, therefore, accounting for their variations in segregation. Examination of 1930 data led to the rejection of this approach.

The classical ecological interest in the outward dispersion and decentralization of immigrant groups and their children was considered for 1930 and 1950. After general socio-economic gradients were found in each city under consideration, the question of where with respect to distance from the center of the city the immigrants and their children located was considered a meaningful one. By and large, the newer immigrant groups locate nearer the center of the city than the older groups and a general outward movement is observed for immigrant groups between 1930 and 1950 as well as an inter-generational dispersion in 1930. The degree of suburbanization of immigrant groups and their children generally fits into the Burgess model of centralization, but only after differences in suburban economic levels are controlled.

A brief investigation was made of differences in residential segregation between Negroes and white ethnic groups in an effort to determine whether the former group could be viewed as varying on a continuum from the situation faced by white ethnic groups. Although several exceptions were found in 1910 and 1920, immigrant groups were far more segregated from Negroes than from native whites--indeed their segregation indexes from Negroes were about the same as that of the native whites from Negroes. Changes within the forty year period indicate that Negroes and immigrant groups have moved in opposite directions, i.e., declining segregation for immigrants and increasing segregation for Negroes. Although this matter is considered as incidental to the central problems under investigation, the results suggest that Negro residential patterns are not to be viewed as simply being more highly segregated than immigrant residential patterns.

Turning to interrelations of segregation with certain other aspects of assimilation (Chapter 5), an association was found between ability to speak English and residential segregation of foreign born groups from the native white population and from each other. Groups highly segregated from native whites tend to have lower proportions able to speak English than the less segregated groups. Similarly, variations between immigrant groups in their segregation from one another are interpreted as reflecting their ability to speak the same language. There is presumably a mutual relationship between segregation and ability to speak English, that is, low segregation leading to a greater tendency to learn English and, on the other hand, knowledge of English leading to lower segregation.

On the basis of an analysis of citizenship in 1900 in the 160 cities with at least 25,000 inhabitants, immigrants' length of residence was found to be the major factor accounting for differences between cities in their proportion naturalized. Since the old-new distinction in 1900 is clearly related to length of residence, the zero-order correlations between per cent of immigrants from old countries and per cent naturalized in each city was positive. However, the partial correlation, after length of residence is controlled, indicates a negative relationship, ie., old immigrant groups are less apt to be naturalized than new immigrant groups. While these inferences are based on "ecological correlations," it is fairly evident that length of residence is related to the propensity to become an American citizen. After taking this variable into account, segregation was still found to have an effect on the propensity of immigrant groups in 1930 to be naturalized. That is, although both segregation and citizenship are influenced by length of residence, control of these interrelationships through the use of partial tau correlations indicate that highly segregated groups are less apt to become naturalized than less segregated groups--regardless of length of residence in the United States.

Using an extremely crude indicator of intermarriage--the proportion of second generation persons with mixed parentage--correlations were found that suggest that groups highly segregated in a city are less apt to marry outside of the group than are members of groups less segregated.

Since the occupational composition of immigrant groups and their children is clearly of considerable significance in determining the participation of ethnic groups in the society, detailed attention was paid to this matter in Chapter 6. Data for metropolitan areas in 1950 indicate that in terms of occupational composition, second generation groups were, on the whole, more like the native whites of native parentage than were the immigrant groups. Moreover, while examination of the relationships between occupational status of immigrant groups in each city and their median education indicates fairly high correlations, they are not as high as those for second generation members of the same ethnic groups. Viewing differences between immigrant groups in their status ranks as a function of their differences in educational attainment, the closer association between occupational status and median education found for second generation groups indicates movement toward status crystallization.

Using unpublished data on occupational mobility between generations, the occupational composition of younger adult male members of second generation groups was considered in terms of what would be expected on the basis of the occupational composition of older first generation males. Although limitations of the data required the use of extremely crude methods, in a number of instances the inter-generational occupational mobility tables proved to be accurate predictors of the occupational composition of second generation groups. Further, the magnitude of the deviations between the actual and "expected" occupational distributions were found to be related to the segregation of the immigrant groups. That is, groups highly segregated in 1950 were also groups that deviated most strongly from the general societal patterns of inter-generational occupational mobility. Thus groups highly segregated in their residential patterns are found to also deviate from the general patterns of the social system.

The detailed results of the study support a general theoretical conclusion highlighted by the difference in approach between this study and certain tendencies in earlier research. There is little doubt that ethnic groups differ in a great many social psychological, cultural, and psychological attributes. Frequently, such variations in a given attribute have been used to explain or interpret ethnic differences in another dimension of their assimilation. That there is much to be learned from these approaches, the author does not deny. The structural and aggregate aspects of ethnic assimilation, however, are often overlooked in studies of ethnic behavior in general and assimilation in particular. This study, applying the perspective of human ecology to the assimilation of immigrant groups and their children in our society, finds fairly orderly and consistent patterns which can best be interpreted on the assumption that the process of assimilation is bound up with the process of residential segregation in American cities.

Chapter 2

Data and Methods

This chapter describes the major methodological problems, sources, and procedures involved in the analysis of ethnic segregation and assimilation in ten United States cities between 1910 and 1950. Since the more specific methodological details are considered later in their most meaningful context, the ensuing discussion may prove of interest to general readers as well as specialists.

Ethnic Groups in the Census

The decennial censuses of the United States vary considerably in the extent and nature of the material tabulated for the foreign born and their children. However, at best, there are no United States census data giving country of origin for third generation Americans and their descendents. Consequently, consideration of ethnic assimilation and segregation is limited to the first and second generations, "foreign born" and "native whites of foreign and/or mixed parentage," respectively. The neglect of later generations in this study is due to the limitations of the census sources and not to any assumption that country of origin is irrelevant in later generations. The lack of data on these generations is not and should not be taken to imply their assimilation or homogenization. Whether the third and later generations can be viewed as a homogeneous entity is, in fact, dubious.

Not only are United States censuses restricted almost entirely to immigrants and their immediate descendents, but it is furthermore

19

usually in terms of their country of birth rather than their ethnic membership. Frequently, a European political entity will have more than one major ethnic group; and, conversely, an ethnic group will have major segments living in more than one country. Consequently, utilization of political rather than ethnic data in this study is solely due to the limitations of the sources. The term "ethnic group" is used in this study to refer to persons born in a specified European country and/or their offspring. The term is used solely for convenience and in no way should be construed as an effort to slur over the important fact that in some cases the ethnic composition of immigrants from a given country may be highly heterogeneous.

This study is thus confined to whites who were either born in Europe or were the offspring of European-born immigrants. Persons born outside of the United States are sometimes referred to as the "foreign born," "first generation," or "immigrants." These terms will be used interchangeably in this study. Persons born in the United States who have one or both parents born in a foreign country are referred to either as "native whites of foreign and/or mixed parentage" or as the "second generation." "Native whites of native parentage" are persons born in the United States whose parents were also born in the United States. In effect, this last category refers to persons who are at least third generation Americans. "Native whites" refers to all persons born in the United States who are white and comprises two subcategories: "native white of native parentage" (at least third generation Americans) and "native white of foreign and/or mixed parentage" (the second generation).

Native white of foreign and/or mixed parentage is the most difficult of the above census categories to use. There are no problems in delineating nationality when both parents are born in the same foreign country. However in cases where the parents were born in different foreign countries, the nationality of the father is used by the Census Bureau for the origin of the person. When one parent is foreign-born and one parent American-born, the nationality of the foreign parent determines the classification.

An additional problem is presented by changes in political boundaries that have occurred in Europe, particularly around World War I. This is very important for eastern and central Europe since a number of new countries were formed as a result of World War I. Although efforts were made in connection with the 1920 Census to estimate for prior census dates the population born in the areas acquired by these newly formed countries, it is not possible to do the same for spatial units as small as wards or census tracts. Therefore no effort was made to determine the spatial segregation in 1910 of the populations born in areas which later became new political entities such as Poland and Czechoslovakia. Further difficulties also exist in analyzing changes between 1910 and 1920 for those countries such as Germany and the Austria-Hungary empire which lost large territories as a result of World War I. These problems are primarily confined to the changes in eastern and central Europe as was noted earlier, and the boundary changes are presented in Appendix A for countries relevant to this study.

A similar difficulty for a northwest European country is encountered as a result of the formation of the Irish Free State. Prior to 1930, data were presented in the censuses under the single category "Ireland." However, beginning with 1930, the Irish were classified as either born in Northern Ireland or Eire. Analyses of the Irish during 1910 and 1920 are based on the entire grouping whereas the 1930 and 1950 analyses are confined to persons from the Irish Free State. It should be added, however, that there apparently was considerable under-reporting of those born in Northern Ireland in the 1950 census owing to changes in instructions to enumerators (U. S. Bureau of the Census, 1954, p. 5).

The total effect of these European political changes has been considered by the United States Bureau of the Census, and their conclusions, based both on the Post-Enumeration survey made after the 1950 census and upon analyses of the figures for earlier years, are summarized below:

it is estimated that the same country of birth was obtained in the census and the survey for approximately 90 per cent of the foreign-born persons properly included in the 1950 Census.
This finding seems to be consistent with evidence derived

from the examination of census to census variations in the
classification by country of birth. An examination of these
figures seems to indicate that a completely accurate count
of the foreign stock from the countries whose boundaries
were changed as the result of World War I has never been
achieved. . . . In 1950 the situation was further complicated
by the fact that, although there were extensive de facto boundary changes as a result of World War II, only a small number
of these changes were officially recognized by the United
States.
       . . . In summary, it appears that where there have been
boundary changes or changes in the official name of the country, classification is far from accurate. However, in the case
of countries which have maintained the same boundaries over
a long period of time and the differentiations are clear cut, a
reasonably adequate classification is made. The classification by country of birth of parents is, of course, subject to
the same limitations and may be presumed to be less adequate
than the classification of the foreign born by country of birth.
(U. S. Bureau of the Census, 1954, pp. 5-6.)

As the political changes discussed above indicate, populations of
political entities are often far from homogeneous in their ethnic composition. Such discrepancies between ethnic and political categories as
well as boundary changes probably contribute to the extraordinarily low
indexes of segregation found between certain foreign-born populations.
Under such circumstances, data indicating the mother tongue of foreign-
born populations in particular cities often afford a means for determining the ethnic composition of a population born in a given country.
These data are not available for all censuses and, although referred to
in this study, must be interpreted with caution. Kiser (1956, pp. 313-
15), for example, has pointed to the changes between censuses in the
usage and determination of mother tongue information.

Selection of Nationalities

For the most part, not all foreign-born populations were considered
in the cities under examination. The study was restricted to whites either born in Europe themselves or who had at least one parent of European nativity. Non-whites as well as immigrants born in countries outside of Europe were excluded, along with their children, from direct
consideration in the examination of the relationships between segregation and assimilation. Perhaps the most significant omission in terms

of white ethnic groups is the exclusion of Canadian born and their children from this study. In general, the United States census classifies Canadian born into two categories; those of French descent ("Canada--French") and a residual for other Canadian born ("Canada--Other"). The latter category is of dubious meaning for interpretive purposes. Although Canadians of British descent are presumably the most numerous ethnic stock in this category, it would be difficult to determine the ethnic composition of the "Canada--Other" category in a given city. Thus it is possible that the Canadian born in one United States city--aside from French Canadians--are predominantly of several non-British stocks and in another city are of primarily other stocks. In short, the "Canadian--Other" population epitomizes the difficulties discussed earlier with respect to the lack of congruence between ethnic and national political divisions. An additional difficulty, faced in dealing with the French Canadians as well as other Canadians, is due to the fact that the length of settlement in North America is undetermined. For example, the great influx of French to Canada came several centuries ago; and it is questionable whether one would consider these groups as falling into a situation comparable to that faced by European immigrants to the United States and their children. The automatic exclusion of Mexicans and Puerto Ricans from this study is not very serious since, as the reader will shortly see, none of the ten cities subjected to intensive study is a major center for these groups.

Although data on the residential distribution of the foreign born are available by census tracts for approximately 60 of the larger cities of the United States in 1950 and 1940 and by wards for cities of 50,000 and over in 1910 and 1920, systematic selection of cities for inclusion in the portion of the study dealing with segregation and assimilation was prevented by the limited residential data available for 1930. The year 1930 is critical because census information for specific groups in specific cities is available for an unusually extensive array of indicators of assimilation and socio-economic position. Moreover, the 1930 census included residential data for the second as well as the first generation by country of birth for a small number of tracted cities. Consequently, selection was limited to cities for which foreign-born and

second-generation residential distributions were tabulated in 1930.
These cities are further limited since most of the tabulations of census-tract data for 1930 were not published, and it was not possible to
obtain the data for all cities. (See Green and Truesdell, 1937.) In
several cases, these 1930 tract data were made available through the
cooperation of private organizations listed in the Preface. The ten
cities that were studied are listed below:

> Boston, Massachusetts
> Buffalo, New York
> Chicago, Illinois
> Cincinnati, Ohio
> Cleveland, Ohio
> Columbus, Ohio
> Philadelphia, Pennsylvania
> Pittsburgh, Pennsylvania
> St. Louis, Missouri
> Syracuse, New York

Data for Chicago, it should be noted, were based on "Community
Areas" which are groupings of census tracts. (See Appendix B.) New
York was the only city for which information on residential distribution
for specific foreign-born groups was available for 1930 but was not used.
New York was excluded because of the magnitude of the computational
work necessary for the derivation of segregation indexes for a city with
such an extraordinarily large number of census tracts. Although no
claims of random sampling can be made on the basis of the selection
procedure indicated above, it seems reasonable to assume that a fairly
representative picture of the patterns of residential segregation and
assimilation in the larger cities of the United States industrial belt can
be obtained from examination of these ten urban centers.

As far as could be determined, standard United States census data
pertaining to the residential distribution of specific ethnic groups within
cities are available only for the period beginning with the 1910 Census.
At least ten ethnic groups were selected for the years of 1910, 1920,
1930, and 1950 in each city with the exception of Syracuse in 1930. (See
Appendix C.) Data from the 1940 census were not utilized simply in the
interest of computational economies. There are special censuses giving residential patterns of immigrant groups for earlier periods for at
least one of the ten cities under consideration here, Boston; and these

earlier censuses are analyzed later in this study.

Emphasis was placed on the larger ethnic groups in each city in part for methodological reasons discussed below and in part to facilitate study of the most important ethnic groups in each city. Since the groups varied in relative numerical importance from census to census and from generation to generation, a somewhat arbitrary method was employed in selecting the groups to be studied in each city. The ten largest European groups in each of the following three categories for a given city were selected: foreign-born whites, 1930; foreign-born whites, 1950; and native whites of foreign or mixed parentage, 1930. In each city there was considerable similarity in these three listings. Nevertheless in most cases it was necessary to select, in order of decreasing number, several other groups in each of the three categories until each listing had at least ten groups that were on the remaining two listings.

The method employed is illustrated in Table 1 for Pittsburgh. It will be noted that nine of the ten largest groups in each of the three categories are the same. These nine groups, listed first and running from England and Wales through Austria, were of course selected for inclusion in the analysis of Pittsburgh. Since Northern Ireland was one of the ten largest groups in only the first two columns and Hungary was one of the ten largest immigrant groups in 1950, it was necessary to consider the 11th largest group in each category (indicated by a "y"). This still failed to yield a tenth group found in all three categories. Consequently the 12th largest group for each category was included (indicated by a "z"). This, however, led to the inclusion of two more groups, Scotland and Lithuania, in the analysis of segregation and assimilation in Pittsburgh between 1930 and 1950.

The ethnic populations to be studied in the 1910 and 1920 analyses of segregation by ward in the city were selected from this list of groups. Generally, not all the groups were classified in the 1910 and 1920 data, and it was consequently necessary to add several nationalities to the 1910 and 1920 analyses to substitute for populations used in the 1930-1950 portion of the study. Poland, for example, was not specified by the Census Bureau in the ward data for 1910, for reasons mentioned earlier.

TABLE 1.--Major European stocks in Pittsburgh, 1930 and 1950

Group	Foreign born 1930	Second generation 1930	Foreign born 1950
England and Wales	x	x	x
Irish Free State	x	x	x
Germany	x	x	x
Poland	x	x	x
Czechoslovakia	x	x	x
Russia	x	x	x
Italy	x	x	x
Yugoslavia	x	x	x
Austria	x	x	x
Northern Ireland	x	x	. . .
Hungary	. . .	. . .	x
Lithuania	y	z	y
Scotland	z	y	z

Key:

    x = Among the ten largest groups in category.

    y = Eleventh largest group in category.

    z = Twelfth largest group in category.

In the selection of substitute groups, the same procedure was used as for the 1930-1950 selections, i.e., decreasing numerical size. Several of the groups selected above--Poland, Czechoslovakia, Yugoslavia, and Lithuania--were omitted from the analysis of segregation and assimilation in 1910 and 1920 in Pittsburgh since they were formed as a result of World War I and consequently do not appear in the ward data for 1910.

    In summary, groups were selected for study in each city on the basis of their relative numerical importance therein. In effect, the categories of foreign-born white, 1930; foreign-born white, 1950; and native white of foreign and/or mixed parentage, 1930, were all given equal weight in determining the numerically most important groups in the city. Generally, a number of groups were among the ten largest in all three categories. It was, however, necessary to continue the selection of groups using the same criterion of numerical size in each category until there were at least ten groups in all three listings. As far as possible, the same ethnic populations were included for the earlier decades.

The groups used in each city, specified by year, are indicated in Table 2. The reader will note that "x" denotes the use of the group or a major portion of the group in all four censuses under consideration; "y" indicates that the group was examined only for the earlier time periods, i.e., 1910-1920; and "z" indicates that the group was considered only for the later censuses of 1930 and 1950. This method yields a number of groups that are studied in each of the cities for either one or both of the censuses. These are:

England and Wales--All censuses (See footnote c of Table 2).

Ireland and Irish Free State--1910-1920 and 1930-1950, respectively.

Germany--All censuses.

Poland--1930-1950 censuses.

Russia--All censuses.

Italy--All censuses.

It was therefore possible to study the variation between cities for the same group in their segregation and assimilation.

Examination of Table 3 indicates that this procedure resulted in the inclusion of a large proportion of the total foreign born or second generation in each city investigated. For example, from nearly 70 per cent to as much as 87 per cent of the foreign-born whites in each city were included in 1930. Similarly, from 71 per cent to 90 per cent of the foreign born in 1950 were included on the basis of the selection procedure discussed earlier. Similarly, high percentages are shown for the second-generation populations in 1930. Similar computations were not made for the foreign-born groups used in 1910 and 1920, but we might expect the figures to be lower since it was impossible to make adjustments for the

TABLE 2.--Foreign-white stocks used in segregation and assimilation analyses, by city and year

Nationalities	Boston	Buffalo	Chicago	Cincinnati	Cleveland	Columbus	Philadelphia	Pittsburgh	St. Louis	Syracuse	Number of cities in which group was included	
											1910-20	1930-50
"Old"												
England and Wales	x[c]	x[c]	x[c]	x[c]	x	x	x	x	x[c]	x[c,d]	10	10
Scotland	x	x		x	y	x	x	x	y	y[d]	9	6
Ireland[a]	x	x	x	x	x	x	x	x	x	x[d]	10	10
Norway	y		y		y						2	3
Sweden	x	y	x	x				y		x	6	3
Denmark			y								1	
France		x			y	y	y		x	y	5	3
Switzerland	x			x					y	y	4	
Germany	x	x	x	x	x	x	x	x	x	x	10	10
"New"												
Poland[b]	z	z	z	z	z	z	z	z	z	z		10
Czechoslovakia[b]			z		z			z	z	z		5

TABLE 2.--Continued

Nationalities	Boston	Buffalo	Chicago	Cincinnati	Cleveland	Columbus	Philadelphia	Pittsburgh	St. Louis	Syracuse	Number of cities in which group was included 1910-20	Number of cities in which group was included 1930-50
Austria	y	x	x	x	x	x	x	x	x	x	10	9
Hungary	x	x	y	x	x	x	x	y			8	6
Yugoslavia[b]					z			z	z			3
Russia	x	x	x	x	x	x	x	x	x	x	10	10
Lithuania[b]	z		z				z	z				4
Rumania				x		z[e]	x	y			3	3
Greece	x			x		x					2	2
Italy	x	x	x	x	x	x	x	x	x	x	10	10
1910-20	10	10	10	10	10	10	10	10	10	10		
1930-1950	10	10	10	11	10	11	11	11	11	9		

Key: x = used for all years; y = 1910-1920 analyses only; z = 1930-50 analyses only.

a Irish Free State in 1930-1950, Ireland in 1910-1920.
b Not elegible for 1910-1920 analyses, see text.
c England only, in 1910-1920.
d Great Britain and Northern Ireland used for 1930-1950 analysis.
e Rumania not available for Columbus in 1910.

boundary shifts between 1910 and 1920.

The Measurement of Residential Segregation

Indexes of dissimilarity were used to determine the degree of a group's residential segregation from other groups in a given city. The index indicates the percentage of one population that would have to re- distribute itself in order to have the same per cent distribution by spa- tial units as another population. Thus, complete dissimilarity, that is, complete segregation between two groups, would yield the maximum in- dex value, 100; complete similarity or absolutely no segregation would yield the minimum index value of 0. (For a fuller discussion, see Duncan and Duncan, 1955b.) In a case where there was no segregation at all between two groups, there would be the same per cent of each group's total city population in each ward or tract. Thus, if the Irish had 2 per cent of their total city population in a particular ward and if the English had the identical residential distribution, then they too would have 2 per cent of their total city population in that ward. Such would be the case for each ward if there was to be absolutely no seg- regation between the two groups. On the other hand, if the Irish were completely segregated from the Italians, then wherever there were Irish there would be no Italians and in whatever wards the Italians lived there would be no Irish. These extremes did not occur for the groups and cities under investigation. However, the importance of the indexes of dissimilarity is that they enable us to measure the extent to which the groups are similarly distributed in their residential patterns for the cases falling between these extremes. These indexes were also used in considering the occupational distributions of ethnic groups, but discus- sion of this is postponed until Chapter 6.

As was already noted, the residential distribution of specific for- eign-born groups within cities is available for a number of cities and groups throughout most of the time span covered in this study. In 1910 and 1920, wards were the spatial units available for use in measuring ethnic segregation. In general, wards are much larger spatial units than the census tracts used for the 1930 and 1950 analyses of segrega-

TABLE 3.--Per cent of total foreign born and second-generation population included in analyses, 1930-1950, by city.

City	Foreign born 1930	Second generation 1930	Foreign born 1950
Boston	68.8	75.1	71.0
Buffalo	77.2	87.3	76.8
Chicago	78.3	82.5	76.7
Cincinnati	87.2	92.3	82.2
Cleveland	82.9	87.1	83.9
Columbus	82.5	84.9	75.6
Philadelphia	86.1	72.8	90.0
Pittsburgh	85.2	86.7	85.6
St. Louis	85.5	88.9	81.6
Syracuse	78.0	83.4	76.9

tion. Since presumably the wards were designed primarily for political
purposes, they are subject to a number of factors that can neither be estimated nor controlled in this study. The problem essentially is that
there is no way of taking into account political efforts to nullify the potential power of ethnic groups by splitting ethnic and racial populations into several wards or concentrating a group into one or more voting units. The effects of gerrymandering are, therefore, not taken into
account in this study although, as we shall shortly see, they are pertinent to the results obtained by the segregation indexes employed in this
study. However, it is unlikely that any gerrymandering that might have
taken place could distort too greatly the magnitude of the segregation
indexes. The breaking up, for example, of an area populated by members of just one ethnic group into segments of several surrounding areas
would, of course, lower the group's segregation index. But, it is almost
impossible to lower it too greatly unless extraordinary and non-contigu-
ous spatial units are formed.

Further, no information was uncovered on the actual boundaries of the wards used in these two census years. This means that it is impossible to compute centralization indexes (discussed later in this chapter) for these two census years. In a number of cases it is clear that the data for 1910 are not directly comparable with the following census. That is, there were increases in the number of wards in the city. Whether this was due to annexation and/or the formation of new ward boundaries was not determined.

In short, minor variations between groups and between censuses for the same groups cannot be taken too seriously in themselves since they could be due to a number of factors not directly relevant to the substantive problems under investigation--ward boundaries being but one of these methodological difficulties.

Census tracts are much smaller spatial units than wards and are designed to include from about 3,000 to about 6,000 persons. Generally speaking, they were laid out without consideration of ward boundaries and were "designed to include an area fairly homogeneous in population characteristics" (U. S. Bureau of the Census, 1952, p. 1). Although census tracts are more desirable spatial units than wards for the purposes of this study, there are several problems which were encountered in dealing with them. In two cities, Cincinnati and Syracuse, rather extensive revisions in the tract boundaries were made between 1930 and 1950; and comparisons between those years are somewhat dubious. Most of the other cities did have a number of minor revisions in their tract boundaries during this twenty-year span, and efforts were made to adjust for these changes so as to keep the segregation indexes comparable. Perhaps the most common revision involved splitting parts of two or more 1930 tracts into a new tract for 1950. Such changes were taken into account by combining the 1950 tracts to make them comparable with several of the 1930 tracts which were also combined into a single spatial unit. These recombinations of census tracts to maximize the comparability between censuses probably had only negligible effect on the magnitude of the indexes of segregation obtained. The changes between 1930 and 1950 in tract boundaries and the additions of tracts because of annexations are indicated in Appendix D as well as the necessary adjustments that were made to have maximum comparability between censuses.

In one respect we may say that higher segregation indexes would be expected in 1930 than in 1950 simply because the tracts were constructed to maximize the homogeneity of the population. Thus the closer the census year is to the time when the tracts were laid out, the greater the degree of segregation that might be expected. However, barring gerrymandering, the inclusion of other factors in delineating tracts such as housing, income, and major arterials indicates that more than merely ethnic homogeneity was used as a factor in forming tracts in 1930. Further, the important fact that census tracts are such small spatial and population units suggests that the efforts to obtain homogeneous areas had little effect on the changes found through time in segregation indexes of the foreign-born groups studied. While the use of spatial boundaries delineated by the Bureau of the Census does not relieve the present investigation from concern over their nature and effect on the results obtained, it does allow with a fair degree of comfort the assumption that the results reported here are not artifacts of the research design or biased towards the hypotheses under investigation.

Effects of Spatial Units and Group Size on Indexes of Dissimilarity

The index of segregation is used in this study in a manner similar to that employed in several recent investigations (Duncan and Duncan, 1955a; Duncan and Lieberson, 1959). However this study presents certain difficulties not encountered in these earlier investigations of only one city (Chicago). These difficulties are in part due to the properties of the index and in part to the nature of the data and problems analyzed with these indexes.

It is impossible to determine the degree and magnitude of segregation within the spatial units used to compute the index. If tracts are the spatial units used, then the index takes into account only differences in the proportions of two groups in each of the tracts of the city involved. Nothing is known about the groups' intra-tract distributions. Thus two

groups may each have the same proportion of their total city populations in a given tract, but be completely segregated within the tract's
blocks. This block segregation would not show up. In short, the smaller
the spatial units the greater the possible index of segregation. (By size,
of course, is meant size of the population units, not simply areal size.)
If tracts were broken down into blocks, then the index based on blocks
would be at least as high as that obtained for tracts (if there was no intra-tract segregation) and could be higher (if there was intra-tract segregation).

The reader will recall that segregation indexes were computed on
the basis of the ethnic groups' tract distributions in 1930 and 1950, but
on the basis of their ward distributions in 1910 and 1920. Here also is
a situation in which if all other factors were constant, that is, if the
groups did not redistribute themselves, one would expect higher segregation indexes for the years that the indexes were computed on the basis
of tracts (1930 and 1950) than for the years in which ward distributions
were used (1910 and 1920). Use of tracts means a more sensitive index
of segregation than the use of wards since the former involves measuring group differences in terms of smaller spatial units. This means
that one cannot blithely compare ward and tract data for the same city
and expect comparable indexes--at least in terms of absolute values.
Thus, for the most part, changes in the magnitude of ethnic segregation
are examined in terms of a split time series. That is, changes in the
degree of a group's segregation can be examined between 1910 and 1920,
since in both years roughly comparable ward data were used, or between 1930 and 1950 where tract data were used to measure segregation, but not between 1920 and 1930 or any other combination involving
ward and tract indexes of segregation. In particular, one cannot infer
from the higher indexes of segregation obtained for 1930 and 1950 than
for 1910 and 1920 that ethnic segregation has necessarily increased.

For 1910, information is available on the spatial distributions of
immigrant and native-white populations by both wards and census tracts
in Chicago. Comparisons between the segregation indexes obtained on
the basis of the two spatial units indicate that the two series are highly
correlated, with the slope of the ward on the tract indexes being close

to unity. Hence, we have some reason to believe that the ranks of segregation indexes between foreign born and native whites or between foreign-born groups are not too greatly influenced by the spatial units used
in this study. Needless to say, the tract measures of segregation yield
higher indexes than the ward measures.

The question of the effect of the spatial units on the segregation index raises another issue when inter-city comparisons of ethnic segregation are considered. Before making comparisons of Italian segregation, for example, in ten cities in the same year, it is necessary to determine whether differences between cities in the delineation of their
spatial units accounts for a significant proportion of the variations in
the segregation indexes. That is, in making inter-city comparisons of
an ethnic group's segregation, the effect of two possible sources of differences in segregation must be considered. First, there may be differences based on the scheme of spatial units used in each; and, secondly, there may be differences due to the actual segregation of the ethnic
group in each city.

Finally, a somewhat different kind of issue is raised in this general
consideration of the effect of the spatial units on the indexes of dissimilarity: just what is the best spatial unit? Should segregation be examined in terms of sectors, zones, wards, tracts, blocks, houses or what
not? In part, this is an academic question since availability of the data
as well as the ease of computing the indexes left no choice in this study.
Nevertheless, it is apparent that there is no single answer independent
of the problem under investigation. Consider, for example, religious
institutions. If we wanted to determine if there was a relationship between the location of a given religious group and their churches, we
would not in all likelihood be concerned with the smallest of spatial
units such as blocks or individual houses since the populations required
to support a church would be much greater than that in individual houses
or blocks (except, of course, skyscraper apartment houses). By contrast, if we were interested in whether ethnic group members borrowed
sugar from each other, we would most certainly want to deal with their
spatial distribution on as small a scale as possible. Thus, in discussing the effect of ethnic segregation on other dimensions of ethnic behavior

we can be sure that tract or ward segregation indexes are not always the ideal measures. For example, in considering the effect of ethnic membership on the location of physicians' offices, one would not particularly want to use census tracts as a measure of the populations served by a physician in a given location since, presumably, this would "confine the mobility of the doctor and the residents of the tract too much." (Lieberson, 1958a, p. 17.)

The relationship between the segregation index and the size of the group under study creates two major types of problems. First, there is a purely methodological matter involved in the effect of group size on the sensitivity of the index of segregation. The second difficulty is both methodological and substantive in nature and is a result of the fact that the index is based on a comparison of per cent distributions and does not take into account the absolute numbers of the groups involved.

In considering the purely methodological problem first, it is important that the reader recall that the range of the index is from 0 to 100 (from complete similarity to complete dissimilarity in the two groups' residential distributions). In practice, it is possible to set out the effect which various group sizes have on attenuating the theoretically possible range of the index of dissimilarity. In cases where the population of a given ethnic group is less than or equal to the total population of the city's smallest spatial unit, the maximum index is equal to $(100 - P_t)/(1 - \frac{E}{T})$, where P_t is the per cent of the total city population living in the city's smallest spatial unit, T is the total city population, and E is the total population of a given ethnic group in the city. For example, if the smallest spatial unit in a given city had a population of 100 and if the smallest ethnic group in the same city had a total population of 50 and if the total city population was 1,000, then the maximum index of dissimilarity for the smallest ethnic group, calculated from this formula, would be roughly 94.7. This maximum value would only occur if the total ethnic population was located in the smallest spatial unit of the city. In cases where the ethnic group's total population lived in a larger spatial unit, the maximum value would even be lower. The minimum index of dissimilarity is limited only in a minor way when the ethnic population is smaller than the total number

of populated spatial units as well as by the problems created by round-
ing errors. Since the larger ethnic groups in each city were selected
for study, it was possible to avoid problems created by using an index
of segregation with an abbreviated and inconsistent range of possible
values. Although it is possible to demonstrate that the maximum index
of segregation also cannot be 100 under certain conditions even when
the ethnic population is larger than the population of the smallest spatial unit, it appears reasonable to use the indexes of dissimilarity for
ethnic groups in a given city at face value for intra-city comparisons
of ethnic groups since the extreme cases of segregation were not found
for the ethnic groups investigated.

The second problem in dealing with the relationship between group
size and the index of segregation is derived from the fact that the segregation index does not take into account variations between ethnic
groups in their absolute number. Since indexes of dissimilarity are
based on per cent distributions, this means that a very large and a very
small foreign-born group could have similar indexes of segregation but
without, presumably, the same expected impact on the two immigrant
groups. For example, if two ethnic groups, one relatively large and
one relatively small in number, were both highly segregated in a city,
the index would be less significant in some respects for the smaller
group in terms of segregation's impact on other aspects of their behavior. All of this is to say that presumably the actual size of the
group is a factor influencing the effect which a given degree of segregation could have on ethnic assimilation. Presumably the sheer number of a group as well as their spatial location would influence a group's
capacity to support certain institutions and services such as ethnic voluntary associations and stores specializing in ethnic foods and grocer-
ies. The absolute number of a given group would be relevant in at least
two ways. First, there would probably be a certain minimum number
of consumers required to support a given service irrespective of the
group's segregation. On the other hand, if a group was sufficiently large
in number it could probably support a given service even if the group
was not segregated at all in the city. Thus, there presumably would be
a numerical threshold necessary for a given ethnic activity to take place

even when there is complete group segregation and, by contrast, a much higher and different numerical threshold necessary for the activity to take place even when the group had no segregation at all. This problem is considered in greater detail later when, for example, the relationship between segregation and ability to speak English is examined since group size, holding segregation constant, would be expected to influence the propensity of immigrants to learn English (Chapter 5).

Independence of Indexes of Dissimilarity

In comparing a number of different populations with another population, for example various immigrant groups with the native-white population, it is reasonable to assume that each comparison is independent of the value obtained for any or all of the remaining comparisons. To illustrate, the extent to which Italians in a city are segregated from the native whites has essentially no limiting effect on the extent to which the Irish are segregated from the same native-white population. That is, from a purely methodological point of view, the segregation index between Italian immigrants and native whites tells us nothing about what the segregation index between Irish immigrants and the native whites could be. The two indexes are completely independent of each other. Such would continue to be the case if we examined the segregation of additional immigrant groups from the native whites.

However these indexes are not completely "independent" of each other when all pairs of indexes for three groups are considered. That is, while the relationship between group A and group B is independent in a predictive sense from the segregation of group A and group C, once we know what the segregation indexes are in these two sets, the relationship between groups B and C is narrowed down in the sense that frequently we can state in advance a possible range for the segregation between groups B and C considerably less than from 0 to 100.

For illustrative purposes, consider an extreme case. Suppose we find that the Irish and native whites have the same residential patterns, that is, their segregation index is 0. We may observe that knowledge of the pattern of segregation between these two groups tells us nothing about what the segregation between the Italians and native whites might be. Suppose however we empirically find that the Italians and native whites also have identical residential patterns, that is, that they too have a segregation index of 0. Before considering the segregation between the Irish and Italians, we ask what is the possible range of the segregation index between these two groups, given our knowledge about their segregation against native whites. Clearly, in this case there would also be no segregation between Italian and Irish immigrants. For if both of these immigrant groups have the same distribution as a third group, the native whites, then they must have the same distribution as each other.

This example involving groups with identical residential distributions is, of course, an unusual situation and one not encountered in this study. However it does serve to illustrate the important methodological fact that the degree of residential segregation between two groups is not independent of their spatial relationship with respect to any third group. Through a series of trial and error experiments with different combinations of segregation indexes, the following general relationship was derived for indexes of dissimilarity (called "deltas" in the formulas) between three groups (called "A," "B," and "C" in the formulas):

Given: delta_{AB} and delta_{AC}; then

Maximum $\text{delta}_{BC} = \text{delta}_{AB}$ plus delta_{AC}, or 100,

whichever is lower;

Minimum $\text{delta}_{BC} = |\text{delta}_{AB} - \text{delta}_{AC}|$.

To illustrate with real numbers and groups, if the native whites (A) and the Irish (B) have a segregation index of 30 and if the native whites (A) and the Italians (C) have a segregation index of 60, then the maximum segregation index between the Irish (B) and the Italians (C) would be 90, i.e., (30 + 60) and their minimum index would be 30, i.e., (60 - 30).

No inference of causality can or should be made with respect to the purely mathematical interrelations of these indexes and their generalized limits. What is important here is that relationships between indexes of dissimilarity in a city can be obtained that are at least partially redundant, i.e., purely a function of the mathematical attributes of the segregation indexes. For example, if we consider whether ethnic groups highly segregated from native whites are more highly segregated from each other than groups more similar to the native-white residential pattern, then the issue of minimum and maximum indexes of dissimilarity would clearly be pertinent. Thus groups with segregation indexes from native whites in the 20's would have segregation indexes from each other of less than 60. By contrast, groups with segregation indexes from native whites running much higher, for example in the 50's, would have maximum possible indexes of 100 from each other. The minimum indexes would, of course, depend on the dispersion within each category of groups, that is, the groups with segregation indexes in the 50's from native whites would not necessarily have higher minimum indexes from each other than the groups with indexes ranging in the 20's. We shall return to this issue later in the study when relevant problems arise.

Centralization Indexes

The index of centralization used in this study has been discussed in detail and used elsewhere (Wilkins, 1956; Duncan, 1957; Duncan and Davis, 1953; Duncan and Lieberson, 1959). Consequently, discussion of centralization indexes is confined to describing briefly their computation and meaning. First, the city is classified into a series of concentric zones with the central business district in the center. Then the percentages of each group living in each zone are determined on the basis of the tracts in each zone. A simple index is used to determine the extent to which an ethnic population is centralized (in towards the center of the city) or decentralized (away from the center of the city) in comparison with another group's spatial distribution. The index is based on the following formula:

$$\sum_{i=1}^{k} X_{i-1}Y_i - \sum_{i=1}^{k} X_iY_{i-1}$$

where X and Y refer to the cumulative proportions of various foreign-born and native-white populations, starting with the center of the city

and moving outward. The range for the index of centralization is from
-1.00 to +1.00. In the case of -1.00, the most decentralized members
of the Y population are closer to the center of the city than the least decentralized members of the X population. Conversely, a result of +1.00
means that the least decentralized member of the Y population is further from the center of the city than the most decentralized member of
the X population. A centralization index of 0.00 would be interpreted as
meaning that both groups had essentially the same distribution with respect to distance from the center of the city, although an index of zero
can be obtained as a consequence of more complex compensating zonal
patterns.

Clearly, the census tracts must be categorized in terms of distance
from the central business district of the city. (It should be noted that
the central business district need not necessarily be the point from
which centralization is computed.) Tracts had already been ordered into concentric zones on the basis of distance from the center of the city
by the Chicago Community Inventory for all ten of the cities studied
here for use in their Urban Analysis project (Duncan and Davis, 1953,
p. 72). The zones used in this study follow, on the whole, the zonal system used in this earlier study of cities in 1940. Since the current study
involved centralization in 1930 and 1950, it was necessary to make a
number of minor adjustments. That is, tract boundaries had been changed
and certain tracts, as noted earlier, were combined in this study to maximize comparability between censuses. Combined tracts that included
tracts falling into two or more zones were allocated to a single zone on
the basis of a weighted average zone obtained from the number of whites
living in each tract in 1940. In addition, data on the central business
districts of the cities which were not available at the time of the Chicago
Community Inventory study were used to insure that all central business
district tracts were included in the innermost zone (U. S. Bureau of the
Census, 1958, Appendix). Consequently, in some cases zones 1 (innermost) and 2 were combined or revised so as to include all or nearly all
of the central business district tracts in the first zone. The census
tracts included in each zone of the ten cities are shown in Appendix E.

Correlation and Tests of Significance

Several measures of correlation were used in this study: Spearman rank order correlations, Kendall's tau and partial tau correlations, product moment correlations (Pearson), and weighted product moment correlations. Although these are largely well-known and common techniques, interpretive problems arose in their application; and these difficulties are discussed where applicable throughout the study.

Turning to the question of tests of significance, we should first observe that in most instances in this study we cannot infer the probability of an association existing in either the larger universe of cities in the United States or in the larger universe of all the ethnic groups within a particular city. That is, neither the cities nor the groups studied were selected randomly. The reader will recall that the ten cities considered through most of the study were selected because they were the only cities for which 1930 residential data were available. With respect to the foreign-born and second-generation groups considered, for the most part these were simply the larger groups in these cities. It should be added, however, that inclusion of thirteen smaller groups with as few as 2,000 members did not alter results obtained in the study of Chicago's ten major ethnic groups by Duncan and Lieberson (1959, p. 365).

Tests of significance are discussed here with respect to the two major styles of analysis employed in the study. First, the analysis of differences between roughly ten groups in a particular city with respect to two or more variables. For example, in Chapter 5, the proportion of each group able to speak English was correlated (using ranks) with the group's degree of residential segregation. Using a 5 per cent level of significance, a Spearman rank order correlation of roughly .56 and a Kendall rank order correlation of roughly .42 are judged as not due to chance. (In both cases a one-tailed test is used.)

The second type of analysis involves simply considering the direction of the association between two variables for the ethnic groups examined in each of ten cities. This is particularly relevant when we consider the crude nature of the data used. Often the researcher is forced to use data which lead to merely crude approximations or representations of the phenomenon to be investigated. Under such circumstances, a "low" correlation is not necessarily very discouraging; that is, it is not clear whether the results are due to the researcher's inability to obtain the data he ideally would want for examination of his hypothesis or whether the correlation obtained is, in fact, a reflection of what the relationship would be if more precise data were used. For example, in considering the relationship between segregation of foreign-born groups and their proportion able to speak English, the measure of segregation was not precisely what one would want to use. Under such circumstances, examination of simply the pattern of relationship is useful; that is, we can look at whether the two variables are associated in the same direction in each city. Under such circumstances a sign test is an appropriate measure of significance. We can ask whether there is a tendancy for two variables to be associated in a given direction--regardless of the magnitude of the association--for the ethnic groups investigated in each city. If correlations were in the same direction in at least eight out of ten cities, then we could conclude that a pattern of association between two variables is significant at the .05 level. Even when as few as five cities were available for analysis, a pattern significant at the .05 level would exist if the correlations were in the same direction in all five cities. (In both illustrations a one-tailed test is used.)

Social scientists are not in full agreement concerning the applicability of significance tests, but we do not wish to go into that issue here. We may simply note that tests of significance cannot for the most part be used in this study to infer the probability of a given association in a larger universe. That is, our concern with tests of significance is based on the necessity for the investigator and the reader to use some objective, if arbitrary, method for deciding whether or not an association between two variables does or does not exist for the groups or cities actually studied.

Chapter 3

Residential Segregation

Among the theoretical issues considered in Chapter 1, two aspects of ethnic residential segregation were emphasized: first, the significance of segregation as an aspect of assimilation in itself; secondly, the impact of segregation on other facets of ethnic behavior. In this and the following chapter attention is directed primarily toward the phenomenon of segregation itself, while the relationships between segregation and other aspects of assimilation are considered in Chapter 5.

Since the existence of immigrant ghettos and ethnic colonies in American cities has long been a subject for sociological investigation as well as popular knowledge, the finding that populations in big cities segregate along ethnic lines is far from surprising. Our concern is not merely with the demonstration of the present and past existence of ethnic segregation, but turns here to examining and understanding the variations between ethnic groups in a systematic and generalizable fashion. In addition, the use of relatively precise measures of segregation allows us to examine residential trends through the years. Emphasis has been placed on the residential patterns of immigrant groups with respect to other white segments of the city population since consideration of racial segregation tends to complicate the analysis of immigrant patterns. However, the relationships between Negroes and the white immigrant groups are treated briefly in Chapter 4.

44

Segregation of Ethnic Groups from the
Native-White Population

It is clear that the general trend has been towards declining residential segregation of ethnic groups from the native white population-- at least as far as can be measured by data primarily based on immigrants. Before bogging down in the details of exceptions and methodological difficulties, inspection of Table 4 indicates that the mean residential segregation of immigrant groups from native whites declined between 1910 and 1920 (columns 2 and 3) and between 1930 and 1950 (columns 4 and 5) in each of the ten cities under consideration. Similarly, in 1930 the ethnic second generations were less segregated than were the first generations from native whites of native parentage (columns 7 and 6). In analyses involving second-generation ethnic groups, native whites of native parentage are used rather than total native whites since the second generation is itself a component of the total native population.

Since the 1910 and 1920 segregation indexes are based on ethnic distributions by wards, while the 1930 and 1950 indexes are, in all but one city, based on tract distributions, it is impossible to compare the absolute values of the indexes of segregation for the two earlier censuses with values for the 1930 and 1950 censuses. As was noted in Chapter 2, tracts are smaller population units than wards; and since the segregation index varies with the number and size of the population units, the larger values for computations based on tract data do not necessarily imply that segregation increased between 1920 and 1930.

Although residential segregation from the native-white population declined through time, there is a remarkably high degree of stability in the relative degree of segregation among ethnic groups. The rankings of the foreign-born groups in each city with respect to their segregation are extremely similar in different years. Column 2 of Table 5 shows the rank-order correlations for selected foreign-born groups in their relative degree of segregation from native whites between 1910 and 1920. The correlations range from .85 in Chicago to .99 for the ten immigrant groups in St. Louis. Similarly, high correlations were found

TABLE 4.--Unweighted mean indexes of residential segregation between ethnic groups and native populations

City	FBW v. NW				FBW v. NWNP	NWFMP v. NWNP
	Wards		Tracts[a]		Tracts[a]	
	1910 (2)	1920 (3)	1930 (4)	1950 (5)	1930 (6)	1930 (7)
(1)						
Boston	33.6	32.3	40.4	37.5	41.8	39.4
Buffalo	41.2	38.8	42.8	38.2	43.4	39.2
Chicago	40.6	34.3	39.4	35.9	42.4	38.6
Cincinnati	38.5	33.8	41.0[b]	39.9[b]	42.5[b]	37.6
Cleveland	35.4	30.8	44.9	40.1	48.4	46.5
Columbus	39.1	38.8	46.7	38.3	47.6	39.6
Philadelphia	39.7	34.4	44.3	40.8	47.3	43.5
Pittsburgh	37.3	34.4	42.6	38.4	45.3	42.5
St. Louis	35.7	31.7	48.8	37.6	42.0	38.0
Syracuse	36.5	31.8	47.6[c]	39.3	49.4[c]	42.9

Abbreviations:

FBW = Foreign-born white
NW = Native white
NWNP = Native white of native parentage
NWFMP = Native white of foreign or mixed parentage

[a]Community areas used for Chicago.
[b]Tracts not comparable between 1930 and 1950.
[c]Based on head of family data.

between the 1930 and 1950 indexes of foreign-born segregation from native whites (column 3) and between first and second generation segregation from native whites of native parentage in 1930 (column 4). The high stability of the rankings of ethnic groups coupled with the trend towards lower segregation indicates a kind of "dynamic equilibrium" in which ethnic residential patterns are gradually becoming less dissimilar to the native population's residences. In short, the results reported for Chicago by Duncan and Lieberson (1959), that is, the tendency for

TABLE 5.--Correlations (Spearman) between censuses of the residential segregation of foreign-white stock from native-white populations

City (1)	FBW v. NW		FBW v. NWNP, 1930 NWFMP v. NWNP, 1930 (4)
	1910-1920 (2)	1930-1950 (3)	
Boston	.96	.98	1.00
Buffalo	.96	.81	.99
Chicago	.85	.99	.96
Cincinnati	.94	.93	.91
Cleveland	.98	1.00	.90
Columbus	.88	.85	.95
Philadelphia	.88	.94	.95
Pittsburgh	.89	.99	.97
St. Louis	.99	.89	.96
Syracuse	.96	.88	.95

Note: See Table 4 for abbreviations.

ethnic groups to become more dispersed through time, appears to be fairly widespread--at least as indicated by nine other United States cities and for the added years of 1910 and 1920.

Viewed in the context of this orderly process, the degree to which each ethnic group is segregated from the native-white population and the factors underlying their variations are of considerable interest. We have already noted that even if there were no differences between ethnic groups in culture and values, we would expect these groups to differ in their residential patterns in cities simply because of their differences in time of arrival and the concurrent changes taking place in American society. If one assumes that the situation at arrival is a relevant variable for considering the segregation of ethnic groups, then we may ask to what extent can immigrant differences with respect to their residential patterns be viewed as a result of differences in their time of arrival.

Since, for the time span covered in this study, only the 1930 U. S. census gives the necessary information on the time of arrival in the United States of European immigrants specified by both present residence and country of origin, it is necessary to restrict the analysis of length of residence to 1930. Table 6 shows Spearman rank-order correlations between the segregation of immigrant groups in each city and two indicators of their time of arrival. The segregation measures likewise refer to 1930. The correlations between the per cent of the groups coming in 1900 or earlier and their degree of segregation from the native population are rather high, running from .55 in Chicago to .88 in Cleveland. Correlations between segregation from native whites and median year of arrival also are positive, although the correlations are for the most part lower. Both sets of correlations suggest that, irrespective of cultural differences between the groups and the native population, recency of arrival is an important factor in influencing the extent to which the groups are segregated from the native population.

At least for the moment, this interpretation must be treated cautiously. First, higher correlations for the measure based on the per cent coming before 1900 suggests the possibility that it is the recency of the establishment of the group in the city in relatively sizable numbers which may be influencing the differences in segregation. Secondly, the correlations could be spurious since immigrants arriving at different times may well have differed in other attributes as well which are, in fact, actually accounting for the correlations reported in Table 6.

Following up on this latter point, it is of interest to consider differences in the socio-economic level of ethnic groups at the time of their migration to the United States. Unfortunately, limitations of the data available prevent the examination of many of the theoretically relevant indexes. There are, however, two measures that we may consider as indicators of the condition of the ethnic groups prior to migration. One index, available for 1930, deals with the proportion illiterate in each immigrant group. The ability to read and write in any language may be viewed as a crude indicator of the differences in the educational levels of the immigrant groups. For 1950, a somewhat different index, number of school years completed, is available and is used for the

TABLE 6.--Correlations (Spearman) between length of residence in
the United States and residential segregation, 1930

| City | Segregation FBW v. NW and: | |
	Median year of arrival[a]	Per cent arriving after 1900
Boston	.39	.70
Buffalo	.35	.58
Chicago	.36	.55
Cincinnati	.65	.75
Cleveland	.84	.88
Columbus	.48	.67
Philadelphia	.57	.68
Pittsburgh	.60	.87
St. Louis	.74	.79
Syracuse[b]	.78	.69

Note: See Table 4 for abbreviations.

[a]Where two or more immigrant groups in a given city in 1930
had more than half of their population arriving before 1900 (an open-
ended category), it was assumed that the larger the proportion in
this category the earlier the median year of arrival.

[b]Sweden not available.

same purpose as the 1930 illiteracy data, i.e., as a rough indicator of
differences between immigrant groups in their general socio-economic
position. To some extent this is a more desirable measure for recent
years since literacy tests, initiated in 1917 as a general prerequisite
for migration to the United States (Kiser, 1956, p. 310), tend to level out
the differences between immigrant groups in their illiteracy. (See Table
16.) For both indexes, data are not available for all ten of the cities.
In 1930, the illiteracy data were not available for the three cities with
less than 500,000 population. In 1950, information on educational

attainment was given for a limited number of immigrant groups and only in Standard Metropolitan Areas with 500,000 or more foreign-white stock.

Similar procedures were followed in using the two measures. Persons under 25 years of age were excluded on the grounds that many of them undoubtedly have been educated since coming to the United States and thus differences between younger members of immigrant groups are reflections of experiences after arrival in the country and not of their status at the time of immigration. Furthermore, since age and sex are both factors influencing educational level and literacy, it was desirable to take these into account as far as possible. The 1930 illiteracy data were available for three separate adult age categories: 25-44, 45-64, and 65 years of age and older. The 1950 data on educational attainment were available separately by sex for persons of ages 25-44 and for those 45 and older. The United States foreign-born rates by age categories (and sex in 1950) were determined and then applied to each immigrant distribution in each city to obtain the expected number (E) illiterate in 1930 or with less than 8 years of schooling in 1950. The actual number (A) illiterate or with less than 8 years of schooling completed was then divided by the respective number "expected" on the basis of the national rates, and the groups were then ranked in terms of this quotient (A/E).

Although the exclusion of foreign-born persons under 25 years of age is a fairly reasonable procedure since their educational attainments may well have been due to training after arrival in the United States, it is not possible to eliminate adults who had migrated years before as children. We do not know how many adult members of a given foreign-born population had arrived as children and whose educational level or literacy is really a reflection of training in the United States. What is important is that differences between immigrant groups in their proportion who had arrived as children are not controlled in this analysis nor are differences between groups in the propensity of their adults to pursue educational programs after arrival. For example, Russians comprised roughly 30 and 60 per cent respectively of the male and female immigrants enrolled in St. Louis evening schools early in 1915.

(Percentages derived from figures reported by Crawford, 1916, p. 56.)

Nevertheless, the rank order correlations presented in Table 7 between these crude and indirect indicators of status prior to migration and variations in ethnic segregation from native whites are of considerable interest. In 1930, there was a fairly close correlation between segregation and the extent to which a group exceeded the national illiteracy rates for their age distributions in each city. Somewhat lower correlations for the educational measure used in examining the residential segregation patterns in 1950 still support the conclusion that variations in ethnic residential patterns with respect to the native-white population may be viewed as a function of differences in the socio-economic levels of the immigrant populations. High segregation is associated with high illiteracy or low educational training, and, in both cases, this is presumed to be a reflection of the effect that the socio-economic position of immigrants has on their ability to compete for housing and on the status position of the ethnic group.

TABLE 7.--Correlations (Spearman) between indicators of socio-economic position and residential segregation, 1930 and 1950

City[a]	Segregation, FBW v. NW and:	
	Per cent illiterate (A/E), 1930	Per cent with less than 8 years school (A/E), 1950
Boston	.82	.64
Buffalo	.77	NA
Chicago	.73	.58
Cleveland	.78	.64
Philadelphia	.95	.89
Pittsburgh	.77	.67
St. Louis	.77	NA

Note: See Table 4 for abbreviations.

NA: Data not available.

[a]Not available for either 1930 or 1950 for Cincinnati, Columbus, and Syracuse.

Given the earlier findings that an immigrant group's length of residence also appears to influence the extent of their segregation from native whites, it seems reasonable to pose the question of whether there are interrelationships between length of residence and our measure of socio-economic status in 1930 which account for one of these variables appearing to influence segregation. It is not at all far-fetched to consider such a possibility since presumably the immigrants coming to the United States changed through time in terms of their skills and training-- not to mention their country of origin. For example, the percentage of skilled workers coming from South East Europe between 1899-1909 was far less than the percentage of skilled workers among migrants from North West Europe during the same period. But, as Paul H. Douglas has shown, the per cent of skilled from "old" sources of migration during the period 1871-82 is rather similar to that for the "new" in the later period between 1899-1909. (See Thomas, 1954, footnote 1, pp. 153-54.) If length of residence and illiteracy are themselves correlated for the immigrant groups in each city, it could be that the inferences made earlier are based on spurious correlations. The matter can be resolved by considering the partial correlation between each of the independent variables (length of residence and actual/expected per cent illiteracy) with segregation while taking the effect of the remaining independent variable into account.

As usual, there are several methodological matters to consider before examining the results. Spearman rank order correlations are not useful for the problem at hand since partial correlations based on the Spearman coefficient cannot be justified mathematically. Consequently another non-parametric measure of correlation, Kendall's tau, which can be used to compute partial correlations was employed for this analysis as well as a number of subsequent analyses in this study. Since in this and on a few other occasions we shall shift from Spearman's to Kendall's rank order correlation, the reader should keep in mind that Spearman's coefficient is generally about 50 per cent higher than tau in cases where neither of the correlations is close to unity (Kendall, 1955,

p. 12). Finally, in the computation of tau, the occasional ties in ranks allow for something of an option in the denominator used to determine tau. That is, the denominator can be adjusted for the number of ties or can be used in the form when there are no ties. The latter method was used whenever the option existed and tends to give lower correlations than the adjusted denominator (Kendall, 1955, Chapter 3).

We can consider only the socio-economic measure used for 1930, that is, illiteracy, since the necessary data on year of arrival are available for that year alone. Median year of arrival of the immigrant groups and illiteracy are, once again, positively correlated with ethnic segregation (columns 2 and 3 of Table 8). The results are roughly comparable to the Spearman correlations of the same data reported earlier in Tables 6 and 7 if we keep in mind that Spearman correlations generally tend to run higher than tau. That is, groups with relatively low segregation from native whites have been in the United States longer and have lower illiteracy rates than those groups more highly segregated from native-white residences. For the most part the association with segregation is higher for illiteracy than for median year of arrival, and this is similar to the results found using Spearman correlations.

Median year of arrival is positively correlated with the actual/expected per cent illiterate (column 4). With the exception of Buffalo, where there was essentially no relationship (-.02), groups coming earlier to the country tended to have relatively low rates of illiteracy in terms of the number expected on the basis of their age distribution in 1930. It therefore appears all the more advisable to take this intercorrelation of independent variables into account when looking at each factor's association with the segregation of immigrant groups.

The partial correlations with segregation for both the indicator of length of residence (column 5) and socio-economic status (column 6) are still largely in the same direction as noted earlier, although for the most part not as strong. For two cities, Boston and Chicago, the effect of length of residence on variations between ethnic groups in their degree of segregation from native whites is essentially eliminated once illiteracy is taken into account. However, for the remaining five cities, time of arrival appears to influence the segregation of groups as

TABLE 8.--Tau, partial tau, and multiple tau correlations between length of residence and socio-economic status and residential segregation, 1930

City	Tau			Partial tau		Multiple tau
	Segregation FBW v. NW and:		Median year of arrival and per cent illiterate (A/E)	Median year of arrival (holding illiterate constant)	Per cent illiterate (A/E) (holding arrival constant)	Median year of arrival and per cent illiterate v. segregation of FBW
	Median year of arrival	Per cent illiterate (A/E)				
(1)	(2)	(3)	(4)	(5)	(6)	(7)
Boston	.18	.64	.27	.01	.62	.64
Buffalo	.29	.60	-.02	.38	.64	.67
Chicago	.24	.51	.56	-.07	.47	.51
Cleveland	.69	.56	.60	.53	.26	.71
Philadelphia	.47	.85	.40	.26	.81	.86
Pittsburgh	.47	.60	.51	.24	.47	.63
St. Louis	.56	.56	.42	.43	.42	.66

Note: See Table 4 for abbreviations

does illiteracy for all seven cities.

For the reader willing to venture into the wilderness of exotic statistical techniques, we may consider the combined effect which length of residence and illiteracy have on the segregation of ethnic groups, using a non-parametric measure of multiple correlation proposed by Moran (1951). The multiple correlation coefficients shown in column 7 range from a low of .51 in Chicago to a high of .86 in Philadelphia. Comparison of the total correlation between each of the independent variables (columns 2 and 3) with the multiple correlation (column 7) indicates that for several cities length of residence adds essentially nothing to improve our understanding of the factors leading to differential ethnic segregation. However, in several cities, Cleveland and St. Louis in particular, length of residence appears clearly to influence the variations between ethnic groups in their segregation from native whites.

In addition, by squaring the multiple correlations shown in column 7, it is possible to determine the per cent of variance in the groups' segregation ranks that can be "explained" by their rank positions with respect to illiteracy and median year of arrival. According to Moran (1951, p. 29), the square of the multiple tau correlation is "the square of the product moment multiple correlation coefficient between the set of scores for the ranking 1 and the sets for rankings 2 and 3." The squares of the multiple correlations shown in column 7, therefore, indicate the total variance in the segregation ranks of each city's immigrant groups accounted for by length of residence and the crude measure of socio-economic status at arrival. The per cent of the variance "explained," ranging from a low of 26 per cent in Chicago to 74 per cent in Philadelphia, generally runs in the low 40's. The reader should keep in mind that the above comments refer solely to variations in rank and not to variations in the absolute magnitude of the groups' segregation indexes.

The correlations between length of residence and illiteracy reported in Table 8 do not necessarily mean that variations in illiteracy are to be largely attributed to length of residence in the United States. There are data indicating rather clearly that the European countries differed considerably in their degree of illiteracy (Chapter 3, Table 15).

Secondly, although this does not, of course, offset the possibilities of differential migration from each country, the evidence points to another conclusion. An examination of the Scots, a group in 1930 with a relatively recent median year of arrival but with relatively little illiteracy, is made later in this chapter in connection with the so-called "Old-New" immigrant differences. Consideration of several other factors is likewise postponed.

Residential Segregation Among Ethnic Groups

With respect to segregation between ethnic groups, a trend similar to that found in segregation from native whites is indicated in Table 9. The mean index of residential segregation of each foreign-born group from each of the remaining immigrant groups is higher in 1910 than in 1920 (columns 2 and 3). Similarly, the foreign-born groups are, on the average, less segregated from each other in 1950 than they were in 1930 (columns 5 and 4) and the second generation is less segregated than the first generation in 1930 (columns 6 and 4). First-generation groups are less segregated from each other in 1950 than were second-generation members of the same groups in 1930 (compare columns 5 and 6). Cincinnati, with non-comparable tracts, is the only exception. The difficulties noted earlier in comparing 1910 and 1920 results with more recent years apply here also.

Since the total number of cases of segregation in each city between the foreign-born groups tends to run to about 50 for each year studied, we can look at the product moment correlations between the intra-ethnic segregation indexes for comparable censuses. The segregation indexes of the foreign-born groups from each other in 1910 were correlated with the corresponding segregation indexes in 1920. The results obtained are presented in Table 10. The product moment correlations, like the rank order correlations for segregation from native populations presented earlier in Table 5, are quite high (columns 4 and 7). That is, the pattern of inter-ethnic segregation found in 1920 is closely associated with that found in 1910 for roughly comparable groups. (The reader

TABLE 9.--Unweighted mean indexes of residential segregation between ethnic groups

| City | Segregation between FBW groups | | | | Segregation between NWFMP groups |
| | Wards | | Tracts[a] | | Tracts[a] |
(1)	1910 (2)	1920 (3)	1930 (4)	1950 (5)	1930 (6)
Boston	46.2	43.0	54.2	50.6	52.7
Buffalo	56.0	53.3	58.4	52.0	56.1
Chicago	54.1	47.7	54.2	50.1	51.5
Cincinnati	50.4	45.2	52.4[b]	48.4[b]	47.9
Cleveland	50.6	43.5	60.8	54.3	60.6
Columbus	51.2	49.4	57.3	49.3	51.4
Philadelphia	51.6	46.5	57.2	53.0	54.6
Pittsburgh	51.8	47.9	57.4	51.6	55.6
St. Louis	48.4	44.2	55.4	49.9	52.6
Syracuse	47.4	45.0	61.4[c]	53.8	57.4

Note: See Table 4 for abbreviations.

[a]Community areas used for Chicago.

[b]Tracts not comparable between 1930 and 1950.

[c]Based on head of family data.

should keep in mind the boundary changes of European countries between 1910 and 1920 that make these comparisons somewhat approximate.) The regression slopes (column 3) are of considerable interest since they are below 1.00 in all cities except Syracuse. This means that the groups relatively low in their segregation from each other in 1910 declined less, on the average, during the ensuing ten years than did the groups more highly segregated from each other in 1910. (For a lengthier statement on the analysis of inter-annual regression slopes, see Duncan and Duncan, 1957, pp. 139-40.)

Similar results were obtained in comparing the segregation indexes

TABLE 10.--Linear regression and product moment correlation of inter-group segregation of the foreign born: 1910 compared with 1920, and 1930 compared with 1950

City	x = FBW, 1910 y = FBW, 1920			x = FBW, 1930 y = FBW, 1950		
(1)	a (2)	b (3)	r (4)	a (5)	b (6)	r (7)
Boston	3.64	.85	.95	2.36	.89	.95
Buffalo	5.23	.86	.88	3.57	.83	.96
Chicago	9.21	.71	.76	.77	.91	.95
Cincinnati	10.44	.69	.85	-2.90	.98	.94
Cleveland	10.95	.63	.85	- .43	.90	.96
Columbus	11.44	.74	.86	15.83	.84	.85
Philadelphia	-1.00	.92	.97	-1.36	.95	.94
Pittsburgh	5.36	.82	.94	3.94	.83	.96
St. Louis	5.07	.81	.94	-3.86	.97	.94
Syracuse	-9.78	1.16	.83	- .87	.89	.89

Note: a = y intercept.
    b = Regression slope of y on x
    r = Product moment correlation coefficient
    See Table 4 for abbreviations.

between the foreign-born groups in 1930 with the comparable indexes for 1950 (Table 5). Thus the correlations for 1930-1950 are also very high (column 7), and the slopes tend to fall slightly below unity (column 6) and therefore indicate a slightly more rapid decline in segregation between the relatively highly segregated groups.

Before delving into the factors accounting for these patterns of inter-ethnic segregation, a brief methodological consideration of the patterns themselves is warranted. The reader will recall the rules of minimum and maximum indexes of dissimilarity presented in Chapter 2 where it was shown that given the segregation index between groups A and B as well as the segregation index between groups A and C, the segregation index between groups B and C could no longer in many cases be conceived of as having a potential range from 0 to 100. This is relevant to the examination here of inter-ethnic segregation since the indexes were computed for each of the ten or so immigrant groups against the spatial patterns of each of the remaining foreign-born groups. Indeed the "fixing" effect is increased when more than three groups are involved. That is, we could select for the maximum index between two groups the lowest maximum obtained from any of the combinations involving eight other groups and, similarly, select the highest minimum from any of the combinations involving eight groups. To illustrate, using actual segregation indexes obtained for Boston in 1910, the highest minimum index of dissimilarity between Germany and Sweden could be obtained by computing the minimum on the basis of their segregation from Norway (42 and 26, respectively) and the lowest maximum by adding their indexes of segregation from Scotland (25 and 17, respectively). This would lead to a minimum of 16 and a maximum of 42 for the index of segregation between Germany and Sweden (it actually is 32). (With further analysis, an even narrower range could be established with the data given.) The point then is that the indexes are not independent of each other in a given set of indexes based on the same groups at the same time in a given city. The interrelation of such a set with another set of indexes for a different year, however, is free to vary. Thus, although there is considerable interdependence between the indexes in a given year, this does not affect either the descriptive validity or the meaning of the comparisons between years of the matrices of inter-ethnic segregation indexes. Having taxed the general reader sufficiently, let us return to the problem at hand.

Given these persistent variations in the segregation between foreign-born groups, their differences in year of arrival become relevant. If segregation from native whites is partially related to the length of residence of the immigrant populations, can the same be said about the differences between foreign-born groups in their segregation from one another? The per cent of each group in 1930 who had arrived in the United States during the following time periods was determined for each city: 1900 or earlier, 1901-1910, 1911-1914, 1915-1919, 1920-1924, and 1925-1930. Immigrants whose year of arrival was unknown were excluded from the analysis. These per cent distributions were then used to compute indexes of dissimilarity between the time of arrival distributions of the foreign-born groups in each city. The indexes in Philadelphia based on time of arrival ranged, for example, from 5.2 for Poland compared with Lithuania and 5.3 for England and Wales compared with the Irish Free State to as high as 58.5 for Germany compared with Lithuania and 54.0 for Germany compared with Poland.

The results presented in Table 11 indicate little if any relationship between the degree of similarity of the time of arrival of immigrant groups in 1930 and the extent to which they were segregated from each other residentially. This is in sharp contrast with the results noted earlier with respect to the segregation of immigrant groups from native whites. The measures employed are somewhat different, i.e., the segregation of immigrant groups from the native whites was examined in terms of the ethnic groups' length of residence in the United States while differences in inter-ethnic segregation were considered in terms of their similarity or dissimilarity in their year-of-arrival distributions. Both investigations, however, are based on the assumption that length of residence affects the residential patterns of the groups. If groups have similar length of residence patterns, then it was expected that they would be similarly affected in their selection of residential locations.

This finding, particularly when contrasted with the earlier findings, poses an interesting and significant problem, namely, accounting for the differences in importance of length of residence in its effect on residential segregation. As we shall shortly see, year of arrival is related to the "old"-- "new" distinction between immigrant groups; and the problem is considered further in the examination of these differences.

The Distinction between "Old" and "New" Immigrant Groups

A classical if not somewhat battered distinction used in analyses

TABLE 11.--Linear regression and product moment correlation of inter-group segregation of the foreign born with similarity in their year of arrival, 1930.

City	x = Similarity in year of arrival y = Inter-group segregation of FBW		
(1)	a (2)	b (3)	r (4)
Boston	41.29	.45	.39
Buffalo	58.05	.01	.01
Chicago	47.39	.26	.31
Cincinnati	49.87	.08	.09
Cleveland	62.35	-.06	-.07
Columbus	55.93	.04	.06
Philadelphia	50.89	.23	.25
Pittsburgh	55.19	.08	.11
St. Louis	55.49	.00	.00
Syracuse	58.90	.08	.11

Note: a = y intercept
b = Regression slope of y on x
r = Product moment correlation coefficient

See Table 4 for abbreviations.

of immigrant groups and their descendents in the United States is that made between the "old" and "new" immigrants. This distinction, in one way or another, purports to divide immigrants into categories based on their geographical origins, time of greatest immigration, cultural dissimilarities with the native population, and alleged differences in the propensity to assimilate. The geographical distinction is the most clear-cut, with northern and western Europeans placed in the old immigrant category and immigrants from southern and eastern Europe in the new immigrant category. Carpenter, writing in the 'twenties, summarized the rationale for the distinction:

About the year 1880, immigrants from the various northern and western European countries, which had previously contributed

the overwhelming majority of this Nation's foreign white
stock, began giving place to migrants originating in eastern
and southern Europe and, latterly, in Asia Minor. Students
have attached great significance to this change, from the
"old immigration" to the "new immigration," as these groups
are generally termed, because of the difference in racial
type, cultural background, and personality traits which dis-
tinguishes--or is believed to distinguish--these two groups.
(Carpenter, 1927, p. 44.)

These behavioral differences based on geographical origins are, of
course, subject to empirical inquiry. The historian Handlin (1957,
Chapter 5) has been highly critical of the Immigration Commission of
1907 and their reports because of both empirical evidence and the Commission's prejudgment of the inherent inferiority of the new groups.
However, it should be noted that Handlin at times appears to be extreme
in his criticisms. Nevertheless, considering the close relationship between immigrant quotas and the old-new distinction, there is little doubt
that the question of old-new differences in behavior is far from ideolog-
ically neutral. Carpenter has examined the issue of differences in time
of arrival and concludes that although in general the geographical distinction holds,

Some northwestern European nationalities fall clearly within
the chronological limits ordinarily assigned the "new" immigration; such are France, Belgium, Luxemburg, and the Netherlands, as well as the Scandinavian countries, and, in some
degree, England. Contrariwise, certain of the central, southern, and eastern Europeans were coming here in large numbers during the years when the "old" immigration was in the
ascendancy. This, certainly, was the case with the Bohemians
and probably with the Poles, while a considerable number of
Italians can also claim enumeration as "old" immigrants. . .
There is, obviously, no such clear-cut distinction between the
"old" and "new" immigration as many students appear to believe. (Carpenter, 1927, p. 85.)

Gavit (1922, p. 197) has noted the shifting meaning of the terms
"old" and "new" in American history and points out that the migration
of the Irish starting in the 1830's and that of the Germans in the 1840's
were at the time viewed as the migration of "new" groups and were a
factor in the formation of the Know-Nothing and Native-American movements of the mid-nineteenth century. Part of Gavit's empirical criticism of the Immigration Commission's conclusions about old-new dif-

ferences is considered later in Chapter 5.

It is clearly important in one's use of the terms "old" and "new" to determine whether the reference is to individuals or to groups coming before or after the arbitrary dividing year of 1880. Distinctions based on the former criterion would increasingly include larger portions of immigrants coming from northern and western European countries the longer the time expired after 1880. On the other hand, the latter distinction would include immigrants coming from northern and western European countries after 1880 as still members of "old" ethnic groups. If there is any utility at all in this old-new distinction, it is necessary to indicate clearly the two sources of variation involved.

Consider, for example, the perhaps classical case of old-new differences in the propensity to farm. Since the new immigrants, using the geographical distinction, came predominantly after the great development and settlement of the nation's agricultural regions, they were not in a position comparable to that of the "old" immigrants coming during the mid-nineteenth century. If we look at immigrants living in urban places in 1930 in comparison with those living on farms or in rural-nonfarm areas, it is clear, as rows 1-4 of Table 12 indicate, that immigrants from all of the major geographic parts of Europe were living predominantly in cities. It is true, however, that immigrants from northwestern Europe and Germany were, on the average, less urban and more rural than immigrants from other sectors of Europe. But, even in 1930, the immigrant groups differed in their length of residence in the United States. Consequently, it is interesting to consider the urban-rural differences between geographical sections of Europe for those immigrants coming to the United States in specific years. To be sure this involves difficulties the further back one goes from 1930 since we cannot take into account the effect of differences between immigrant groups in their age distributions at their time of arrival or differential internal migration.

The best data in 1930 for analyzing differences between immigrants coming to the United States from different parts of Europe are those for the period between 1925 and 1930 (rows 5-8), since presumably the vast majority of persons immigrating during this period were still alive in

TABLE 12.--Urban-rural differences in location of immigrants, by geographical origin, 1930

Geographical origin and year of migration from Europe	Per cent living in:			
	Urban	Rural farm	Rural nonfarm	Total
All years				
Northwestern and Germany (1)	75.0	11.5	13.5	100.0
Eastern (2)	86.9	6.6	6.5	100.0
Southern (3)	87.5	3.1	9.4	100.0
Central, except Germany (4)	81.6	6.6	11.8	100.0
1925-1930				
Northwestern and Germany (5)	88.5	3.7	7.8	100.0
Eastern (6)	93.2	2.3	4.5	100.0
Southern (7)	90.9	1.3	7.8	100.0
Central, except Germany (8)	90.7	2.4	6.9	100.0
1901-10				
Northwestern and Germany (9)	75.1	11.8	13.1	100.0
Eastern (10)	86.9	7.0	6.1	100.0
Southern (11)	86.9	3.4	9.7	100.0
Central, except Germany (12)	80.6	6.8	12.6	100.0
1900 and earlier				
Northwestern and Germany(13)	69.6	15.0	15.4	100.0
Eastern (14)	81.8	10.1	8.1	100.0
Southern (15)	86.7	4.1	9.2	100.0
Central, except Germany (16)	77.1	10.6	12.3	100.0

1930. All of the immigrants are highly urban in location, and there is but a slight difference between those coming from "old" countries (northwestern Europe and Germany) and immigrants from other geographic subdivisions of Europe. In short, from a gross point of view, immigrants from "old" and "new" countries coming to the United States at a time well after the great settlement of agricultural areas of the country differ only slightly in their propensity to live in urban areas.

It is necessary to point out that different results were obtained when considering immigrants alive in 1930 who had migrated to the United States in 1900 or before as well as those migrating between 1901 and 1910. The results, shown in rows 13-16 and 9-12 of Table 12, indicate a sharper difference between northwestern European immigrants and others in their propensity to locate in urban as opposed to rural areas. It should be noted, however, that the central Europeans other than those from Germany (this includes Poland, Czechoslovakia, Austria, Hungary, and Yugoslavia) are not too different from the Northwestern Europeans. Further, we have difficulties created by the use of the open-ended category "1900 and earlier" since the groups may differ in how long before 1900 they came; and presumably this would be related to the proportion engaged in agriculture.

At any rate, the fact remains that immigrants in 1930 were primarily urban, irrespective of what geographic area of Europe they had come from. To be sure, there are wide variations between nationalities in a given geographic category. Nevertheless, we shall be careful to keep in mind the significance of distinguishing between year of arrival and European region when analyzing the differences between old and new immigrant groups. It is fairly clear that by 1950 the application of such a distinction on any basis of the differences between immigrant groups in the proportion arriving before or after 1880 is untenable. That is, by 1950, nearly all immigrants in the United States would have come after 1880. The regional distinction is used below.

The old-new distinction is still of considerable interest long after 1880. The reader will note in Table 13 that the old foreign-born groups in all cities are less segregated on the average from native whites than are the new immigrant groups. This relationship holds for all time periods in the cities investigated. Similar results were found in the differences between old and new second-generation groups in their segregation from native whites of native parentage (column 7 of Table 13). Since almost all immigrants by 1950 had arrived after 1880--exceptions

TABLE 13.--Mean indexes of residential segregation of ethnic groups, 1910-1950

City and groups (1)		FBW v. NW				FBW v. NWNP, 1930 (6)	NWFMP v. NWNP, 1930 (7)
		Wards		Tracts[a]			
		1910 (2)	1920 (3)	1930 (4)	1950 (5)		
Boston	Old	20.6	23.2	26.2	25.4	23.5	20.2
	New	53.3	45.8	54.6	49.6	60.0	58.6
	All	33.6	32.3	40.4	37.5	41.8	39.4
Buffalo	Old	28.4	27.9	30.0	28.4	27.6	20.7
	New	60.3	55.2	55.7	48.1	59.3	57.6
	All	41.2	38.8	42.8	38.2	43.4	39.2
Chicago	Old	32.6	29.8	27.7	27.8	23.7	18.8
	New	52.6	41.1	47.1	41.4	54.9	51.8
	All	40.6	34.3	39.4	35.9	42.4	38.6
Cincinnati	Old	22.4	21.5	28.4	28.7	29.5	21.7
	New	54.6	46.0	51.6	49.2	53.4	50.8
	All	38.5	33.8	41.0	39.9	42.5	37.6
Cleveland	Old	24.2	22.6	28.8	27.0	25.0	18.8
	New	52.2	43.1	51.8	45.7	58.4	58.4
	All	35.4	30.8	44.9	40.1	48.4	46.5
Columbus	Old	25.6	26.9	28.4	24.3	28.5	17.7
	New	52.7	50.6	57.2	46.3	58.5	52.2
	All	39.1	38.8	46.7	38.3	47.6	39.6

TABLE 13--Continued

City and groups (1)	FBW v. NW				FBW v. NWNP, 1930 (6)	NWFMP v. NWNP, 1930 (7)
	Wards		Tracts^a			
	1910 (2)	1920 (3)	1930 (4)	1950 (5)		
Philadelphia						
Old	21.6	21.1	29.3	28.4	27.2	20.0
New	57.8	47.7	52.9	48.0	58.7	56.9
All	39.7	34.4	44.3	40.8	47.3	43.5
Pittsburgh						
Old	23.5	20.9	25.1	24.1	24.8	20.3
New	51.0	47.9	52.7	46.6	57.0	55.2
All	37.3	34.4	42.6	38.4	45.3	42.5
St. Louis						
Old	21.3	21.8	26.1	27.6	26.4	19.2
New	57.2	46.5	61.9	43.4	51.0	48.7
All	35.7	31.7	48.8	37.6	42.0	38.0
Syracuse						
Old	28.4	23.6	33.2	27.2	34.9	24.2
New	55.6	50.9	59.2	48.9	61.1	57.9
All	36.5	31.8	47.6	39.3	49.4	42.9

Note: See Table 4 for abbreviations.

^aCommunity areas used for Chicago.

would be at least 70 years old--it is clear that the differences between old and new groups in their degree of residential segregation from native whites are due to something other than differences in their proportions arriving before 1880.

Although the pre- and post-1880 migration streams are completely irrelevant for distinguishing betwen the old and new immigrant groups by 1950 and probably barely relevant for some of the earlier time periods, it is nevertheless necessary to consider the hypothesis that their differential segregation from native whites is still to be explained in terms of differences in such factors as length of residence in the United States, degree of illiteracy, and educational achievement. That is, are the old-new differences in segregation consistent with the effects which immigrant opportunity and socio-economic position appear to have for the segregation of groups with respect to the native whites? Data given in Table 14, showing the unweighted means by city of these three indicators of status for the old and new immigrants separately, indicate that even in 1950 there would be reason to expect the old immigrant groups to be less segregated from native whites than the new immigrant groups.

In all cities, the unweighted mean indexes for the old foreign born indicate earlier year of arrival (column 6 and 7), greater literacy (columns 2 and 3), and higher educational attainment (columns 4 and 5) than those for the new immigrant groups studied in the same city. Thus in each city we would expect to find, on the basis of the differences between old and new groups reported in Table 14, the old foreign-born groups less segregated from native whites. Indeed for two of the variables, illiteracy and per cent with less than eight years of schooling, there is absolutely no overlap between old and new groups in each of the cities studied. Further, the unweighted means for these two variables are in all cases less than 1.0 for the new groups. This indicates that on the average the old foreign-born groups had rates less than that of the total foreign-born population and the new groups had rates higher than the immigrant population. Such results are in the direction expected on the basis of the earlier analyses of factors influencing segregation. Not only was there no overlap in each city between old and new

TABLE 14.--Unweighted means of selected socio-economic indicators of foreign-born status at their time of arrival and median year of arrival

City (1)	Per cent illiterate (A/E), 1930		Per cent with less than 8 years school (A/E), 1950		Median year of arrival, 1930	
	Old (2)	New (3)	Old (4)	New (5)	Old (6)	New (7)
Boston	.0878	1.8451	.5182	1.2847	1904.0	1909.6
Buffalo	.0728	1.2310	NA	NA	1906.4	1908.5
Chicago	.1254	1.6153	.4804	1.1014	1903.7	1908.6
Cincinnati	NA	NA	NA	NA	1901.9	1907.7
Cleveland	.2278	1.5570	.6916	1.3312	1903.8	1909.1
Columbus	NA	NA	NA	NA	1903.1	1909.7
Philadelphia	.0892	1.3009	.7389	1.3791	1904.6	1908.0
Pittsburgh	.1674	1.5922	.8586	1.4683	1902.0	1907.6
St. Louis	.1200	1.1684	NA	NA	1900.0	1905.3
Syracuse	NA	NA	NA	NA	1900.4	1908.3

Note: For a number of the old immigrant groups, the medians are earlier than 1900 and consequently old-new differences are understated. All medians earlier than 1900 were conservatively taken as 1900.

NA: Data not available.

groups but, further, there was no overlap in means for the old immigrants of any of the cities compared with the new means for any of these cities. For example, the highest mean actual/expected per cent illiterate for the old foreign born groups in the cities investigated in 1930, .2278 (column 2) in Cleveland, was considerably lower than the lowest comparable figure for the new groups, 1.1684 (column 3) in St. Louis.

The relationships between median year of arrival and segregation from native whites are similar, but there are some exceptions with respect to "overlap." That is, although the unweighted means indicate that the new foreign-born groups were more recent immigrants than the old in each city investigated, there are several old immigrant groups in some cities whose median years of arrival are more recent than some of the new groups in the same city. Further, there is not the same persistent difference in magnitude for all of the cities. Old immigrant groups in Buffalo, for example, are more recent immigrants than new immigrant groups in St. Louis.

The adequacy of such indicators for measuring socio-economic status differences between immigrant groups coming to the United States can not be fully determined. However, differences between European countries in illiteracy as well as differences between immigrants coming to the United States at specified times can at least be shown to be in the direction of the results reported above. Table 15, based largely on data for male army recruits in selected European countries in the last decade of the nineteenth century, clearly indicates not only a great range among European countries in the extent of illiteracy, but also shows that illiteracy was much higher in the eastern and southern European countries, that is, the countries sending the "new" immigrants.

Similarly, the proportions of immigrants coming to the United States in the fiscal year ending 1910 who were unable to read and write is much higher for the new immigrant groups (Table 16). In addition, with few exceptions, immigrants coming from the new countries brought less money with them than the old immigrants. The effect of the passage of literacy tests in 1917 on the ensuing differences between old

TABLE 15.--Illiteracy rates in selected European countries, circa 1890

Country	Number illiterate per 1,000 population	Year
German Empire	1.1	1896
Sweden and Norway	1.1	1893
Denmark	5.4	1891
Finland	16.0	1892
Switzerland	3.0	1897
Scotland	35.7	1893
Netherlands	40.0	1897
England	58.0	1893
France	49.0	1897
Belgium	128.0	1897
Ireland	170.0	1893
Austria	238.0	1895
Hungary	281.0	1894
Greece	300.0	1897
Italy	383.0	1895
Spain	681.0	1889
Portugal	790.0	1890
Russia	617.0	1894
Servia	860.0	1890
Roumania	890.0	1892

Source: Department of Commerce and Labor, Bureau of the Census, Illiteracy in the United States, Bulletin 26 (Washington: Government Printing Office, 1905), p. 9.   In most cases, data refer to male army recruits.

and new immigrant groups is illustrated by data for 1920 shown in columns 3 and 5. Although the proportions unable to read or write have declined radically, the old immigrants appear still to have, on the whole, proportionately fewer members unable to read or write than the new

TABLE 16.--Literacy and financial condition of selected immigrant
groups: 1910-1920

Origin	Per cent unable to read or write		Ratio of immigrants with less than $50 to those with more than $50 at arrival	
(1)	1910[a,b] (2)	1920[c,d] (3)	1910[a] (4)	1920[c] (5)
Bohemian and Moravian (Czech)	1.1	0.0	4.68	1.07
Croatian and Slovenian	33.5	4.7	22.92	1.00
Dalmatian, Bosnian and Herzegovinian	39.3	1.8	14.20	1.30
Dutch and Flemish	2.7	0.8	1.84	0.26
English	0.5	0.2	0.97	0.36
French	10.8	1.8	1.07	0.48
German	5.7	0.6	1.96	0.37
Greek	24.0	3.2	13.37	1.57
Hebrew	28.8	6.7	6.80	0.45
Irish	1.4	0.3	4.27	0.78
Italian (north)	7.2	1.7	5.24	0.62
Italian (south)	51.8	13.9	12.21	2.11
Lithuanian	50.0	4.2	21.07	0.18
Magyar	11.8	0.7	8.82	0.44
Polish	35.0	2.6	30.92	0.47
Roumanian	36.5	3.2	16.69	0.46
Russian	38.1	2.0	14.28	0.56
Scandinavian	0.1	0.1	5.91	0.44
Scottish	0.4	0.2	1.28	0.43
Slovak	21.3	2.9	16.63	1.55
Welsh	0.6	0.7	0.90	0.26

Sources: Annual Report of the Commissioner-General of Immigration, 1910 (Washington: Government Printing Office, 1910), Table VIII, pp. 20-21; U. S. Department of Labor, Bureau of Immigration, Annual Report of the Commissioner-General of Immigration, 1920 (Washington: Government Printing Office, 1920), Table VII, pp. 95-97.

[a]Fiscal year ending June 30, 1910.

[b]Persons 14 years of age and older.

[c]Fiscal year ending June 30, 1920.

[d]Persons 16 years of age and older.

immigrants. Similarly, although the proportions bringing less than fifty dollars with them appear to have declined between the fiscal years of 1910 and 1920, the old immigrant groups still seem to maintain some advantage over the new immigrants.

Thus these data, derived from other sources, seem to support the inference based on census data of socio-economic differences between old and new immigrants.

The European Origins of the Native White Population

The Scottish immigrants are a striking exception to these general associations involving the new and old dichotomy. Although they were not studied in all ten cities in 1930, consideration of their ranking with respect to median year of arrival in the cities in which they were included is most interesting. Out of ten immigrant groups in Boston and Buffalo, the Scottish had the ninth and tenth most recent median year of arrival respectively. Of the eleven immigrant groups investigated in the cities of Cincinnati, Columbus, Philadelphia, and Pittsburgh, they were respectively tenth, eighth, eleventh, and ninth in the length of residence of their population as measured by medians for 1930. Yet in the four cities above for which illiteracy was computed in 1930--Boston, Buffalo, Philadelphia, and Pittsburgh--the Scottish had the lowest actual proportion illiterate as measured against the proportion "expected." These two sets of ranks for the Scots are consistent with Brinley Thomas' examination of emigration from the British Isles to the United States in which he noted: "An interesting feature of Scottish emigration is its fairly substantial proportion of professional and entrepreneurial grades throughout the period; and after the turn of the century nearly a fifth of English emigration was of this class." (Thomas, 1954, p. 64.)

The unusual position of the Scots, i.e., high literacy but recent year of arrival, leads into a rather interesting problem. Presumably this is a group which formed a significant portion of the population of the United States long before the twentieth century. For example, according to the United States Census Bureau estimates of 1909 and the

American Council of Learned Societies estimates of 1932, the Scots
comprised about 7 to 8 per cent of the population of the United States
in 1790. (See Kiser, 1956, p. 308.) In looking at the residential patterns of the foreign-born groups in relation to the residential distribution of the native whites, the ethnic composition of the native-white
population has been essentially ignored. Since the native-white population includes all the American-born children of immigrants as well
as the further removed descendents of immigrant groups, we cannot
assume that the degree of segregation which foreign-born groups show
from native whites is independent of the composition of the native-white
population. To phrase the problem somewhat differently, if immigrants
from the so-called old European countries in part settled in the city by
following the residential patterns of native whites of the same origin,
then their degree of segregation from native whites would be a function
of the proportion of the native-white population that had the same origin as these immigrants as well as the extent to which the predecessors
from a given European country had dispersed residentially. In short,
the residential patterns of the immigrants can not be viewed as taking
place in a vacuum. Immigrants enter a city which already has a system of population and housing distributions.

For the 1910, 1920, and 1930 analyses of immigrant segregation
from native whites, we can consider the possible influence of the ethnic
composition of the native white population in an indirect--although a
significant--manner. For each spatial unit in the cities, the native
white population in each of the three censuses was classified into two
subcategories: those whose parents were foreign born (native white of
foreign or mixed parentage); and those who were the children of native
parents (native white of native parentage). If our hypothesis is correct,
then we would expect to find immigrants from old sources less segregated from the native whites of native parentage than immigrants from
new sources, i.e., immigrants from countries with relatively small
numbers of third or later generation natives in the United States population. Examination of Table 17 partially supports this contention. The
reader will note that, with the exception of St. Louis in 1930, the mean
index of segregation for the new immigrant groups is higher when com-

pared with the residential distributions of the native whites of native parentage (third generation or later) than with the total native white population. By contrast, in roughly half of the cases, the old foreign-born populations were less segregated from native whites of native parentage than from the total native white population. In Buffalo, for example, immigrants from old sources have lower segregation indexes in all three decades when compared with native whites of native parentage. By contrast, the new immigrants are even more segregated when compared with the native whites of native parentage.

Suggestive as these findings may be, they are nevertheless inconclusive in so far as they could be due to the fact that the old immigrants had a smaller proportion of the second generation in each city than did the new immigrant groups. Therefore, let us probe further into the influence of the ethnic origins of the native white population on the residential patterns of European immigrants.

Another means for getting at this problem is to consider old immigrants in comparable conditions, that is, to examine the situation faced by the old immigrant groups when they first arrived in the United States in sizable numbers during the mid-nineteenth century. One of the difficulties constantly encountered in this study is the lack of comparable data on the so-called "old" immigrant groups, that is, although the statistical information enabling us to determine the residential patterns of the immigrant groups goes back to 1910, it does not go back sufficiently far to determine the residential patterns of old immigrants during their early influxes into American city life. Boston is consequently of special interest since residential data going back as far as the mid-eighteen hundreds are available for this city. As might be expected, these data are not quite comparable with later census information utilized in the analyses of Boston's immigrants between 1910 and 1950.

Keeping in mind the question of what effects the composition of the native population would have on the degree of segregation of new immigrants as well as the rare opportunity to consider in quantitative terms the residential patterns of immigrant groups from northern and western Europe when they themselves were "new," the special censuses taken of Boston in the eighteen hundreds are of great value. Table 18 gives

TABLE 17.--Unweighted mean indexes of old and new foreign-born residential segregation

City		1910 FBW v.		1920 FBW v.		1930 FBW v.	
		NW	NWNP	NW	NWNP	NW	NWNP
Boston	Old	20.6	22.7	23.2	21.4	26.2	23.5
	New	53.3	58.6	45.8	50.3	54.6	60.0
Buffalo	Old	28.4	25.5	27.9	25.8	30.0	27.6
	New	60.3	65.7	55.2	59.8	55.7	59.3
Chicago	Old	32.6	35.2	29.8	28.7	27.7	23.7
	New	52.6	64.4	41.1	50.0	47.1	54.9
Cincinnati	Old	22.4	21.8	21.5	22.4	28.4	29.5
	New	54.6	55.9	46.0	47.3	51.6	53.4
Cleveland	Old	24.2	24.2	22.6	19.9	28.8	25.0
	New	52.2	58.3	43.1	48.7	51.8	58.4
Columbus	Old	25.6	26.3	26.9	27.4	28.4	28.5
	New	52.7	53.7	50.6	51.6	57.2	58.5
Philadelphia	Old	21.6	23.1	21.1	20.4	29.3	27.2
	New	57.8	62.5	47.7	52.6	52.9	58.7
Pittsburgh	Old	23.5	24.9	20.9	20.9	25.1	24.8
	New	51.0	56.5	47.9	52.0	52.7	57.0
St. Louis	Old	21.3	20.6	21.8	23.5	26.1	26.4
	New	57.2	58.8	46.5	47.9	61.9	51.0
Syracuse	Old	28.4	31.5	23.6	25.3	33.2	34.9
	New	55.6	60.4	50.9	55.4	59.2	61.1

Note: See Table 4 for abbreviations.

the residential segregation indexes for the native-white and colored populations as well as that for two of the more important immigrant groups in 1850 for the twelve wards of Boston. The great influx of immigrants from Ireland to Boston had begun in 1840, and by 1850 there were approximately 50,000 Irish born and their children in the city, comprising well over a third of the total population of 137,000. Roughly half of the 14,500 Irish working in Boston in 1850 were laborers. (See Handlin, 1959, p. 253.) The index of Irish segregation from native whites, 20.7, is rather high considering the small number of wards used. (See the discussion in Chapter 2 for the effect of the number of spatial units on the index of segregation.) The Germans, then number- ing roughly 2,500 persons, were even more segregated from the native population. The 2,000 colored, largely American-born Negroes, were the most segregated of the groups specified in the census.

Between 1850 and 1855, the Irish had a net increase of roughly 15,500, the German net increase was close to 2,000, the other foreign elements' net increase was close to 4,500, and the colored population barely changed in number--increasing only by 131. The segregation in- dexes based on the census conducted in Boston in 1855 (Table 18, below diagonal) show that all the immigrants increased in their segregation from the native-white population with the colored remaining constant. The Germans increased in their segregation from the Irish, the other foreign born, and the colored. By contrast, Irish segregation from the colored and foreign born other than the Germans remained fairly con- stant, as did the segregation between the colored and the other foreign born. Considering the small number of wards involved, the segregation indexes for the Irish and the Germans were fairly high. Handlin's (1959, p. 91) comment that there were no German districts similar to that of the Irish appears to be true only because of the smaller numbers of Germans. That is, the Germans were also rather highly segregated, although no district was probably formed because of their relatively small number. Presumably the rapid influx of recent immigrants from Europe accounts for the changes in segregation in such a short span of time as five years.

By 1880, Irish segregation from the native whites had declined con- siderably, particularly when we consider that Boston was then subdivided into 25 wards and therefore, if anything, there would be a tendency to get higher segregation indexes. German segregation from native whites also declined from 1850--although not as sharply. This is precisely in line with our expectation since presumably the descendents of Irish

TABLE 18.--Indexes of residential segregation between selected populations of Boston, 1850 and 1855 (1850, above diagonal; 1855, below diagonal)

Group	Group (see stub)				
	(1)	(2)	(3)	(4)	(5)
(1) Native white	. . .	20.7	31.0	20.5	51.2
(2) Ireland	26.0	. . .	36.1	20.2	64.6
(3) Germany	38.6	44.7	. . .	34.8	67.9
(4) Other foreign white	26.4	21.2	49.3	. . .	61.6
(5) Colored	51.2	64.9	73.1	61.7	. . .

Source: Josiah Curtis, Report of the Joint Special Committee on the Census of Boston, May, 1855 (Boston: Moore and Crosby, City Printers, 1856), pp. 7-8.

Note: Data on foreign population includes the children under 21 years of age of foreign parents. Washington Village, annexed to Boston, May 21, 1855, excluded in analyses above.

immigrants had already begun to comprise a sizable proportion of the native population. Irish and German segregation from each other also declined as did their segregation from the colored population. The Irish migration to Boston had already reached its peak and the immigrants from Italy had yet to arrive in sizable numbers. The 1,300 Italians in Boston in 1880 were, however, highly segregated from the native whites as well as the other ethnic and racial segments of the city's population investigated, except for the Russians and Poles. Thus the English, Scottish, Irish, and native white populations are all relatively similar in their residential distributions. The German, Norwegian, and Swedish groups were moderately segregated from the native white population and the vanguards of the Italian, Russian, and Polish waves were already highly segregated.

Given this background of ethnic residential patterns in Boston during the second half of the nineteenth century, what relevance does it

TABLE 19.--Indexes of residential segregation between selected populations of Boston, 1880

Group	(1)	(2)	(3)	(4)	(5)	(6)	(7)	(8)	(9)	(10)
(1) Native white										
(2) Colored	50.6									
(3) England	12.5	50.4								
(4) Scotland	11.8	50.7	6.9							
(5) Ireland	14.7	54.0	16.4	16.6						
(6) Germany	30.7	53.9	28.4	30.8	33.0					
(7) Norway	39.5	60.6	34.6	35.7	37.8	45.2				
(8) Poland	61.5	53.8	61.6	60.6	55.9	63.6	57.3			
(9) Russia	53.8	57.8	53.9	54.1	50.1	53.8	49.3	38.5		
(10) Sweden	26.8	50.2	23.0	25.2	28.7	31.9	26.6	55.0	43.8	
(11) Italy	73.8	79.1	74.4	74.1	68.7	77.9	65.7	48.0	34.4	65.4

Group (see stub)

have for our examination of ethnic groups in the twentieth century? It
is apparent that in many respects the "old" immigrants from at least
some of the northern and western European countries during the mid-
nineteenth century were perhaps no different from the "new" immigrants who came around the turn of the nineteenth century, in terms of
their propensity to form ethnic colonies, to live in the least desirable
sections of the city, to participate in the lower end of the occupational
structure of the city, and to arouse strong reactions against them on
the part of the native population. As Gavit (1922, p. 197) has described
the situation:

> Each phase of immigration has been "the new immigration" at
> its time; each has been viewed with alarm; each has been de-
> scribed as certain to deteriorate the physical quality of our peo-
> ple and destroy the standards of living and of citizenship.

Although far from conclusive, it is pertinent to compare Irish and
German segregation from the native-white population in a heavily Irish
city such as Boston with cities heavily settled by Germans such as Cincinnati and St. Louis. Using our segregation indexes for 1910, in Boston
the German foreign born had an index of 30.5 from the native whites
while the Irish had an index of 19.0 from the same native-white population. In the two cities where presumably the Germans comprised a
much larger segment of the native population, Cincinnati and St. Louis,
the Germans are less segregated from the native-white population than
are the Irish. In Cincinnati, the indexes are 17.9 and 28.2 and in St.
Louis the indexes are 18.3 and 22.7 for the German and Irish immigrants respectively in 1910.

Taking our cue from these Irish-German comparisons, let us attempt a systematic analysis of the effect of the ethnic composition of
cities on the variations in the degree of segregation for a given foreign-
born group. For the ten cities under study, the per cent of foreign born
in 1870 who were members of each of six groups was determined. The
results, shown in Table 20, indicate wide variations between groups in
their proportion of the total immigrant population. The Irish and German immigrant groups were the largest, Austrians and Italians the
smallest, and immigrants from England and Wales and Scotland occupied
intermediate positions. Additional groups are not considered, although

data were available, since their proportions of the total foreign-born populations of these cities are even smaller than those for the Austrians and Italians. Since the great waves of migration from eastern and southern Europe had not begun, these figures for 1870 are hardly surprising. The fluctuations between cities in the per cent a given foreign-born group is of the total immigrant population are, however, of considerable interest. For example, in 1870, the Irish immigrants comprised roughly 65 per cent of the foreign born living in Boston, but only 23 per cent of Buffalo's immigrant population. By contrast the Germans were less than 10 per cent of Boston's foreign born, but more than 60 per cent of Cincinnati's immigrants. England and Wales ranged from roughly 5 per cent of the foreign-born population in Cincinnati and St. Louis to more than double that percentage in Pittsburgh.

The correlations shown in Table 21 indicate that in cities where the foreign-born group was a relatively large proportion of the immigrant population in 1870, the immigrant members of the group were less segregated in 1910 from native whites than in cities where the group was a relatively small proportion of the total foreign-born in 1870. These correlations range from -.77 for the Irish to -.08 for the Italians in ten cities, and the direction of the correlation is negative for each of the six groups considered. To be sure, there are a number of vital factors that are not considered. For example, the proportion that all the foreign-born are of the city's total population as well as the ethnic composition of the native whites in 1870 should also be considered. But in so far as the foreign-born percentages reported earlier in Table 20 reflect to some extent the ethnic composition of the native whites in 1910, we may infer that the residential segregation of a foreign-born group from native whites varies between cities at least partially because of differences in the ethnic origins of the city's native white population.

The Old-New Distinction and Segregation Among Ethnic Groups

Similar differences between old and new immigrant groups are found in the inter-ethnic segregation patterns of each city. This is

TABLE 20.--Selected foreign-born groups as a percentage of the total
foreign born in a city, 1870

City	Per cent of city's immigrants born in:					
	Ireland	England & Wales	Scotland	Germany	Austria	Italy
Boston	65.2	6.4	2.0	6.4	0.1	0.3
Buffalo	22.7	9.0	2.6	48.1	0.3	0.1
Chicago	28.1	7.2	2.6	36.2	0.5	0.4
Cincinnati	23.9	4.6	1.0	62.1	0.7	0.5
Cleveland	26.3	11.8	1.7	40.9	5.6	0.1
Columbus	25.3	11.1	1.7	52.3	0.3	0.2
Philadelphia	54.4	10.8	2.1	27.6	0.3	0.3
Pittsburgh	48.5	12.5	2.1	31.3	0.4	0.3
St. Louis	28.6	5.0	1.1	52.6	0.7	0.7
Syracuse	37.7	9.6	1.0	36.2	0.3	0.1

Note: Persons born in Great Britain and Ireland given in combined number and not separately for Ireland, England and Wales, and
Scotland. Since the number of persons engaged in all classes of occupations in each city in 1870 are given separately for these three
ethnic groups, the occupational figures were used as weights for esti-
mating the proportion of the combined per cent of the foreign born
from Great Britain and Ireland that came from each of the three segments. These estimates are based on the crude assumption that the
same proportion of each group were engaged in occupations.

indicated in Table 22 by comparing rows 1 and 3 for each city. Without exception, in each of the census years investigated, the unweighted
mean index of residential segregation between the new immigrant groups
is higher than that between the old groups. The same results are obtained for the second generations of each city in 1930 (rows 1 and 3 of
column 5). The mean index of segregation between old and new groups
(row 2) are generally quite high and closer in magnitude to the segregation between the new groups (row 3) than the old immigrant groups
(row 1). In cities such as Cleveland, Columbus, and St. Louis the new

TABLE 21.--Correlations (Spearman) between segregation in 1910 and per cent of the immigrant population in the cities in 1870

Foreign-born group	Correlation
Ireland	-.77
England and Wales	-.28
Scotland	-.37
Germany	-.34
Austria	-.43
Italy	-.08

immigrant groups were consistently more segregated from the other new immigrant groups than they were from the old immigrants. In other cities there was no consistent pattern.

In short, the old-new distinction appears to be significantly related to the residential segregation of ethnic groups from one another. This is, of course, to be expected, given the fact that the old-new distinction is related to the segregation patterns between immigrants and the native-white population, if only because of the minimum-maximum segregation rule set out earlier. Thus if old immigrant groups are quite similar to the native whites in residential distribution, then they can not be too highly segregated from each other. By contrast, if two groups are highly dissimilar from the native-white population in their residential distributions, there is little or no limitation on how high their segregation from each other could be. However, it is true that two groups highly segregated from native whites could have a rather low minimum index of segregation between each other.

Housing Costs and Segregation: A Null Hypothesis

In endeavoring to understand the factors accounting for the residential patterns of ethnic groups, it is necessary to consider as an alterna-

TABLE 22.--Mean indexes of residential segregation between selected white ethnic groups

City	Comparison	Tracts[a]			Wards	
		FBW, 1950	FBW, 1930	NWFMP, 1930	FBW, 1920	FBW, 1910
(1)	(2)	(3)	(4)	(5)	(6)	(7)
Boston	Old v. Old (1)	28.5	29.8	23.9	27.2	27.0
	Old v. New (2)	55.0	61.2	59.5	52.5	56.7
	New v. New (3)	61.5	61.2	64.4	44.2	52.2
Buffalo	Old v. Old (1)	33.2	36.9	29.0	35.3	37.2
	Old v. New (2)	55.4	62.2	60.7	61.8	65.4
	New v. New (3)	62.3	70.4	71.6	64.4	64.8
Chicago	Old v. Old (1)	34.0	35.3	27.8	39.7	43.5
	Old v. New (2)	52.1	57.9	55.0	52.6	61.4
	New v. New (3)	53.3	55.8	55.3	47.7	51.2
Cincinnati	Old v. Old (1)	35.8	38.9	27.1	28.7	29.1
	Old v. New (2)	51.3	56.2	53.3	48.8	56.1
	New v. New (3)	51.0	53.9	51.1	52.8	57.4
Cleveland	Old v. Old (1)	30.3	35.5	27.3	27.9	31.9
	Old v. New (2)	53.9	59.8	59.9	50.8	58.3
	New v. New (3)	58.1	65.4	66.2	53.6	66.9
Columbus	Old v. Old (1)	36.3	41.1	24.7	37.9	34.9
	Old v. New (2)	49.7	59.2	52.9	50.9	52.3
	New v. New (3)	52.4	59.4	57.0	57.2	65.0

TABLE 22--Continued

City	Comparison	Tracts[a]			Wards	
		FBW, 1950	FBW, 1930	NWFMP, 1930	FBW, 1920	FBW, 1910
(1)	(2)	(3)	(4)	(5)	(6)	(7)
Philadelphia	Old v. Old (1) Old v. New (2) New v. New (3)	32.9 56.9 53.4	35.2 62.1 57.1	25.5 58.7 57.4	24.6 54.3 49.0	27.2 61.2 52.0
Pittsburgh	Old v. Old (1) Old v. New (2) New v. New (3)	32.0 53.4 54.8	33.3 58.7 62.5	26.8 56.8 62.2	28.1 54.0 52.6	32.2 56.1 60.8
St. Louis	Old v. Old (1) Old v. New (2) New v. New (3)	35.6 48.5 56.0	35.8 55.2 61.3	25.9 52.3 60.6	30.0 49.9 57.0	28.0 58.3 59.3
Syracuse	Old v. Old (1) Old v. New (2) New v. New (3)	39.6 56.5 57.0	47.9 63.5 65.5	37.0 60.4 63.6	31.7 55.3 65.3	38.5 56.3 47.7

Note: See Table 4 for abbreviations.

[a]Community areas used for Chicago.

tive hypothesis the effect that the different income levels of the immigrants and the native whites might have on their residential patterns. If housing of a given cost or value is not randomly distributed through a city and if the groups differ in their housing expenditures, then one would expect some segregation between the various ethnic groups and the native-white population irrespective of the factors investigated in this chapter. Consider, for example, the differences between families having Polish and English-born heads in Cleveland. The median value of their homes in 1930 was $6,576 and $7,088 respectively, and the median rental was, respectively $25.34 and $40.92 for families renting. Further, the ethnic groups differ in their propensity to own homes. Thus, in Cleveland, 37.1 per cent of the English families owned their own homes while 53.5 per cent of the Polish-born heads of families owned their homes in 1930. Since rented dwellings presumably are not spatially distributed in the same fashion as owned dwellings in a city, this would be an additional factor leading to segregation--even if the groups had the same median home values and rentals. (It has been necessary to use family data in this section because of the limitation of the available data to family units.)

In order to consider the effects which differences between groups in housing expenditures and tenure have on the residential patterns of immigrants, an indirect standardization procedure was used for examining the residential patterns in Cleveland in 1930. Owned homes were divided into the following value categories: under $1500; $1500-2999; $3000-4999; $5000-7499; $7500-9999; $10,000 and over; and value unknown. Rented homes were similarly classified by rent into the following categories: under $15; $15-29; $30-49; $50-99; $100 and over; and rent unknown. In addition, there was a category for cases where the tenure was unknown. Using data for the city of Cleveland, the proportion each ethnic group comprised of the population living in a given type of housing was computed. Thus, for example, the Polish-born heads of families comprised roughly 16 per cent of the families living in homes with rentals of under $15 per month, while families whose head was born in Great Britain and Northern Ireland account for somewhat less than 1 per cent of the families living in rented homes with such values. These rates were then applied to the value and rental distribution of residences in each tract of Cleveland to obtain the number of each ethnic group "expected" to reside in the particular tract. The expected residential distributions of all the groups were then compared with each other as well as with the actual distributions of these groups in Cleveland in 1930.

The results are summarized in Table 23, which shows the actual indexes of residential segregation of foreign-born, native, and Negro families above the diagonal. Indicated below the diagonal are the indexes expected on the basis of the differences in tenure and housing expenditures of these groups. It is readily apparent that the actual segregation is much greater than would be expected solely on the basis of differences in housing patterns. Secondly, when the data are plotted on a scatter diagram, it appears that there is no systematic co-variation of the magnitudes of the actual and expected residential segregation of the foreign-born groups from each other.

To be sure, the method used has certain shortcomings since the indirect standardization fails to take into account variations between groups in the quality of their housing. Since the immigrant groups vary considerably in the size of their families, two groups may pay the same rent for housing of different quality. If one makes the assumption that houses of a given cost but of different quality and size are not distributed similarly in the city, then this would mean that the analysis understates the "expected" segregation. Similarly, value of housing fails to take into account the number of dwelling units involved. Thus two groups could have the same distribution of housing in terms of value, but differ in terms of the degree to which they owned multiple dwelling units which were being partially rented but to other families. Finally, these results are based on housing expenditures rather than income.

Irrespective of these methodological difficulties which might understate the expected degree of segregation between immigrant groups, the sheer magnitude of the differences between actual and expected segregation clearly suggests that something much more significant than mere economic differences is operating to produce the degree of ethnic segregation found in Cleveland and, presumably, in the other cities under

TABLE 23.--Actual and expected indexes of residential segregation, foreign-born and native families, Cleveland, 1930 (Actual, above diagonal; expected, below diagonal)

Group	Group (see stub)						
	(1)	(2)	(3)	(4)	(5)	(6)	(7)
NWNP (1)	. . .	21.6	18.7	33.3	32.8	68.2	63.5
NWFMP (2)	7.3	. . .	24.0	35.3	22.8	56.9	48.8
Britain and No. Ireland (3)	5.8	3.1	. . .	30.8	35.5	65.9	63.4
Irish Free State (4)	12.3	5.7	6.9	. . .	41.3	69.3	67.2
Germany (5)	14.6	8.1	9.1	3.0	. . .	60.4	51.2
Poland (6)	19.0	11.8	14.2	9.1	8.3	. . .	61.0
Czechoslovakia (7)	19.8	12.7	14.6	8.5	6.5	4.0	. . .
Austria (8)	11.8	4.9	6.4	2.3	3.6	8.8	8.6
Hungary (9)	15.0	7.7	10.1	5.3	5.4	4.3	6.0
Yugoslavia (10)	20.4	13.6	16.2	11.5	10.8	3.0	5.9
Russia (11)	4.4	6.5	4.4	10.3	12.4	17.9	18.2
Lithuania (12)	12.6	5.5	7.7	3.3	4.6	7.7	8.1
Roumania (13)	14.2	7.1	9.6	5.5	6.0	5.0	6.9
Greece (14)	13.9	10.2	12.5	13.5	15.3	13.8	16.7
Italy (15)	13.9	7.0	9.5	5.7	6.6	6.1	8.0
Canada (16)	2.7	6.2	4.5	10.6	12.8	17.9	18.3
Other FBW (17)	10.0	3.3	6.0	5.4	7.5	9.4	10.8
Nonwhite (18)	24.0	19.2	22.0	19.5	20.3	14.2	17.8

Note: See Table 4 for abbreviations.

TABLE 23.--Continued

Group (see stub)										
(8)	(9)	(10)	(11)	(12)	(13)	(14)	(15)	(16)	(17)	(18)
41.0	59.8	68.2	65.8	60.0	50.0	54.7	64.6	12.6	26.4	85.6
31.8	53.7	66.2	61.9	57.4	43.4	53.7	60.8	26.6	22.4	86.8
39.6	60.0	67.8	61.7	56.8	51.7	57.9	64.1	19.8	28.1	86.7
47.8	60.0	69.7	66.7	61.0	46.5	61.0	68.3	32.7	31.4	88.8
33.7	54.7	65.8	65.2	57.3	43.0	56.0	66.3	36.5	27.7	87.9
56.9	75.2	74.0	66.4	59.2	67.0	62.9	74.5	69.5	60.5	90.0
51.0	52.3	73.4	70.7	75.3	50.5	68.2	63.6	66.9	56.4	88.1
. . .	53.7	60.6	51.2	50.5	43.4	56.3	59.9	42.0	35.3	83.8
5.0	. . .	78.0	72.3	75.4	38.1	72.7	71.8	60.6	51.6	86.5
11.3	6.5	. . .	80.8	57.7	70.1	70.9	72.7	67.7	66.1	91.5
9.9	13.8	20.0	. . .	57.0	65.8	73.0	64.5	65.4	61.3	85.0
2.5	3.6	9.9	10.8	. . .	63.5	65.2	70.6	58.8	55.5	89.7
4.9	1.4	6.8	13.3	3.6	. . .	64.2	65.8	50.9	41.2	88.4
12.7	11.4	13.3	15.3	11.8	10.5	. . .	69.9	55.5	48.6	80.7
5.6	2.8	7.0	13.3	4.4	2.8	9.7	. . .	66.5	61.3	76.2
10.2	13.8	19.8	2.7	11.2	13.2	14.7	13.2	. . .	27.7	86.0
4.5	5.5	10.8	9.6	4.2	4.6	8.7	4.2	9.3	. . .	83.0
19.0	15.0	12.2	25.0	17.5	14.5	11.0	14.1	24.7	16.3	. . .

TABLE 24.--Actual and expected residential segregation of foreign-
born families from selected native populations and degree
of dissimilarity of the group, Cleveland, 1930

Group (1)	Actual (y)			Expected (x)			Dissimilarity between actual and expected distribution (8)
	Non-white (2)	NW NP (3)	NWF MP (4)	Non-white (5)	NW NP (6)	NWF MP (7)	
Great Britain and Northern Ireland	87	19	24	22	6	3	25.5
Irish Free State	89	33	35	19	12	6	39.7
Germany	88	33	23	20	15	8	26.1
Poland	90	68	57	14	19	12	52.2
Czechoslovakia	88	64	49	18	20	13	42.1
Austria	84	41	32	19	12	5	29.0
Hungary	87	60	54	15	15	8	52.9
Yugoslavia	91	68	66	12	20	14	61.5
Russia	85	66	62	25	4	7	55.9
Lithuania	90	60	57	18	13	6	57.4
Rumania	88	50	43	15	14	7	43.0
Greece	81	55	54	11	14	10	45.7
Italy	76	65	61	14	14	7	53.1
Nonwhite							70.6
NWNP							21.4
NWFMP							14.1
Correlations, actual v. expected							
a	84	32	27				
b	.14	1.53	2.51				
r	.14	.45	.56				

Note: a = y intercept
b = Regression slope of y on x
r = Product moment correlation coefficient

investigation.

With respect to the segregation of foreign-born groups from non-whites, native whites of native parentage, and native whites of foreign or mixed parentage, the results are similar to that for inter-ethnic segregation. As might be expected, there is no relationship between the actual and expected segregation from nonwhites. (Data are not available for Negro families separately; however, almost all nonwhites in Cleveland in 1930 were Negro.) The product moment correlation for the actual and expected segregation indexes of thirteen immigrant groups from the nonwhites is .14, with the unweighted actual and expected mean indexes of segregation being 86 and 17 respectively. There is a moderate correlation between the actual and expected segregation of foreign-born groups from the two native-white components of the population. (See Table 24.) The unweighted mean indexes of actual segregation of these immigrant groups from the native components of the population, however, are far in excess of the degree of segregation expected on the basis of housing costs of these groups. In short, it appears that differences in housing costs fail to account for the inter-ethnic segregation in Cleveland, either in terms of magnitude or pattern of variation. Such is also the case with respect to ethnic segregation from nonwhites. However, although ethnic segregation from native whites appears to be mildly related to the differences in housing costs of the groups, the magnitude of the segregation of these ethnic groups from native whites again is hardly accounted for by differences in housing expenditures.

Still making use of the results obtained by the indirect standardization discussed above, we may approach the question of residential location of these groups from a somewhat different line of inquiry. Namely, to what extent does the actual location of each group resemble the residential distribution expected on the basis of their housing costs? The results, shown in column 8 of Table 24, indicate that the groups varied considerably in the extent to which they were actually distributed according to the pattern expected on the basis of their housing expenditures. We may note that the nonwhites have the greatest degree of displacement whereas the native whites of foreign or mixed parentage have the lowest degree of displacement.

Chapter 4

Further Analyses of Ethnic Segregation

In Chapter 3 considerable evidence was presented to indicate that the differential segregation of ethnic groups in the ten cities could be viewed largely as a function of such factors as length of residence in the United States, socio-economic status at their time of migration to the country, and ethnic composition of the native population of these cities. To be sure, a number of other approaches to the differential assimilation of ethnic groups are plausible and undoubtedly have merit. Presumably economic, cultural, and social-psychological differences between ethnic groups do operate to some extent in influencing the propensities of groups to assimilate. However, to say that many factors operate is, in one very important sense, to say nothing. Since the issue here is not to demonstrate that everything is related to everything else, but is to see how far one can go in dealing with ethnic differences in behavior by using a consistent approach, we are obliged to spell out what are the more significant factors or variables from the standpoint of this approach. In this chapter, we shall expand on the findings reported earlier and consider, as well, several alternative interpretations of these results.

Economic Factors and Segregation

We observed in the last section of Chapter 3 that although housing of a given quality or cost is not randomly distributed in a city, the fact that ethnic groups differ in their expenditures for housing largely fails to account for either the segregation between ethnic groups or that of ethnic groups with respect to the native whites. If, however, variations in segregation are at least partially indicative of the relative desirability of ethnic groups as neighbors or renters in an area, then we would expect to find segregation associated with variations in housing costs. To select an extreme case, that of the Negro, it is clear that since the group is relatively undesirable from the standpoint of most whites as either owners or renters, the Negro must often pay more than whites for housing of a given quality and, it is argued, it is sometimes easier for the Negro to purchase a home than to rent a dwelling in a predominantly white area. (See Duncan and Duncan, 1957, pp. 9, 234.) The problem therefore becomes rather complex for analysis. There are both economic effects and economic causes of segregation. That the causes are of rather limited significance is suggested by the Cleveland results in Chapter 3 which indicated that the segregation of ethnic groups from native whites or among themselves is largely due to non-economic factors. Yet such economic factors as family income do have some influence, although apparently a limited one, on the residential patterns of an ethnic group. Thus in examining economic correlates of residential segregation, we shall be confronted with the difficult task of separating the economic effects from the economic causes of segregation.

Turning again to the housing costs of ethnic groups, we shall consider the members of immigrant groups who rent dwellings separately from the home owners although the median rent of immigrant families in each city usually is correlated rather highly with the median value of the homes of immigrant families (Table 25, column 2). There is a persistent positive correlation between segregation from native whites and immigrant differences in median housing costs from that of the native whites. Thus the closer an immigrant group's rent is to that of the city's native-white population, the less segregated the total immigrant group is from the native population (Table 25, column 4) and, similarly, for the segment of the immigrant group owning their homes, the closer their median home value is to that of the home-owning native whites, the lower the segregation of the total immigrant group from the native-white population (Table 25, column 3). Ideally, we should like to consider the residential segregation patterns of the renters and home owners separately, but such data are not available.

Since most of the immigrant groups have lower median rents and home values than do the native whites of their city, it is possible that the correlations presented in columns 3 and 4 of Table 25 merely reflect an association between immigrant income--as measured by housing costs--and the propensity to segregate from native whites. Fortunately, some of the immigrant groups in these cities have higher median rents and values than that of the native populations of their cities. (The only exception is Syracuse where all eight of the immigrant family groups investigated have lower median rents than that of the native whites.) Thus we can rank the immigrant groups in terms of their housing costs, independent of their similarity to that of the native whites, and observe what these rankings of immigrant housing costs yield when correlated with segregation. These correlations are presented in columns 5 and 6 of Table 25 for median value and rents, respectively. With respect to rental cost, in all but one of the cities, the groups with low segregation from native whites tend, as expected, to pay higher rents than those groups more highly segregated from native whites (column 6). Since, as we have already observed, the rental ranks for foreign-born groups are fairly strongly associated with the groups' ranks for home owning members (Table 25, column 2), we would expect similar results when considering the relationship between segregation and median values for those owning homes. Thus the correlations between immigrant housing value and segregation shown in column 5 are of considerable interest since in three of the nine cities (Boston, Buffalo, and Cincinnati), there is, if anything, a positive association between the value of homes of immigrant groups and the magnitude of their segregation from native whites. (See note under Table 25 for ranking procedure).

In summary, there are two important findings to consider in the correlations presented in Table 25. First, the correlations with segregation from native whites are either higher or more often positive when immigrant costs are compared to native-white costs than when immigrant costs are merely ranked from high to low (compare columns 3

TABLE 25.--Correlations (Spearman) between residential segregation of immigrants and housing costs, 1930

City[a]	Median value v. median rent	Segregation of FBW v. NW and:			
		Similarity in value	Similarity in rent	Median value	Median value rent
(1)	(2)	(3)	(4)	(5)	(6)
Boston	.27	.14	.54	-.67	.20
Buffalo	.64	.12	.76	-.07	.58
Chicago	.95	.47	.62	.33	.54
Cincinnati	.74	.26	.55	-.64	-.32
Cleveland	.90	.62	.48	.20	.39
Philadelphia	.70	.18	.65	.16	.57
Pittsburgh	.84	.60	.66	.22	.45
St. Louis	.55	.55	.75	.05	.41
Syracuse	.69	.19	.57	.19	.57

Note: See Table 4 for abbreviations. Median value and median rent ranked from high to low. All other variables ranked from low to high. Groups with median home values given as $10,000 and over were computed as having medians of $10,000. In all but one case this gave the group the greatest foreign-born difference from the native white population, and thus there was no distortion of the results.

[a]Data not available for Columbus.

and 5; 4 and 6). Thus we can infer that immigrant similarity in housing costs to that of the native whites is associated with relatively less segregation from the native white population. Further, this relationship exists independently of the fact that most immigrant groups have lower housing costs than natives, i.e., such correlations are in part merely correlations between the housing costs of immigrants and segregation when the variables are ranked inversely. Secondly, we observe that similarity in rents is more highly associated with similarity to native-white residential patterns than similarity in housing values is with segregation (for each city, the correlation in column 4 is higher than in column 3).

These findings call for further analysis. We shall, for the moment, postpone consideration of the fact that correlations with group
segregation are higher for rented than for owned dwellings and turn to
the finding that low segregation and similarity of immigrant housing
costs to that of the native-white population are associated. We still
can not determine whether housing costs are merely a reflection of
differences between ethnic groups in income or whether the association is due to differences in costs which groups more highly segregated
must face. An examination of the relationship between ethnic income
and residential segregation offers hope of determining whether the association between housing costs and segregation can be viewed as
merely a reflection of differential incomes of immigrant groups. That
is, if ethnic groups that are similar to native whites in income are also relatively similar to native whites in residential location, then we
would have no reason not to interpret the association between similarity in housing costs and in residential patterns to that of the native
white population as merely a reflection of differences between groups
in their economic capacity to live in areas where native whites reside.
If, on the other hand, ethnic similarity to native white residential patterns is not a function of ethnic similarity in income, then housing
costs of ethnic groups can not be viewed as merely an intervening variable that reflects the association between income and residence.

Since we do not have the necessary income data for 1930, we must
use 1950 foreign-born income in the larger Standard Metropolitan Areas. The correlations involve the use of 1950 segregation data for five
of the central cities of these metropolitan areas and are shown in Table
26. The results--far from conclusive--do suggest that foreign born
similarity to native-white median income is, if anything, associated
with higher segregation from the native-white population. Since there
are only five cities investigated and because the correlations are neither particularly high nor consistent, no conclusions can be drawn on
the basis of the results obtained except that there appears to be no
strong relationship between income and segregation. To be sure, fail-
ure to take into account such factors as age, family size, and the fact

TABLE   26.--Correlations (Spearman) between residential segregation and median income of foreign-born males, 25 years
old and over, 1950

City	Number of groups	Correlation
Boston	7	.43
Chicago	9	-.38
Cleveland	8	.40
Philadelphia	7	.42
Pittsburgh	8	.29

that the segregation data are based on the political city whereas the income data are drawn from a SMA sample, would no doubt be relevant
for further analysis. However, with the exception of the metropolitan
area matter, it is worth noting that these factors were not taken into
account when the correlations between residence and rent were computed. Therefore we can suggest that for the housing cost problem at
hand the correlations between housing cost and segregation are not
merely a reflection of economic differences between ethnic groups in
their ability to match the housing expenditures of the native-white population. A similar problem is encountered when segregation and occupational similarities between immigrant groups and the native-white
population are considered. (These results are reported in Chapter 6.) In
short, it appears that the association between housing costs and residence
for immigrant groups compared with native whites is due to the differential competitive ability of ethnic groups. Since the residential patterns in
1950 are highly correlated with those in 1930, the use of housing cost data
in 1930 with segregation data for that year and the use of income and segregation data for 1950 does not pose as much of a handicap as might otherwise be the case as long as we assume there were no major shifts in the
income ranks of the ethnic groups between 1930 and 1950.

Turning now to the question posed by the finding that similarity in
rent is more closely associated with similarity in residence than is
ethnic-native white similarity in values of homes, several interpreta-

tions are possible. One, merely methodological in nature, concerns the fact that while segregation was measured on the basis of the total group involved--irrespective of whether they owned or rented their homes--the correlations between housing costs are based on only parts of the total group. Thus, to use an extreme case, if only 1 per cent of each group owned homes, then we would of course expect a greater deviation in the home value-segregation correlation than the rent-segregation correlation. Ideally, if we could combine both home values and rental costs to compute a total housing cost measure for each group, then this would be the most reasonable measure to be examined in terms of segregation. Since we cannot equate very readily a given rental value with housing value, such a procedure has been omitted. No further analysis is offered for these findings.

Segregation and Home Ownership

In first analyzing the relationship between home ownership and segregation for Chicago, it was assumed that segregation and home ownership would be inversely related, that is, a group highly segregated from native whites would have a relatively small proportion of its members owning homes. This expectation was based on the assumption that home ownership is an indication of an immigrant's commitment to remain in the United States and, further, that home ownership is directly associated with socio-economic level and that, in turn, socio-economic level is inversely related to segregation. Further, the more highly segregated groups were those living closer to the center of the city and therefore in neighborhoods where a relatively small proportion of the housing was owner-occupied. The findings for Chicago were rather surprising. The Spearman rank order correlation between the segregation of foreign-born groups in 1930 from native whites and the proportion of these groups owning homes (using 1940 data) indicated an inverse relationship between these variables (Duncan and Lieberson, 1959, p. 372). Although the correlation was not significantly different from zero, it was in the opposite direction to that expected. Whether indeed immigrant groups differ in their propensity to own homes is a matter to be considered shortly. However, Duncan and Lieberson (1959) noted that the foreign born generally had higher home-ownership rates than the second generation who, in turn, had larger proportions owning homes than did the native whites of native parentage. In addition to Chicago, such differences between first, second, and later generations were observed for Detroit, Los Angeles, and Philadelphia in 1930, although they did not occur in New York City.

If immigrants in general have greater propensities to own their homes and if one assumes that home ownership as contrasted to home rental is a deterrent to residential mobility, that is, that home owners are less mobile spatially than renters, can it be that the patterns of eth- nic segregation are largely due to differences between immigrant groups in their degree of home ownership? Such a finding would fit in neatly with an approach to ethnic segregation giving emphasis to the cultural differences between immigrant groups. If immigrant cultures differed in the value placed on home ownership and if home ownership was then related to the propensity to segregate, then the key factor in the differ- ential segregation of ethnic groups could be cultural in nature.

Using data available for 1930, the degree of home ownership of each immigrant group was examined in relationship to its residential segregation from the native-white population for each of the ten cities under consideration. The results, presented in Table 27, indicate that, if anything, groups with low home ownership tend to be more highly segregated than groups with high home ownership, and the Chicago re- sults are seen to constitute an exception. However, since these corre- lations are neither significant in themselves nor persistently in one di- rection (Chicago and Philadelphia have low positive correlations), it would appear unlikely from a static cross-sectional point of view that the variations between immigrant groups in their degree of home owner- ship account for differences in segregation from native whites.

Further, we may observe that ownership of homes is negatively rather than positively related, in an aggregate sense, to variations be- tween groups in their housing costs. Groups with high proportions of home owners are also groups that tend to have lower median home val- ues and lower median rents (Table 28, columns 2 and 3, respectively)

TABLE 27.--Correlations (Spearman) between per cent of foreign-born families owning homes and their residential segregation, 1930

City[a]	Correlation
Boston	-.10
Buffalo	-.18
Chicago	.31
Cincinnati	-.05
Cleveland	-.28
Philadelphia	.04
Pittsburgh	-.41
St. Louis	-.40
Syracuse	-.05

[a]Data not available for Columbus.

than groups with smaller proportions owning their homes. Since the rental and home value ranks are fairly highly correlated (column 4), that is, groups with high median rents are also groups with high median home values, it was of interest to consider whether the relationship between high home ownership and low home values exists independently of the propensity for immigrant groups with high proportions owning homes to spend less money even for their rented dwellings. The partial tau correlations between home ownership and median value of homes owned (Table 28, column 5) indicate that the negative relationship exists independently of the fact that groups with high home ownership also spend less on rented dwellings. Thus we must reject any notion that home ownership for the foreign born is an indication of higher socio-economic status. Further, we may conclude that although ethnic groups differ in their propensities to own homes, such differences--whether cultural or not--fail to account for their differential residential segregation.

TABLE 28.--<u>Tau</u> correlations between home ownership, home value, and rental costs of foreign-born families, 1930

City[a]	Tau			Partial <u>tau</u>
	Per cent owning homes and:		Median value v. median rent	Per cent owning homes and median value (holding rent constant)
	Median value	Median rent		
(1)	(2)	(3)	(4)	(5)
Boston	-.07	-.16	.20	-.04
Buffalo	-.42	-.20	.51	-.38
Chicago	-.40	-.44	.87	-.04
Cincinnati	-.13	.00	.58	-.16
Cleveland	-.51	-.33	.73	-.42
Philadelphia	-.42	-.27	.56	-.34
Pittsburgh	-.24	-.13	.67	-.20
St. Louis	-.05	-.20	.42	.03
Syracuse	-.43	-.07	.50	-.45

Note: All variables ranked from high to low.

[a]Data not available for Columbus.

Centralization

One of the approaches most frequently utilized by human ecologists and others in the study of immigrant residential patterns in American cities stems from the work of Burgess (1928) and Cressey (1938) on the settlement of new immigrant groups near the center of Chicago followed by their dispersion outward from these slums as newer groups succeed the older immigrants and their children. Wirth describes the Jewish ghetto of Chicago as but one phase in a long history of immigrant settlements in the area:

> The near West Side has been the stamping-ground of virtually every immigrant group that has come to Chicago. The occupation of this area by the Jews is, it seems, merely a passing phase of a long process of succession in which one population group has been

crowded out by another. There seems to be more regularity in this process, however, than at first sight appears. . . .

In the course of the extension of the Jewish settlement they encountered the Irish and the Germans. As these groups moved on, the Jews followed, only to be succeeded by the Italians, the Poles and Lithuanians, the Greeks and Turks, and finally by the Negroes. Such observations as have been made in other large American cities, notably New York and Philadelphia, indicate that a similar order of succession is to be seen there. This phenomenon seems to be due, not merely to the chronological order of immigration of these various groups, but also to the relation of the standards of living of the various nationalities to one another, and to the attraction and tolerance of the successor by the predecessor. (Wirth, 1928, pp. 226-28.)

This process of initial immigrant settlement in toward the center of the city followed by dispersion outward has been well documented for Chicago, with Ford (1950) and Duncan and Lieberson (1959) following up the earlier work of Cressey and Burgess with improved methods and more recent data. We are in a position here to examine the extent to which this process of outward movement from the center of the city is found in other cities besides Chicago. Unlike the earlier examinations of residential segregation in general, which spanned the period between 1910 and 1950, this analysis of ethnic centralization is limited to 1930 and 1950. Methodological limitations, in particular the lack of information about the location of the wards with respect to the center of the cities in 1910 and 1920, necessitated this somewhat abbreviated examination of centralization.

Examination of the decentralization of ethnic groups poses certain interpretive problems. First, it is based on a general assumption about the concentric distribution of dwellings of varying quality in a city. That is, if Burgess' model of a positive association between quality of residential community and distance from the central business district fails to fit the facts about a given city, then to that extent we must re-evaluate our findings. For example, if the better residential areas tend to be centralized in a particular city, as Collison and Mogey (1959) report is the case for Oxford, England, or if dwellings are randomly distributed in a given city with respect to their quality, then we could not interpret the process and status of centralization in the same manner as when a city's housing fits into the Burgess model of quality and desirability increasing with greater distance from the central district. The residential pattern of the Dutch in Chicago illustrates another caution necessary in dealing with the analysis of ethnic centralization.   Duncan and Lieberson (1959) noted that the highly decentralized position of the Dutch in Chicago is not due to a process of dispersion from the center of Chicago. Rather it is accounted for by their agricultural settlement in an outlying area before it became one of the built-up residential areas of the city. As a consequence, the decentralized position of the Dutch in Chicago is due to the expansion of the city rather than to a peculiarly rapid decentralization of the immigrants.

All of this points to the fact that it is not the symmetry of concentric zones that concerns us, but rather that centralization is a device for summarizing the form or pattern of residential segregation, albeit one of many possible patterns. If housing in a given city is adequately described by Burgess' characterization of increasing socio-economic status associated with increasing distance from the center of a city, then we can infer the relative positions of ethnic groups by considering their centralization in such a city. It is therefore well to consider the existence of such a socio-economic gradient in each of the ten cities under investigation before turning to the residential patterns of ethnic groups. A rather crude method was utilized, to wit, the decentralization or centralization of the employed professional, technical, and kindred males in each city was compared to that of all employed males. As Table 29 indicates, in each city the professional males were relatively decentralized when compared with all employed males in their city.   The reader will recall that the centralization index used in this study ranges from -1.00 (maximum decentralization) to + 1.00 (maximum centralization).   Since the professional males comprise an appreciable proportion of the total employed males in each city, the figures shown in Table 29 actually understate the decentralization of professionals compared to other employed males.   In any case, the socio-economic gradient suggested by these results supports an approach to the ethnic residential patterns in each city in terms of their centralization or decentralization.

TABLE 29.--Index of centralization of males in professional, technical, and kindred occupations with respect to all employed males, 1950

City	Index
Boston	-.089
Buffalo	-.136
Chicago	-.150
Cincinnati	-.227
Cleveland	-.157
Columbus	-.271
Philadelphia	-.171
Pittsburgh	-.176
St. Louis	-.224
Syracuse	-.163

The process of decentralization noted for Chicago appears to hold up fairly well for the remaining nine cities. In general, foreign-born groups in 1950 are less centralized than in 1930 when compared to the positions of the native white in the respective years (Table 30, columns 3 and 2). Similarly, the second generation in 1930 is less centralized than the first generation in the same year when the groups are compared with native whites of native parentage (Table 30, columns 5 and 4). With the exceptions of St. Louis and Cincinnati, the foreign born are somewhat more centralized when compared with native whites of native parentage (column 4) than when compared with the total native-white population (column 2). This is no doubt due to the fact that second generation whites are more centralized than whites of the third generation or later.

The exceptions found in Cincinnati and St. Louis are possibly due to the fact that descendents of German immigrants account for rather large proportions of both cities' second generation in 1930, 59 and 47 per cent respectively, and these groups were only slightly decentralized in com-

TABLE 30.--Mean indexes of centralization of foreign-white groups, 1930 and 1950

City	FBW v. NW		FBW v. NWNP, 1930	NWFMP v. NWNP, 1930
	1930	1950		
(1)	(2)	(3)	(4)	(5)
Boston	.04	-.02	.06	.00
Buffalo	.07	-.02	.12	.08
Chicago	.13	.06	.20	.13
Cincinnati	.10	NA	.10	.05
Cleveland	-.02	-.04	-.01	-.03
Columbus	.24	.15	.27	.20
Philadelphia	.12	.06	.19	.15
Pittsburgh	.09	.02	.13	.11
St. Louis	.07	-.05	.06	.04
Syracuse	.14	.06	.15	.13

Note: See Table 4 for abbreviations.
NA: Data not available.

parison with native whites of native parentage (-.02 and -.03, respectively). Consequently removal of the second generation from other native whites in these cities had relatively little effect on the centralization indexes for the foreign born in 1930. While this explains the methodological aspects of the finding, it of course leaves for further inquiry the propensity of second-generation Germans to be so similar to that of the native whites of third or later generations in their cities. Such a finding can be reasonably interpreted, however, if we keep in mind the ethnic composition of these native whites of native parentage. In the two cities involved, presumably Americans of German origin comprise major portions of the native white of native parentage population. Thus, just as in the case of ethnic segregation, if the second generation Germans merely follow the locational patterns of Americans of German ancestry, then we would expect a fairly close approximation to the centralization position of native whites of native parentage in these cities

TABLE 31.--Mean indexes of centralization of old and new foreign-
white groups, 1930 and 1950

City	Group	FBW y. NW		FBW y. NWNP, 1930	NWFMP y. NWNP, 1930
		1930	1950		
(1)	(2)	(3)	(4)	(5)	(6)
Boston	Old	-.06	-.10	-.05	-.13
	New	.15	.06	.17	.12
Buffalo	Old	.02	-.03	.07	.02
	New	.12	-.01	.17	.14
Chicago	Old	-.03	-.06	.04	-.05
	New	.23	.14	.30	.26
Cincinnati	Old	.01	NA	.02	-.01
	New	.18	NA	.18	.11
Cleveland	Old	.04	-.03	.05	.01
	New	-.05	-.05	-.04	-.05
Columbus	Old	.10	.01	.12	.07
	New	.33	.23	.35	.27
Philadelphia	Old	-.09	-.11	-.02	-.04
	New	.25	.16	.32	.26
Pittsburgh	Old	-.05	-.07	-.01	.00
	New	.17	.07	.21	.17
St. Louis	Old	-.03	-.11	-.04	-.07
	New	.13	-.02	.12	.10
Syracuse	Old	-.01	-.08	.00	.00
	New	.27	.18	.27	.24

Note: See Table 4 for abbreviations.
NA: Data not available.

where Germans are so predominant.

Given this decentralization of ethnic groups through time, i.e., the
immigrant groups are more decentralized in 1950 than in 1930 when
compared to the native whites in the respective years and the second

generation is less centralized than the first in 1930, we may look at variations between ethnic groups in their propensities to centralize in location. With the exception of Cleveland, new ethnic groups are more centralized than old groups in both 1930 and 1950 and for both first and second generations in 1930. (See Table 31.) By "old" and "new" is meant
the distinctions based on geographic location in Europe, that is, "old"
refers to northern and western Europe and "new" refers to southern and
eastern Europe.

Since the data in Table 31 refer to unweighted mean indexes of centralization, it does not, of course, follow that every old ethnic group is
less centralized than every new ethnic group. Turning to the degree of
centralization for specific groups and considering the extent to which
the groups systematically vary in their length of residence in the country, we observe relationships in eight of the ten cities that are similar
to the association between length of residence and segregation observed
in Chapter 3. With the exceptions of Buffalo and Cleveland, groups with
recent median years of arrival tend to be more centralized than groups
with longer median years of residence in the United States (Table 32).

TABLE 32.--Correlations (Spearman) between centralization of foreign-
born groups and their median year of arrival, 1930

City	Correlation
Boston	.54
Buffalo	-.32
Chicago	.75
Cincinnati	.29
Cleveland	-.43
Columbus	.24
Philadelphia	.38
Pittsburgh	.09
St. Louis	.47
Syracuse	.71

Note: Centralization computed against native-white population,
1930. Centralization ranked from most decentralized to most centralized, and year of arrival ranked from oldest to most recent.

TABLE 33.--Linear regression and product moment correlation between inter-group zonal segregation of the foreign born
and similarity in their year of arrival, 1930

City (1)	x = Similarity in year of arrival y = Inter-group zonal segregation of foreign born		
	a (2)	b (3)	r (4)
Boston	25.09	.21	.22
Buffalo	36.79	-.14	-.11
Chicago	22.95	.22	.27
Cincinnati	30.04	-.01	-.01
Cleveland	31.27	-.10	-.12
Columbus	31.35	.03	.07
Philadelphia	17.93	.29	.48
Pittsburgh	27.16	.02	.03
St. Louis	29.34	.07	.10
Syracuse	17.77	.26	.44

Note: a = y intercept
b = Regression slope of y on x
r = Product moment correlation between y and x

Just as similarity in length of residence failed to account for very
much of the variations between immigrant groups in their segregation
from one another, so does similarity in year of arrival fail to account
for the zonal segregation between immigrant groups. The low correlations between inter-zonal immigrant segregation and similarity in the
year of arrival distribution of the 1930 foreign-born populations, Table
33, indicate that not only do groups tend to segregate on a tract basis
from one another independently of their similarity or dissimilarity in
years of arrival in the United States, but they also segregate from each
other on a broader zonal basis independently of their similarity in years
of arrival.

Centralization and Suburbanization

Before considering the relationship between centralization within the central city and suburbanization, it is worth summarizing the findings reported above. We have observed that examination of the centralization or decentralization of ethnic groups in a city is meaningful in so far as the city's residential pattern is such that there is a socio-economic gradient with distance from the central business district. In each city, a crude measure of this gradient was used--the proportion of males in professional and allied occupations--and it was found that this proportion increased on the average with distance from the center of the city. Thus the Burgess model seems to hold for the cities under consideration. Given this socio-economic gradient, the hypothesized pattern of gradual immigrant movement outward from the center of the city was considered. The results largely supported the hypothesis. That is, in 1930 the second generation tended to be less centralized in residence than the first generation. In addition, the foreign born in 1950 were less centralized than the foreign born in 1930 when both groups were compared with the native white populations for their respective years. Further, the old-new differences held for the most part; new groups were more centralized than old groups in each city. Finally, in eight of the ten cities there was some association between length of residence and the degree of decentralization, that is, groups with more years of residence in the United States tended to be more decentralized than the relatively recent immigrants.

Given these general patterns with respect to centralization within the central city of the metropolitan area, that is, the major urban center, we would expect a group's centralization to be closely related to the proportion of its total metropolitan population that resides in the central city. If the suburbs are crudely considered as the outermost ring or zone, then we would expect those groups showing centralized residential patterns within the city to have relatively fewer members residing in the suburbs than a group whose members select residences near the periphery of the central city. That is, viewing suburbs as merely continuations of the gradients in living patterns found as one moves from the center of the city outward implies that the proportions of various groups residing in these suburbs would be associated with the centralization of the groups within the main political city of the metropolitan area. The term "suburbs" is used herein to refer to all communities in the ring of the Standard Metropolitan Area, i.e., all communities in a metropolitan area except the central city. It is not used to denote a particular style of life or socio-economic level of a community's population.

The procedure utilized in studying the suburbanization of selected ethnic groups involves determining the number of foreign born living in the Standard Metropolitan Area of each of the ten cities under study. Then the per cent of this total number who reside in the central city was computed for 1950. Again using the foreign-born population in the Standard Metropolitan Area as the base, the proportion in 1950 of each group living in the urbanized area was also computed. Although the Standard Metropolitan Area concept was first introduced in the federal census for 1950, it was possible to reconstruct these metropolitan areas for 1930 for all cities but Boston where the Standard Metropolitan Area includes segments of counties. In 1930, the proportions of both the first and second generations residing in the central city were computed since data for the second generation groups were also available for 1930.

The results, indicating the unweighted mean per cent of ethnic groups living in the central areas as well as the per cent of native white living in these areas, are shown in Table 34. First, we may note that no inferences can be made about differences between cities in the percentage of a given group residing in the central city--at least without additional analysis. For example, the fact that less than 60 per cent of the native whites in Cincinnati lived in the central city in 1930 whereas close to 80 per cent of the same group resided in the central city of the Columbus metropolitan area (column 3) could merely be a reflection of the arbitrary nature of the political and social delineations involved. That is, metropolitan areas vary in the proportions of their total population residing in the central city. However comparisons between segments of the population of a given metropolitan area are reasonable. Without exception, the proportion of each metropolitan area's native-

TABLE 34.--Unweighted mean per cent of foreign-white stock and native-white population in standard metropolitan areas who reside in the central city or urbanized area, 1930 and 1950

Standard metropolitan area (SMA)	Group	Mean per cent		In urbanized area of SMA
		In central city of SMA		
		1930	1950	1950
(1)	(2)	(3)	(4)	(5)
Boston	FBW	NA	40.4	95.8
	NWFMP	NA	NA	NA
	NW	NA	31.8	93.8
Buffalo	FBW	69.1	60.4	77.7
	NWFMP	67.7	NA	NA
	NW	62.3	51.5	72.6
Chicago	FBW	80.0	75.8	93.7
	NWFMP	76.7	NA	NA
	NW	69.2	61.8	87.8
Cincinnati	FBW	77.2	73.4	94.4
	NWFMP	72.6	NA	NA
	NW	56.7	51.9	88.8
Cleveland	FBW	82.0	69.9	96.5
	NWFMP	78.4	NA	NA
	NW	67.7	56.4	93.5
Columbus	FBW	89.6	81.7	94.1
	NWFMP	87.6	NA	NA
	NW	78.8	72.6	85.6
Philadelphia	FBW	75.2	69.8	86.5
	NWFMP	72.4	NA	NA
	NW	58.1	51.2	77.0
Pittsburgh	FBW	36.4	34.6	74.0
	NWFMP	35.7	NA	NA
	NW	31.9	28.3	67.8
St. Louis	FBW	68.2	59.2	89.3
	NWFMP	65.0	NA	NA
	NW	57.9	47.4	81.1

TABLE 34--Continued

Standard metropolitan area (SMA)	Group	Mean per cent		In urbanized area of SMA
		In central city of SMA		
(1)	(2)	1930 (3)	1950 (4)	1950 (5)
Syracuse	FBW	77.5	72.2	83.9
	NWFMP	75.8	NA	NA
	NW	70.6	63.2	76.6

Note: See Table 4 for abbreviations.
NA: Data not available.

white population living in the central city is less than the proportion of the foreign born living in the central city. This holds for 1930 (column 3) and 1950 (column 4) and for the proportions living in the urbanized area in 1950 (column 5). In each case the foreign born, as measured by the groups selected for analysis, are less likely to live in the suburbs of the metropolitan area than are the native whites. Analysis of the second generation is possible only for 1930, but the results are also consistent. First, in each city a smaller per cent of the second generation than of the first generation are located in the central city (column 3). Secondly, in each community examined, the proportion of the total native-white population living in the central city is even lower than that for the second generation. Since the second generation is one segment of the total native-white population (the other being native whites of native parentage) we can conclude with a fair degree of certainty that the native whites of native parentage, i.e., persons whose parents were also born in the United States, are even less prone to live in the central city than are native whites whose parents are foreign born, i.e., the second generation. Finally, we may observe that the proportion living in the central city goes down between 1930 and 1950 for both the foreign born and the native-white population.

The suburbanization of ethnic groups classified into the old and new distinction is largely consistent with the pattern noted above. The new immigrants and their children have a larger proportion living in the central city than do the old immigrants or their children. Pittsburgh provides the major exception to these generalizations, and we shall consider this city later. Ignoring Pittsburgh for the moment, we may observe that in all other cases the proportion in the central city is higher for the new immigrants (Table 35). This applies to the foreign born in both 1930 and 1950 (columns 3 and 5, respectively), the second generation in 1930 (column 4), and to the foreign born in 1950 when the proportion living in the urbanized area is considered (column 6). The cross-sectional differences between the foreign born and second generation in 1930 as well as the shifts for the foreign born between 1930 and 1950 form fairly consistent indications of a decline in the segment of each ethnic group residing in the central city of each metropolitan area. Lower per cents living in the central city are found for all second generation groups in 1930 when compared with the foreign born in that year--with the sole exception of old ethnics in Pittsburgh where there is a minor increase.

If we were to view the central city as an inner ring and all of the other political units of each metropolitan area as an outer ring, then we have in a sense observed in the results shown in Tables 34 and 35 a process of metropolitan decentralization similar to that found in the earlier analysis of decentralization within the ten political cities. In both cases, not only where there general tendencies for the groups to move outward, but the total native-white population exceeded the second generation who, in turn, exceeded the first generation in the proportions living in the areas more distant from the central business district. Similarly, the old ethnic groups showed greater distance from the central business district than did the new ethnic groups in both situations, that is, for both the within-city analysis and the central city

TABLE 35.--Unweighted mean per cent of old and new foreign-white stock in standard metropolitan areas who reside in the central city or urbanized area, 1930 and 1950

Standard metropolitan area (SMA) (1)	Group (2)	Mean per cent			
		In central city of SMA			In urbanized area of SMA
		FBW, 1930 (3)	NWFMP, 1930 (4)	FBW, 1950 (5)	FBW, 1950 (6)
Boston	Old	NA	NA	34.6	94.3
	New	NA	NA	46.2	97.4
Buffalo	Old	67.3	64.8	56.1	73.0
	New	70.9	70.6	64.7	82.5
Chicago	Old	78.4	72.8	73.9	91.4
	New	81.1	79.3	77.0	95.2
Cincinnati	Old	68.6	62.7	63.9	92.6
	New	84.3	80.8	81.2	95.9
Cleveland	Old	72.8	67.4	60.9	95.6
	New	86.0	83.1	73.8	96.9
Columbus	Old	86.7	84.9	78.9	92.3
	New	91.3	89.2	83.4	95.2
Philadelphia	Old	69.8	65.9	62.0	86.2
	New	78.3	76.1	74.2	86.6
Pittsburgh	Old	42.6	44.0	38.4	79.8
	New	32.8	30.9	32.4	70.6
St. Louis	Old	65.3	61.9	56.0	87.4
	New	69.8	66.8	61.1	90.3
Syracuse	Old	77.0	74.4	71.7	83.0
	New	77.8	76.7	72.5	84.4

Note: See Table 4 for abbreviations.

NA: Data not available.

suburb study. This conclusion is, of course, based on the assumption
that the political suburbs of the metropolitan areas are all more distant from the business district than is any significant segment of the
political city. Since no city is a perfect circle or segment thereof, we
can be sure that this assumption is far from a perfect description. That
is, there undoubtedly are suburbs outside of the central city that are
closer to the central business district of the metropolitan area than are
some outer segments of the central city itself. However, we can reasonably assume that these inconsistencies are relatively minor and, if
random, merely work against finding the results reported above. An
additional methodological problem is less easily avoided. This hinges
on the fact that finding the various groups declining in their per cent
living in the central city is different from noting the decline in centralization within the city. In the latter case, a base population--the native
whites or a segment of that group--was used and a decline in the centralization index indicates that the ethnic groups decentralized even
when compared with a group that either had themselves moved outward
through time or were at least free to do so.

An alternate and perhaps more direct approach to the relationship
between centralization within a city and suburbanization in the metropolitan area involves correlating the positions of each ethnic group with
respect to these two variables. The results, shown in Table 36, are far
from fully consistent. For selected foreign-born groups in 1950, there
is for most cities the expected positive correlation between the groups'
ranks in centralization within the political city's zones and the per cent
living in the central city of the metropolitan area (Table 36, column 4).
Pittsburgh is an exception, having a correlation of -.39, and this is precisely the exception we should expect on the basis of the old-new differences in central city residence indicated earlier in Table 35. In St.
Louis there is a zero correlation and for the remaining seven cities
there are, for the most part, mildly positive correlations. However, in
1930, for both the first and second generations, the results are less
consistent (columns 2 and 3). In addition to Pittsburgh, St. Louis and
Cleveland also fail to show positive relationships between centralization within the central city and low suburbanization. In addition to these

TABLE 36.--Correlations (Spearman) between centralization within central city and the per cent of the standard metropolitan area's ethnic population living in the central city or urbanized area, 1930 and 1950

Central city (1)	Centralization and per cent in central city			Centralization and per cent in urbanized area
	FBW, 1930 (2)	NWFMP, 1930 (3)	FBW, 1950 (4)	FBW, 1950 (5)
Boston	NA	NA	.05	.32
Buffalo	.67	.73	.24	-.31
Chicago	.30	.33	.20	.73
Cincinnati	.43	.31	NA	NA
Cleveland	-.02	-.08	.10	-.10
Columbus	.67	.36	.42	.74
Philadelphia	.54	.73	.65	.27
Pittsburgh	-.01	-.24	-.39	-.55
St. Louis	-.26	-.03	.00	-.32
Syracuse	.24	.31	.02	.36

Note: See Table 4 for abbreviations.
NA: Data not available.

three cities, Buffalo in 1950 shows a negative relationship in the proportions living in the urbanized areas of the metropolitan area (column 5).

There are three cities, if we exclude Buffalo's negative relationship for its urbanized area in 1950, that are exceptions to the expected association between propensity to live in the central city of a metropolitan area and the centralization of the group. These cities are Cleveland, Pittsburgh, and St. Louis. That is, at one time or another groups centralized within the central city were also the groups more highly suburbanized. Before rejecting the original hypothesis which predicted a positive association between centralization and concentration within the central city, it behooves us to consider the conditions under which these negative relationships take place. As we have already observed, the term "suburbanization" has been applied to two different situations. First, there is a strictly technical definition in which the term is applied to all communities in a metropolitan area outside of the central city. In other instances, it is used primarily with reference to selected communities of the metropolitan ring, that is, those communities having a certain style of life that may be called middle class or higher--without defining terms. Given the fact that suburbs, used here in the less exclusive sense, include many communities that are primarily industrial in nature as well as communities of working class composition (Schnore, 1956), it is of relevance to consider not merely whether groups centralized in the city are also relatively less apt to reside in the outer ring of the metropolitan area but, in addition, whether these centralized groups are apt to differ from the less centralized groups in the kinds of suburbs they live in. It is clear that for many cities a large number of their suburbs are heavily industrial in function. Thus, it may well be that the Cleveland, Pittsburgh, and St. Louis deviations can be understood if we examine the suburbs themselves that the ethnic groups live in.

In addition to the three cities showing deviations from the expected relationship between centralization and suburbanization, Cincinnati and Philadelphia were included to serve as informal control cities. Since, as the reader will shortly see, partial correlations were computed, it is necessary to use Kendall rather than Spearman rank order correlations. The correlations between concentration in the central city and centralization are shown in column 2 of Table 37. For selected foreign-born groups in 1930, we observe inverse relationships in three cities where high centralization within the central city is associated with groups that have relatively small proportions of their total metropolitan populations living in the central city. For the second generation in 1930, Pittsburgh presents the only inverse case, and, for the foreign born in 1950, Pittsburgh and St. Louis are the two cities with inverse relationships. Except for the second generations in Cleveland and St. Louis (where the results have shifted from slightly negative to slightly positive correlations), these results using Tau are consistent with the Spearman correlations indicated in Table 36. The reader should, of course, keep in mind that the correlations are for the most part not statistically significant. However, since we have been analyzing these results in terms of the consistency of patterns, that is, directions of the correlations, our concern here is with interpreting the results for cities that disrupt the general patterns of positive correlation between centralization and concentration.

The contract or estimated rent in 1940 of every suburb that had 10,000 or more inhabitants in both 1930 and 1950 was used as a measure of the socio-economic level of the suburbs. The year 1940 was used as a compromise since our analysis pertains to suburbanization in both 1930 and 1950. For each foreign-born group in both 1930 and 1950 and for the second-generation groups in 1930, a suburban housing cost measure was computed that was weighted for the number of members of a specific ethnic group residing in each suburb of 10,000 or more inhabitants. Thus if all members of a given ethnic group resided in a single suburb, their suburban housing cost measure would merely be the average monthly contract or estimated rent in that suburb. If, to take a somewhat more complex illustration, 25 per cent of a group resided in suburb A, 50 per cent in suburb B, and 25 per cent in suburb C, then each percentage would be multiplied by the average housing cost in the suburb and a summary figure obtained. Although such a method does not tell what are the actual costs of the immigrant or second generation group involved, it does give an index of the kinds of suburbs they reside in.

The relationships between the socio-economic level of the suburbs that ethnic groups live in--as measured by the suburban housing costs ranked from high to low--and the groups' centralization and concentration are of considerable interest. In five of the six instances where there is a negative relationship between centralization and concentration (Table 37, column 2), high concentration in the central city is associated with high suburban rental value (column 3). That is, groups with small proportions residing in the central city tend to be groups whose suburban segment live in relatively low cost areas. By contrast, this

TABLE 37.--Tau correlations between per cent in central city of standard metropolitan areas, their centralization, and contract or estimated suburban rent, 1930 and 1950

	Tau			Partial tau (holding suburban costs constant)
	Per cent in central city and centralization	Contract or estimated suburban rent and:		Per cent in central city and centralization
Group, year, and city		Per cent in central city	Centralization	
(1)	(2)	(3)	(4)	(5)
Foreign born, 1930				
Cincinnati	.33	.29	-.20	.41
Cleveland	-.07	.29	.20	-.14
Philadelphia	.42	.42	.42	.29
Pittsburgh	-.04	-.45	.51	.25
St. Louis	-.16	-.49	.67	.26
Second generation, 1930				
Cincinnati	.27	-.20	-.42	.21
Cleveland	.02	.38	.29	-.10
Philadelphia	.53	.38	.56	.42
Pittsburgh	-.15	-.49	.51	.13
St. Louis	.02	-.51	.47	.34
Foreign born, 1950				
Cincinnati	NA	NA	NA	NA
Cleveland	.11	.24	.07	.09
Philadelphia	.45	.27	.31	.40
Pittsburgh	-.31	-.31	.49	-.20
St. Louis	-.05	-.31	.53	.14

Note: Suburban rental value based on all cities in S.M.A. other than central city that had 10,000 or more population in both 1930 and 1950. Rental values are from 1940 figures and include owned as well as rented dwellings. Suburban rental values ranked from high to low; other variables from low to high. NA: Data not available.

negative relationship is found in only two out of the eight cases where centralization and concentration are positively associated. It appears therefore that consideration of the nature of the suburbs in which ethnic groups live may account for the deviations encountered earlier between concentration and suburbanization. Since there are, of course, suburbs with less than 10,000 population, the reader should keep in mind that the measure of the quality of suburbs in which the selected ethnic groups reside is merely a crude indicator.

The partial tau correlations between per cent of selected groups living in the central city (ranked from low to high) and centralization (ranked from decentralized to centralized)--with suburban housing costs "held constant"--reduces the number of cases of negative correlation between centralization and concentration (compare columns 2 and 5 of Table 37). These results, although far from conclusive, suggest that if groups centralized within the central city of a metropolitan area are also concentrated in the outer ring of the metropolitan area, then it is due to their residing in areas in the outer ring that have lower rentals than those of the groups that are less centralized (column 4).

White Ethnic Groups and Negroes

The relationship between white ethnic groups and Negroes in northern cities is one that has received attention both in efforts to distinguish between the problems faced by these groups and, on the other hand, to show that they are in comparable positions. That the factors leading to these groups' migration to the urban north and midwest were similar is fairly clear. Negroes as well as many of the foreign-born groups were low in skills and training but were nevertheless able to move into a more favorable economic position by taking the occupational opportunities offered in urban centers--even if they were the lowest jobs available in these cities. Indeed, the great flow of southern Negroes to northern industrial centers is in no small way presumably related to the decline of new immigration from Europe. The Negroes replaced the European whites in serving the rapidly expanding industries of the northern urban centers. The first great influx of Negroes during World War I was due to the demands for labor created by the War combined with the decline in migrants from European sources. (See Drake and Cayton, 1945, and Duncan and Duncan, 1957.)

In contrast to this similarity in factors leading to migration, the color barrier has often been cited as the great limiting factor in keeping the Negro in the United States from assimilating as rapidly as the European white immigrant. The relationships between Negroes and white ethnic groups receive rather scanty attention in terms of their residential patterns. Burgess (1928) noted in Chicago a propensity for certain ethnic groups to have their residential areas invaded by Negroes more readily than other white ethnic groups. Duncan and Lieberson (1959) found little substantive support for Burgess' observations although, to be sure, the white ethnic groups did vary slightly in their degree of residential segregation from Negroes. However, in all cases, the white ethnics were highly segregated from Negroes and always less segregated from the native-white population or from each other. The question of interest here is therefore whether Negroes and white ethnics can be viewed as belonging on a continuum with respect to their housing experiences or whether they must be viewed as relatively discrete types.

Before discussing the gross relationships between the residential segregation of the foreign born from Negroes and native whites, it is important to warn the reader that the average indexes of segregation do not, of course, tell us anything about the range of the indexes for individual foreign-born groups. There are, in fact, a number of exceptions to the generalizations noted below and these groups will be considered shortly.

In each city, the foreign-born groups' segregation from native whites (Table 38, row 3) is lower than the immigrants' segregation from Negroes (row 2). Further, with the exception of Columbus in 1910, the native whites are less segregated from the foreign born than they are from Negroes (rows 3 and 1). These findings, coupled with the fairly similar degree of segregation which both native and foreign-born whites show from Negroes, suggest that the foreign born are quite different

TABLE 38.--Unweighted mean indexes of residential segregation of
selected foreign-born white groups from native whites
and Negroes, and Negro residential segregation from
native whites

City	Comparison	Row	Areal unit and year			
			Wards		Tracts[a]	
			1910	1920	1930	1950
Boston	NW v. Negro	(1)	64.1	65.3	77.9	80.1
	FBW v. Negro	(2)	65.1	65.8	79.9	81.5
	FBW v. NW	(3)	33.6	32.3	40.4	37.5
Buffalo	NW v. Negro	(1)	62.6	71.5	80.5	82.5
	FBW v. Negro	(2)	72.1	71.6	77.4	82.7
	FBW v. NW	(3)	41.2	38.8	42.8	38.2
Chicago	NW v. Negro	(1)	66.8	75.7	85.2	79.7
	FBW v. Negro	(2)	74.8	78.2	88.1	83.4
	FBW v. NW	(3)	40.6	34.3	39.4	35.9
Cincinnati	NW v. Negro	(1)	47.3	57.2	72.8	80.6
	FBW v. Negro	(2)	45.7	56.8	77.9	85.3
	FBW v. NW	(3)	38.5	33.8	41.0	39.9
Cleveland	NW v. Negro	(1)	60.6	70.1	85.0	86.6
	FBW v. Negro	(2)	65.7	68.1	86.7	86.9
	FBW v. NW	(3)	35.4	30.8	44.9	40.1
Columbus	NW v. Negro	(1)	31.6	43.8	62.8	70.3
	FBW v. Negro	(2)	44.1	46.7	67.0	75.5
	FBW v. NW	(3)	39.1	38.8	46.7	38.3
Philadelphia	NW v. Negro	(1)	46.0	47.9	63.4	74.0
	FBW v. Negro	(2)	57.6	57.0	72.0	78.4
	FBW v. NW	(3)	39.7	34.4	44.3	40.8
Pittsburgh	NW v. Negro	(1)	44.1	43.3	61.4	68.5
	FBW v. Negro	(2)	52.9	48.7	66.2	74.2
	FBW v. NW	(3)	37.3	34.4	42.6	38.4
St. Louis	NW v. Negro	(1)	54.3	62.1	82.1	85.4
	FBW v. Negro	(2)	56.2	63.3	82.0	87.7
	FBW v. NW	(3)	35.7	31.7	48.8	37.6
Syracuse	NW v. Negro	(1)	64.0	65.2	86.7	85.8
	FBW v. Negro	(2)	69.6	67.9	83.6	84.2
	FBW v. NW	(3)	36.5	31.8	47.6	39.3

Note: See Table 4 for abbreviations.

[a]Community Areas used for Chicago.

from Negroes with respect to the native white residential patterns. Thus, with only one exception in Columbus, Negro segregation from both the foreign-born and native elements of the white population is greater than the average segregation between white immigrant groups and the native whites.

The pattern of variation between the foreign-born groups in their segregation from Negroes is fairly stable through time--at least in rank order terms. The Spearman correlations of the segregation of foreign-born groups from Negroes in two time periods in a given city are rather high. Although there are several exceptions, such as Buffalo between 1910 and 1920, for the most part foreign-born groups tend to persist through time in their relative segregation from Negroes of a given city (Table 39, columns 2 and 4). Similarly the intra-group generational changes noted for the first and second generations in 1930 (column 3) indicate high stability in the degree of segregation from native whites.

Keeping in mind the temporal stability noted earlier for foreign-born groups in their segregation from native whites, we may ask whether there is any relationship between the rankings of foreign-born groups in their segregation from native whites and Negroes. The rank order correlations between these two variables for each time period and for the second generation in 1930 are presented in Table 40. Although there are several cases of low negative correlations (none of which is significant at the 5 per cent level), the predominant pattern of association between segregation from native whites and from Negroes is positive for the foreign-born and second-generation groups under study. The majority of these positive correlations are not significant, but the general pattern of correlations suggest that groups least segregated from native whites are also least segregated from Negroes. Therefore the correlations shown in Table 40 fail to support any "continuum" hypothesis with respect to white immigrant groups and Negroes. That is, if immigrants and Negroes were simply segregated along a continuum, one would expect to find the immigrant groups most dissimilar in residential distribution to the native whites to be closer to the Negro residential pattern than immigrant groups whose residential patterns are relatively

TABLE 39.--Correlations (Spearman) between different years of the
residential segregation of foreign-white stock from
Negroes

City (1)	FBW v. Negro 1910-1920 (2)	FBW v. Negro and NWFMP v. Negro 1930 (3)	FBW v. Negro 1930-1950 (4)
Boston	.85	.71	.73
Buffalo	.26	.94	.50
Chicago	.48	.98	.92
Cincinnati	.87	.73	.65
Cleveland	.60	.99	.78
Columbus	.71	.95	.96
Philadelphia	.72	.81	.88
Pittsburgh	.77	.95	.75
St. Louis	.85	.94	.79
Syracuse	.84	.93	.85

Note: See Table 4 for abbreviations.

similar to that of the native whites. The very opposite appears to be
the case, that is, in most cities the foreign-born and second-generation
groups highly segregated from native whites also tend to be most segregated from Negroes.

Similarly, differences between old and new groups in their segregation from Negroes form no clear-cut pattern. To be sure, in 36 of the
50 comparisons between old and new immigrant groups shown in Table
41, the old immigrant groups have lower average segregation from Negroes than do the new immigrant groups. Although there are a number
of cases in which old immigrant groups are more segregated than new
immigrant groups from the Negro population, the general pattern is one
where the new immigrant groups are more highly segregated from both
native whites and Negroes.

Attention is now shifted to the individual exceptions noted in some

TABLE 40.--Correlations (Spearman) between Negro and native-white
residential segregation from foreign-white stock

City	FBW v. NW and Negro				NWFMP v. NWNP and Negro, 1930
(1)	1910 (2)	1920 (3)	1930 (4)	1950 (5)	(6)
Boston	.76	.50	.47	.52	.50
Buffalo	.90	.50	.20	.21	.01
Chicago	.77	.56	.71	.53	.71
Cincinnati	-.03	-.12	.37	.74	.49
Cleveland	.22	-.33	.13	.02	.20
Columbus	.90	.52	.42	.49	.38
Philadelphia	.92	.81	.27	.05	.42
Pittsburgh	.22	-.28	.30	.67	.46
St. Louis	.39	.15	-.26	-.01	-.35
Syracuse	.41	.22	-.10	-.40	.28

Note: See Table 4 for abbreviations.

of the generalizations given above. First, it was pointed out that the
unweighted averages used for examining foreign-born segregation from
native whites and Negroes conceal a number of cases in which individual
foreign-born groups are more segregated from native whites than they
are from Negroes. Secondly, there are individual foreign-born groups
whose members are more segregated from the native-white population
than are the Negroes in the city. All cases were recorded in which a
foreign-born group had a higher segregation index from native whites
than it did from Negroes or in which Negroes were less segregated from
native whites than were the foreign born of a given nationality. Once a
group was found to fall in one of these classifications, then its segregation indexes were presented for later decades until the group no longer
fit into either of these situations. Before turning to the data given in
Tables 42 and 43, the reader should remember that the data for 1910

TABLE 41.--Mean indexes of residential segregation between ethnic groups and Negroes

| City (1) | Group (2) | FBW v. Negroes | | | | NWFMP v. Negroes, |
		1910 (3)	1920 (4)	1930 (5)	1950 (6)	1930 (7)
Boston	Old	62.1	65.5	78.6	80.4	79.8
	New	69.6	66.3	81.2	82.7	83.0
Buffalo	Old	64.8	72.9	79.6	82.5	80.4
	New	83.0	69.6	75.2	83.0	78.4
Chicago	Old	69.5	77.2	86.6	82.5	86.8
	New	82.7	79.7	89.0	84.0	89.5
Cincinnati	Old	41.7	55.8	76.9	84.1	75.8
	New	49.7	57.9	78.6	86.3	78.7
Cleveland	Old	64.8	72.7	87.5	87.2	87.6
	New	67.1	61.2	86.3	86.7	86.4
Columbus	Old	34.5	44.5	64.4	74.8	63.2
	New	53.7	49.0	68.5	75.9	67.6
Philadel-phia	Old	49.1	52.6	70.0	77.6	70.1
	New	66.2	61.3	73.2	78.8	73.4
Pittsburgh	Old	50.4	49.1	63.8	70.4	64.2
	New	55.4	48.3	67.6	76.3	70.2
St. Louis	Old	51.5	61.2	82.5	86.4	83.7
	New	63.4	66.6	81.6	88.4	82.9
Syracuse	Old	69.0	70.8	89.3	88.1	85.1
	New	71.0	61.2	79.1	81.0	79.8

Note: See Table 4 for abbreviations.

and 1920 are based on wards while the data for 1930 and 1950 are based on tracts. Thus, once again, it is necessary to remember that no comparisons of the magnitude of the segregation indexes can be made between either of the first two censuses and the later censuses.

In all of the cities except Syracuse, at least one of the foreign-born groups studied was in 1910 more segregated from the native whites than were the Negroes (Table 42). To be sure, in a number of cases, the white immigrant group was barely higher than the Negroes of the city in segregation from the native whites. Nevertheless, even roughly similar segregation indexes are of considerable interest. First, we may observe that in a number of cases there is a reversal by 1920, that is, the same foreign-born groups are less segregated than are the Negroes when compared with the residential distribution of their city's native white population. Thus by 1920, no cases of higher foreign-born segregation were observed in Boston, Buffalo, Chicago, Cincinnati, Cleveland, or St. Louis. In Columbus, the Germans and Austrians were no longer more segregated by 1920, but it was not until sometime in the 1920's that the Italians, Hungarians, and Greeks became less segregated than the Negroes of Columbus. And the Russians were still higher than the Negroes in 1930, although this was reversed by 1950. In Philadelphia, although all four of the foreign-born groups declined in their segregation from native whites between 1910 and 1920 while Negro-white segregation increased slightly, it was not until the 1930 census that these groups were less segregated. Similar to Columbus, Pittsburgh's Russian born were still more segregated than Negroes until 1930 when they were roughly the same and were, by 1950, less segregated. Segregation indexes were not computed for Roumanians in 1930 and 1950 and it is, therefore, impossible to say when and if the Roumanians of that city became less segregated than Negroes from the native whites.

Still using the data presented in Table 42, it is of interest to consider what groups were more segregated at one time or another from the native whites than were Negroes. There are very few cases in which members of old immigrant groups are so classified. Indeed, the Germans in Columbus in 1910 are the only case for the old immigrant groups studied. By contrast, the Italian immigrants were more segregated than Negroes in 1910 in all cities except Pittsburgh and Syracuse. The Russians also show up in a number of cities, namely Cincinnati, Columbus, Philadelphia, Pittsburgh, and St. Louis.

Since a number of the groups were examined in only several of the ten cities, no systematic analysis is implied here. Nevertheless, we may conclude that at least in 1910 there were several immigrant groups

TABLE 42.--Foreign-born groups more segregated than Negroes from native whites, 1910-1950

City and group (1)	Ward		Tract	
	1910 (2)	1920 (3)	1930 (4)	1950 (5)
Boston				
Negro	64	65	. . .	. . .
Italy	66	56	. . .	. . .
Buffalo				
Negro	63	72	. . .	. . .
Italy	72	70	. . .	. . .
Hungary	65	61	. . .	. . .
Chicago				
Negro	67	76	. . .	. . .
Italy	68	57	. . .	. . .
Cincinnati				
Negro	47	57	. . .	. . .
Russia	65	54	. . .	. . .
Roumania	63	54	. . .	. . .
Italy	56	52	. . .	. . .
Hungary	56	42	. . .	. . .
Cleveland				
Negro	61	70	. . .	. . .
Italy	75	52	. . .	. . .
Columbus				
Negro	32	44	63	70
Germany	40	37	. . .	. . .
Austria	42	35	. . .	. . .
Russia	64	59	67	63
Italy	36	46	56	. . .
Hungary	64	55	49	. . .
Greece	58	58	52	. . .
Philadelphia				
Negro	46	48	63	. . .
Russia	58	50	57	. . .
Roumania	67	51	53	. . .
Italy	61	53	61	. . .
Hungary	60	52	49	. . .
Pittsburgh				
Negro	44	43	61	68
Russia	56	55	61	59
Roumania	80	70	NA	NA

TABLE 42--<u>Continued</u>

City and group (1)	Ward		Tract	
	1910 (2)	1920 (3)	1930 (4)	1950 (5)
St. Louis				
Negro	54	62	. . .	. . .
Russia	66	50	. . .	. . .
Italy	69	61	. . .	. . .
Syracuse	. . .	. . .	. . .	. . .

NA: Data not available.

more segregated from the native whites than were the Negroes of their cities. Further, it was largely the recent immigrant groups that were so highly segregated. By 1920, for a number of cities, the Negroes had become the most segregated of the groups. Presumably, the large-scale migration of Negroes to these urban centers during World War I, combined with the decline in new European immigrants, contributed to this shift. Nevertheless, there were some groups that were not less segregated than Negroes until sometime after 1930.

Still another way of considering Negro-white ethnic group similarities is by examining those groups that were less segregated from Negroes than from native whites. To be sure, the lack of independence between segregation indexes makes the analysis somewhat redundant; nevertheless it is of interest to consider what groups, if any, tend to be particularly associated with Negroes. The results reported in Table 43 indicate, on the whole, that although there were a number of groups less segregated from Negroes than from native whites, these situations occurred more frequently in the earlier years than in more recent years. For the groups investigated, there were only two cases in which a group not more highly segregated than Negroes in 1910 became so later. These two exceptions are the Russians in Buffalo and the Greeks in Columbus. In both of these situations, the groups were less segregated from native whites than from Negroes in 1910, but had switched by 1920. Needless to say, oscillations that might occur between censuses would not be

TABLE 43.--Foreign-born groups more segregated from native whites than from Negroes, 1910-1950

City and group (1)	Wards				Tracts			
	1910		1920		1930		1950	
	Negro (2)	NW (3)	Negro (4)	NW (5)	Negro (6)	NW (7)	Negro (8)	NW (9)
Boston								
Greece	61	62	49	56	73	51	..	..
Buffalo								
Russia	..	..	49	53	54	56	84	54
Chicago	..	..	..	..	..	..	..	..
Cincinnati								
Russia	45	65	48	54	81[a]	70	..	..
Roumania	44	63	65	54	..	..	..	..
Italy	34	56	44	52	74[a]	47	..	..
Cleveland								
Italy	66	75	50	52	78	58	..	..
Columbus								
Ireland	28	30	28	31	56[b]	37[b]	..	..
Russia	59	64	66	59	..	..	..	..
Italy	30	36	35	46	56	56	71	46
Greece	..	..	42	58	52	52	64	29

TABLE 43.--Continued

City and group (1)	Wards				Tracts			
	1910		1920		1930		1950	
	Negro (2)	NW (3)	Negro (4)	NW (5)	Negro (6)	NW (7)	Negro (8)	NW (9)
Philadelphia	..	..	..	..	..	..	..	..
Pittsburgh								
Russia	48	56	37	55	56	61	79	59
Roumania	49	80	36	70	NA	NA	NA	NA
St. Louis								
Russia	61	66	54	50	..	..	..	..
Italy	62	69	65	61	..	..	..	..
Syracuse								
Russia	52	61	36	66	51	64	59	60

Note: See Table 4 for abbreviations.

[a]Nonwhite used rather than Negro.

[b]Irish Free State used rather than All Ireland.

NA: Data not available.

ascertained. Once again, we may observe that it is the more recent
immigrant groups who are less segregated from Negroes than from
native whites. Columbus' Irish during 1910 and 1920 are the only old
group represented in Table 43. Similar to the results reported earlier,
the Russians and Italians are particularly prominent among the new
immigrant groups, although the same caution with respect to the un-
systematic inclusion of specific ethnic groups is warranted.

In summarizing the findings about Negro-European immigrant
housing patterns, we may observe that although at one time certain
specific immigrant groups in a city have been somewhat less segregated from Negroes than from native whites or more segregated than
Negroes were from the native whites, the general summary figures
indicate that Negroes and immigrant groups have moved in opposite
directions, i.e., declining segregation for immigrants and increasing
segregation for Negroes. In terms of sheer magnitude, the Negroes
are far more highly segregated than are the immigrant groups. The
old-new distinction that has been so meaningful in earlier analyses is
not particularly significant with respect to segregation from Negroes.
That is, the old and new immigrants are on the average similar in being highly segregated from Negroes--although the new immigrant
groups were most apt to deviate from these general tendencies. Whether
these differences in trends between Negroes and European immigrants
are due to the added color problem for Negroes or to the fact that the
peaks of migration for these groups came at different times is a matter
for further research and beyond the scope of the present study. It
would perhaps be more correct to say that undoubtedly both factors are
relevant, but the significance of each is yet to be weighed. The pre-
dominance of exceptions during the period before World War I suggests
that the added color problem faced by Negroes is not the sole factor to
be considered.

Chapter 5

Residential Segregation
and Assimilation

The concept of assimilation is, as we have seen, one of the more elusive terms used in studies of race and ethnic relations. The plethora of definitions given to this term as well as the divergent ways in which it has been operationally defined were mentioned in Chapter 1. In this chapter, attention turns to the relationship between residential segregation and other aspects of ethnic behavior with respect to this complex concept of assimilation. The point of view outlined earlier may be briefly summarized as involving the hypothesis that the degree to which an ethnic group is residentially segregated affects other dimensions of ethnic behavior and that, further, this effect exists irrespective of covariations between factors which may be said to influence both segregation and other attributes of immigrant behavior. At times, the complexities of the indicator of assimilation and the difficulties of the data make our task much more difficult and the conclusions less clear-cut than might be desired, but such is the nature of the world.

Ability to Speak English and Segregation

Holding everything else constant, one would expect a certain interaction between ability to speak English and segregation from native whites. If we assume for the moment that all native whites are able to speak English and no other language, then one would expect immigrant groups whose members speak English to be less hampered or handicapped by language differences in their location near native whites than immigrant groups with large proportions of non-English speaking members. Such would also be the case for native whites if we continue our assumption that they all speak English but no other language. From this point of view, ability to speak English can be used as an independent variable in considering the variations between immigrant groups in their segregation from native whites in a given city. On the other hand, one could easily enough reverse the line of reasoning and assume that isolated foreign-born groups would have less reason and opportunity to learn English than a group widely dispersed among the native-white population. Thus, in the latter case, ability to speak English would be the dependent variable. If one assumes that ability to speak English may be at least partially a function of length of residence in the United States, then the matter becomes more complicated since segregation also appears to be related to length of residence. Consequently it would be necessary to partial out variations which could be explained by variables other than residential segregation.

Actually, the residential segregation factor is not so easily isolated. Other variables, such as the size of a group, enter into the situation. Contrast the situation faced by two foreign-born groups, both highly segregated from native whites in the same city, with one group being very small in absolute numbers and the other group very large. Under such circumstances, one would expect the numerically larger group to be slower in adopting English irrespective of their similarity in segregation if we assume that the frequency of contact with fellow members of the immigrant group is greater for the larger than for the smaller group. It would therefore seem that segregation and density of a given immigrant group would be the relevant variables here. Moreover, it is necessary to consider not merely a given ethnic group's segregation from native whites, but also from other immigrant groups. That is, some members of groups other than the one under study may be assumed to speak English and thus play a role in influencing the propensity of members of other groups to speak English. We cannot even consider here the significance of such factors as the occupational patterns of immigrant groups, their age distribution, and other variables which would also influence the propensity of a group to adopt English.

Finally, the assumption that all native whites speak English and only English is obviously an over-simplification.

Given the limitations of the available data and the complexities of the problem, analysis of the relationship between segregation and the ability to speak English can, at best, be carried out in a rather approximate manner. Segregation from native whites and segregation from other foreign-born groups are analyzed separately. The reader will recall that length of residence in the United States has an effect on the extent to which foreign-born groups are segregated from native whites, that is, the longer the group's residence in the country the lower their segregation from native whites. By contrast, similarity or dissimilarity in the time of arrival of two immigrant groups appeared to have little or no effect on their segregation from each other. In considering the proportion of an immigrant group able to speak English it would seem reasonable to take into account their length of residence in the United States. That is, all other factors being constant, length of residence would presumably affect the ability of immigrants to speak English. Thus in considering the relationship between ability to speak English and segregation, it would seem advisable to take into account length of residence in dealing with segregation from native whites, although not necessarily in considering the segregation of ethnic groups from each other since time of arrival appears to play no important role in influencing inter-ethnic segregation.

The tau correlations presented in Table 44 indicate that ability to speak English and segregation from native whites (column 2) are correlated in the direction expected, that is, the more highly segregated a given group is from the native whites, the larger the proportion unable to speak English. These tau correlations run from .29 in Cincinnati to .84 in Philadelphia. Similarly, median length of residence for the immigrant groups in each city is positively related to their ability to speak English (column 3). There is but one exception, Buffalo, where the correlation is nil. Column 4 gives the correlations considered earlier which indicate some relationship between length of residence and degree of segregation. Taking into account the findings that both segregation and ability to speak English are in part functions of length of

TABLE 44.--Tau correlations between ability to speak English, segregation from native whites, and length of residence, 1930

City	Per cent of FBW unable to speak English and:		Segregation FBW v. NW and:	
	Segregation FBW v. NW	Median year of arrival	Median year of arrival	Ability to speak English (holding arrival constant
(1)	(2)	(3)	(4)	(5)
Boston	.71	.42	.18	.71
Buffalo	.53	.00	.29	.55
Chicago	.44	.44	.24	.38
Cincinnati	.29	.47	.42	.11
Cleveland	.40	.49	.69	.10
Columbus	.40	.40	.31	.32
Philadelphia	.84	.49	.47	.79
Pittsburgh	.49	.44	.47	.35
St. Louis	.51	.47	.56	.34
Syracuse	.64	.75	.50	.47

Note: See Table 4 for abbreviations.

residence in the United States, the partial tau correlations between segregation and ability to speak English were computed (column 5). Although these partial correlations are generally lower than the correlations found without taking into account length of residence (compare columns 2 and 5), they are nevertheless all positive and indicate an association between ability to speak English and segregation from native whites even after length of residence is held "constant."

In considering residential segregation between immigrant groups, length of residence was not a discernably relevant factor according to the findings presented in Chapter 3. Consequently the indexes of foreign-born segregation from each other were correlated in each city only with the proportion of each group able to speak English. For each pair of immigrant groups, the per cent of one group able to speak English was multiplied by the per cent of the second immigrant group able to speak English. Use of this measure is analogous to the combination of independent probabilities. To illustrate with data taken from Boston in 1930, 89.0 per cent of the Italian-born population were able to speak English while 93.3 per cent of the Polish born were able to speak English. These two figures were then multiplied and compared with the results of similar steps taken for each combination of foreign-born groups in the city. The results were then ranked from high to low and compared with the segregation indexes of the pairs of foreign-born groups also ranked from high to low. The variations in numbers between different foreign-born groups in a given city have been essentially controlled in the computations of the segregation indexes since, as the reader will recall from the discussion in Chapter 2, the measures of segregation are based on per cent distributions. The correlations have a wide range (Table 45), from -.10 for Cincinnati to -.82 for Buffalo; but they consistently indicate that ability to speak English is inversely related to the magnitude of segregation between these foreign-born groups. Thus, although we are not in a position to attribute causal priority to either variable--the proportion of immigrants knowing English and the segregation of ethnic groups from each other--there does appear to at least be some connection between the two. That is, groups highly segregated from other groups are less likely to have as a common language of discourse the dominant tongue of the host society, i.e., English.

Consideration of Mother Tongue

Looking further, it appears that mother tongue is a factor in the residential patterns between immigrant groups although it has not been systematically examined in this study. It is fairly evident that national origin statistics in some cases hide significant ethnic similarities between persons born in the same country. Consider, for example, the Austrians in the United States of whom roughly half gave German and roughly 25 per cent gave Yiddish as their mother tongue in 1930. Thus, irrespective of their ability to speak English, one would expect a fairly close residential association between the Austrians and the Germans as

TABLE 45.--Correlations (Spearman) between indexes of inter-group segregation and combined proportions able to speak English, foreign born, 1930

City	Correlation
Boston	-.57
Buffalo	-.82
Chicago	-.41
Cincinnati	-.10
Cleveland	-.50
Columbus	-.20
Philadelphia	-.58
Pittsburgh	-.38
St. Louis	-.50
Syracuse	-.37

Note: Ability to speak English and segregation both ranked high to low.

well as between the Austrians and the Russians (of whom over 60 per cent gave Yiddish as their mother tongue.) The Polish and Roumanian foreign born in 1930 also had important proportions giving Yiddish as their mother tongue and the Hungarians had somewhat more than 15 per cent of their immigrants reporting German as their mother tongue. To be sure, per cents based on national data can not be applied haphazardly to individual cities since undoubtedly these proportions vary from community to community. Nevertheless some of the surprisingly low indexes of segregation which have turned up between pairs of immigrant groups may be accounted for in these terms. For example, in Philadelphia in 1930, out of 55 combinations of pairs of foreign-born groups, the Russians and Roumanians had an index of segregation which was the second lowest in the city between two foreign-born groups. Although the Roumanian-born population of Philadelphia was roughly 7,500 in 1930, only 2,000 in the city reported Roumanian as their mother tongue.

Similarly, although there were 81,000 Russian born in Philadelphia, only 13,500 foreign born in 1930 gave Russian as their mother tongue. That this is not solely due to errors of reporting is suggested by the close similarity between the number of Italians in Philadelphia and the number reporting Italian as their mother tongue.

In short, although residential segregation between immigrant groups appears to be related to the extent they can both speak English, other factors such as their mother tongue and, in turn, ethnic similarities hidden by the use of country-of-birth statistics are probably also influential in the resulting patterns of immigrant segregation. It should be added that the old immigrant groups, which are usually the least segregated from each other, include a number of groups that are English speaking to begin with. In computations, foreign born from England, Scotland, and Eire were assumed to all be able to speak English. The census did not provide data on these groups, presumably, for this reason. However, it should also be noted that some of the old immigrant groups, particularly the Germans, who were studied in all ten cities, tend also to have very high proportions speaking English and low segregation indexes from other old immigrant groups.

Citizenship

Naturalization is by no means a perfect indicator of an individual's state of assimilation. Thus some naturalized immigrants later return to their country of origin whereas not all immigrants remaining in the United States for twenty or more years adopt American citizenship. (For example, see the figures shown in U. S. Department of Labor, 1919, pp. 106-12.) Nevertheless it seems reasonable to use naturalization in dealing with aggregates "as an indication that the assimilative process has proceeded to a moderate extent at least. The fact of naturalization is indicative of an attitude towards the country very different from that of the immigrant who shows no desire to take out naturalization papers." (Hurd, 1942, p. 662.) It is clear that differences between immigrant groups in citizenship status are related to such factors as length of residence in the United States, literacy, changes in citizenship laws, age, and sex. That there are even more subtle factors involved is readily illustrated, although less easily measured. For example, Fordyce (1937, p. 121), writing about the participation of ethnic groups in political activity in Cleveland, reports a case of mass naturalization of immigrants shortly before an election as well as the conducting of naturalization examinations by a disbarred judge around the turn of the century. Crawford, in comparing Massachusetts and Missouri voting laws, indicates clearly the complicated relationships between voting, political groups, and variations in citizenship between groups and cities as well:

> The United States has laid down a very definite list of requirements which all prospective citizens are expected to fulfill; but the actual political privileges accorded an American citizen, in reality, depend far more upon the laws of the individual state than upon the laws of the nation. In Massachusetts, for instance, "a citizen can not vote unless he is able to read the Constitution of the Commonwealth in the English language." Missouri puts up no bars; any man may vote on state questions who has declared his intention of becoming a citizen. Complete naturalization is an expensive as well as a lengthy process. The temptation which comes as a result, to obtain declaration papers with state political franchise, rather than full citizenship, is thoroughly appreciated and exploited by political schemers locally. (Crawford, 1916, p. 66.)

Under such circumstances, one would like to take these factors into account in considering the effect of segregation on citizenship status, that is, these additional factors influencing citizenship status could hinder our chances of isolating a relationship with segregation and in other cases it might be difficult to determine whether any relationship was spurious. Thus, for example, if length of residence is related to citizenship status and is also related to the degree of segregation of a group, it would be necessary to take this factor into account in determining whether there was indeed an independent relationship between the degree of a group's segregation and its citizenship status. Just such an approach will be considered presently. However, the issue nevertheless remains, as indeed it remains for most sociological studies, that not all of the presumed sources of influence have been taken into account. Under the circumstances we can only note the existence of evidence tending to either support or disrupt the hypothesis under consideration.

Length of Residence and Citizenship

It is fairly reasonable to assume that length of residence in the United States is an important factor in influencing the propensity of immigrants to obtain United States citizenship. Although the citizenship laws have changed through the years and there are exceptional cases, for the most part a minimum of five years residence in the United States is required. Ideally, for each immigrant group in a city, we should like to have data giving citizenship status cross-classified by length of residence, that is, telling us what proportion of immigrants from each country who had come to the United States at a specific time were naturalized. Under such circumstances, it would be possible to compare immigrant groups in terms of their citizenship rates based on comparable chances. It is only for 1900, a year in which no segregation data are available, that we can take a somewhat direct approach to determining the relationship between citizenship status and length of residence. To be sure, for 1930 there are data giving the length of residence of specific immigrant groups in each city and, although these data are used below in examining the relationship between segregation and naturalization, they are only indirectly relevant. However, in 1900 for the 161 United States cities that had a population of at least 25,000 information is available on the number of foreign-born males 21 years of age and over who were aliens, cross-classified by their length of residence in the United States. While such data could not yield any true type of incidence rates since they fail to take into account such factors as mortality and return migration, they are highly useful for our purposes. The proportion of males at least 21 years old who were aliens is presented below for the aggregate of all 161 cities by specific length of residence categories.

Length of residence	Proportion alien
Less than 1 year	.7111
1 year	.7728
2 years	.7695
3 years	.7435

Length of residence	Proportion alien
4 years	.6991
5 years	.6279
6-9 years	.4111
10-14 years	.2427
15-19 years	.1385
20 years and over	.0709
Unknown	.0446

Except for those in the United States less than one year, there is an orderly decline in the proportion alien as length of residence increases. The lowest proportion alien is found among those not reporting their length of residence in the country. Perhaps it is due to their incorrect reporting of citizenship status or perhaps in part to the fact that these are persons who have been in the United States for an extremely long time. The relatively low proportion alien among those in the United States less than one year is difficult to account for, except on the supposition of gross reporting errors.

We are in a position to apply these rates based on all 161 cities to the males in each of the cities separately to determine how much of the inter-city variations in their proportions alien is accounted for by the differences between cities in the length of residence of their immigrants. Several matters, as usual, complicate the analysis. First, since foreign-born Orientals were largely not eligible for citizenship, although "A small number of Chinese may have been naturalized prior to 1882 . . . and a few more Chinese and some Japanese may have been illegally admitted to citizenship prior to 1916" (U. S. Department of Commerce, 1933, p. 402), it would not be fair to compare directly the immigrant citizenship behavior in cities with relatively large Oriental populations, for example, San Francisco, with cities having only a small proportion of their foreign born from the Orient. Consequently the "expected rates," that is, the proportions alien by length of residence shown above, were applied only to the proportion of the foreign-born population born outside of the Orient. The actual number of persons born in the Orient was added to the expected number alien and thus a grand total was obtained. To illustrate, consider San Francisco in which 16 per cent of the foreign-born males 21 and older were born

in Asia. The per cent of all foreign-born males 21 and over expected
to be alien was 17.5 per cent based on the rates shown above applied
to the length of residence distribution of males in San Francisco. This
expected per cent was multiplied by .84 (the proportion of San Francisco's foreigners born outside of Asia) to which was added the per
cent of all foreign-born males who were Asian-born aliens (15.1) leading to an expectation that 29.8 per cent of all foreign born males would
be alien (the actual per cent in San Francisco is 28.8 in 1900). This
method then applies expected rates to the non-Asiatic population and
adds on the actual number of Asiatic aliens to obtain a grand total expected per cent alien. That is, both the actual and expected rates for
a given city take into account the actual number of Asiatic males who
are aliens; the differences between the actual and expected rates is
therefore based on the degree to which the actual number of non-Asiatic
males differ in their propensity to remain aliens from what would be
expected on the basis of their length of residence in the United States.

There are several minor methodological difficulties involved in
this approach to the Oriental problem. First, undoubtedly a small number of whites were born in Asiatic countries and a small number of
Asiatics were born outside of the Orient. Secondly, the length-of-residence distribution for each city includes Asiatics as well as other races
and therefore the analysis is carried out with the awkward but unavoid-
able assumption that the length-of-residence distribution for Asiatics
in each city is the same as for the non-Asiatics. A similar criticism
may be made of the overall rates shown above, that is, that they include
Asiatics as well as other races. It was decided, nonetheless, to apply
the analysis to all but one of the 161 cities, Honolulu, where the proportion Asiatic is extremely high.

A product moment correlation, weighted for the proportion in each
city of the total number of foreign-born adult males in the aggregate of
160 cities, was computed between the actual and expected per cent of
immigrant males who were alien. Use of weights meant that the behavior found in each city was not given equal significance in influencing
the results of the regression and correlation coefficients. Instead, the
immigrant population in cities with larger numbers of foreign born was

more important than that of cities with very small absolute numbers of immigrants in terms of influencing the regression and correlation obtained.
(For computational formulas and an exposition of the rationale behind the
use of weights in regressions, see Robinson, 1956.)

The weighted correlation between the actual and expected per cent
alien is .838, with a slope and intercept of 1.675 and -17.18 respectively,
taking the expected per cent as the independent variable. This indicates
that a considerable amount of the variance, 70 per cent, between cities in
their proportions who are alien can be interpreted as a function of differences between cities in the length of residence of their immigrants in the
United States--ignoring the factor of the proportion Asiatic, which affects
only a few cities.

It appears that, irrespective of differences between cities in the origins of their non-Asiatic immigrants, length of residence in the United
States is a critical factor in determining the extent to which the immigrants are aliens. Although the weighted actual and expected mean per
cent alien are not identical because of the adjustments for Orientals, they
are sufficiently similar (21.4 and 23.0, respectively) to warrant consideration of the deviation of the regression slope from unity. In this case, the
slope of 1.675 indicates that in cities where the per cent of immigrants expected to be aliens is low then the actual per cent who are aliens is even
lower. In cities where the expected per cent is roughly above 25 per cent,
the actual per cent is even higher. This suggests that there may be some
kind of "interaction" between length of residence and proportion acquiring
citizenship.

There are, of course, a number of plausible hypotheses to pursue
further on the basis of this finding, but the most important one in terms
of the issues raised in this study are the differences between the behavior of the old and new immigrant groups. The reader will recall the difficulties involved in separating out any differences between old and new
groups without taking into account their differences in such matters as
length of residence in the United States. Since we have knowledge about
the country of birth of immigrants in each of these cities, we can examine
this old-new effect on alien status, in an indirect manner, to see if country of origin plays a role in influencing the propensity of immigrants to

remain aliens while holding constant length of residence. Persons born in the following European countries in each city were classified in a somewhat arbitrary manner as belonging to the old immigrant groups: Belgium, Denmark, England, France, Germany, Holland, Ireland, Luxemburg, Norway, Scotland, Sweden, Switzerland, and Wales. In addition, immigrants from Australia as well as both French and non-French immigrants from Canada were classified as belonging to the old immigrant groups. Immigrants from all other sources were classified as new groups. The percentage of immigrant adult males from old immigrant countries varied considerably from city to city, from a little above 40 per cent in Johnstown, Pennsylvania to well over 95 per cent in Quincy Illinois. The regression and correlation are computed on the basis of weights mentioned earlier, as were all of the data to be discussed in this analysis of citizenship status in 1900. The results are in the direction expected if one assumes that the old immigrants in 1900 had resided in the United States for a longer time than the new immigrants. The correlation is -.318, the slope is -.320, and the intercept is 45.15 for the regression of the actual per cent alien on per cent old immigrants. That is, the greater the proportion of a city's immigrant population from old countries, the lower the proportion who are aliens. The correlation is not, however, very high. Similar results are obtained when the per cent of immigrants from old countries is correlated with the per cent expected to be aliens. In this case a correlation of -.602, a slope of -.303, and an intercept of 45.52 were obtained when the per cent old was used as the independent variable to estimate the per cent expected to be alien. This testifies to the fact that the old immigrants had been in the country for a longer period of time than the new immigrant groups. Thus the larger the proportion of the old in a given city is, the lower is the proportion expected to be aliens. The multiple regression where Y is the actual per cent alien, X_1 is the expected per cent alien, X_2 the per cent old is: $Y = -47.18 + 2.029X_1 + .295X_2$. The multiple correlation is .868, with 75 per cent of the variance taken into account.

The critical question is what effect if any does the old-new difference have on the propensity of immigrants to remain as aliens once old-new differences in length of residence has been taken into account. The partial correlation between per cent alien and per cent old, when length of residence is taken into account is actually positive ($r = .428$). Holding constant the differences between cities in the time of arrival of their immigrants, the greater the proportion of the immigrants in the city from old countries is, the greater is the proportion of the immigrants who are aliens. To be sure this is an aggregative correlation and we can not conclude that the specific alien length-of-residence rates for old immigrants are higher than that for new immigrants. In many cases it is possible for such results to be obtained if new immigrants were more apt to give up their alien status when living in cities where they were large in relative number and less apt to give up their alien status in cities where they were but a small proportion of the immigrant population. Nevertheless, the results are certainly surprising when we consider the general tendency to assume that "new immigrants are less likely to assimilate.

As is the case for almost any conclusion, it is possible to find mention in the literature of additional evidence for justifying the new empirical findings. In this case, however, the evidence provided by Gavit (1922, Chapter 8) and based on immigration statistics is rather impressive. Working with somewhat more than 25,000 naturalization petitions filed during the fiscal year 1913-1914, which amounted to a little more than 20 per cent of all the petitions filed during that time, Gavit showed clearly, first, the primary significance which length of residence in the United States has for citizenship status and, secondly, the differences between immigrants in their propensity to become naturalized based on their age when arriving in the United States. Looking separately at petitioners who arrived in the country when they were 21 and over, 15 to 20, and under 15 years of age, Gavit found in each case that immigrants born in the new countries tended to have shorter average intervals between their reaching the age of 21 and attainment of citizenship than those from old sources of immigration. Although a criticism of Gavit's work is not germane to the present study, the interested reader should note that apparently there were no data on differences, if any, between immigrant groups in those not applying for citizenship at all. Such differences could affect the over-all conclusions if they were in the direction of more new immigrants refraining from applying. Nevertheless, the general tenor of Gavit's work is supported by the analysis presented here for 1900 which is, furthermore, based on census returns.

Segregation and Citizenship Status

In turning our attention now to the question of whether segregation influences the propensity of groups to give up their old citizenship, it is apparent that variations between groups in their length of residence must be taken into account. The citizenship status of immigrants can be placed into three categories: aliens, persons with first papers, naturalized citizens. Since the laws generally provide both a waiting period between the time first papers are obtained and the time the immigrant is eligible for naturalization as well as a certain minimum length of residence in the United States, it was decided to consider as far as possible just the per cent of each group who were aliens and, in addition, to exclude from the analysis immigrants whose citizenship was unknown. At one time there was a tendency to assume that immigrants not reporting their citizenship status were largely not naturalized. However, a study made after the 1950 census (U. S. Bureau of the Census, 1954, p. 6) indicated that members of a given immigrant group not reporting their citizenship status had about the same proportion naturalized as those who had reported their citizenship status, although there was some tendency for an overstatement of citizenship on the part of those reporting their status. The use of data pertaining to alien status reduces somewhat the effect of year of arrival differences between immigrant groups since naturalization requirements generally involve a certain minimum length of residence, but obtaining first papers does not. Nevertheless, since the chances of having taken out first papers is clearly related to length of residence, this factor is far from fully taken into account.

For each of the four census years under study, citizenship data are available for at least some of the ten cities. For 1910, data pertaining only to the citizenship status of males 21 and older are reported by the Census Bureau. Although additional data were available for later censuses, as far as possible the analysis was restricted to the per cent of each immigrant group's males 21 and older who were aliens. Such data were not available for 1950, and it was necessary to shift to a citizen-non citizen type of analysis. The results given in Table 46 indicate

TABLE 46.--Correlations (Spearman) between immigrant segregation
from native whites and immigrant citizenship status,
1910-1950

City[a]	Per cent of FBW males, 21 and older, alien			Per cent of FBW males, all ages, not naturalized
	1910	1920	1930	1950
Boston	.59	.65	.54	-.04
Buffalo	.62	.67	.30	NA
Chicago	.61	.50	.49	-.04
Cincinnati	.73[b]	.75	.35	NA
Cleveland	.76	.86	.81	.32
Columbus	.52	.55	.43	NA
Philadelphia	.73	.76	.29	-.28
Pittsburgh	.61	.68	.82	.55
St. Louis	.81	.85	.75	NA
Syracuse	.35	.27	.79[c]	NA

Note: See Table 4 for abbreviations.

[a]Citizenship based on Standard Metropolitan Areas in 1950.

[b]Roumania not available.

[c]Sweden not available.

NA: Data not available.

a positive relationship between the degree of segregation of immigrant
groups in a given city and their proportions who are aliens. The correlations in 1910 and 1920 are the most comparable of the sets of correlations, although they are subject to the difficulties noted elsewhere
in so far as the boundary changes after World War I affected comparability. For the most part the correlations do not differ greatly as between 1910 and 1920. There is a general upward trend, however, toward a closer relationship between segregation and citizenship status
during the later period. The relationship continues to hold for 1930,
although not as strongly as in the previous decade.

However, it should be noted that neither the segregation indexes
nor the groups are completely comparable with earlier periods. By

1950, for the smaller number of groups available and for the reduced number of cities there are both negative and positive correlations between segregation of a group and the proportion who are aliens (in this case, persons having first papers only are included). The relationships appear to be only moderate at best in 1950. One factor in the decline of the correlations between 1930 and 1950 is that with the declining numbers of new immigrants the average length of residence in the United States is greater for the foreign-born population by 1950 and very high proportions of all the groups are citizens. This is illustrated rather clearly in Table 47 which gives the unweighted mean per cent of aliens for all of the groups considered in the preceding table. Omitting the results reported for 1950 for a moment since they are not directly comparable, it is fairly clear that the mean per cent of the foreign-born groups who are alien in each city declined from 1910 through 1930. The decline between 1910 and 1920 is fairly sharp and may well be due to the drop in immigration during the decade because of World War I. The decline between 1920 and 1930 is somewhat less comparable because of the use of somewhat different ethnic groups in the respective analyses. However, in only two of the ten cities was there a mild rise, although many of the declines were also only slight. The data for 1950 are not directly comparable since they include persons having first papers as well as persons who are aliens. Therefore the decline noted between 1930 and 1950 actually understate the drop in the proportions who are aliens. It must, of course, be added that the 1950 data reported in Table 47 are based on the standard metropolitan area rather than the city rates used for earlier decades.

In short, these findings suggest a general relation between segregation and citizenship status. Since citizenship is related to other factors which are in turn related to segregation, the results presented in Table 46 are possible spurious in the sense that they may be due solely to interrelated variables not taken into account. As we shall shortly see, this is probably not the case. However, irrespective of the extent to which the interplay between citizenship status and segregation is due to other variables which jointly influence both, the fact remains that residential segregation of foreign-born groups is associated with their

TABLE 47.--Unweighted mean per cent alien among immigrant groups: 1910-1950

| City[a] | Unweighted means | | | |
| | Per cent of FBW males, 21 and older, alien | | | Per cent of FBW males, all ages, not naturalized |
	1910	1920	1930	1950
Boston	40.1	29.2	28.5	12.3
Buffalo	37.5	19.1	14.4	NA
Chicago	34.9	17.2	16.0	8.3
Cincinnati	31.3[b]	22.5	12.2	NA
Cleveland	37.9	19.5	20.0	10.5
Columbus	42.1	29.9	24.9	NA
Philadelphia	43.9	25.3	18.5	9.8
Pittsburgh	41.3	27.8	18.5	9.4
St. Louis	31.5	17.4	20.3	NA
Syracuse	30.4	24.3	22.5[c]	NA

Note: See Table 4 for abbreviations.

[a]Based on Standard Metropolitan Areas in 1950.

[b]Roumania not available.

[c]Sweden not available.

NA: Data not available.

movement toward participation in a formal legal sense, at any rate, in the new country and a step toward permanent residence in the United States.

Segregation, Citizenship, and Year of Arrival

As was noted earlier, citizenship is affected by length of residence in the United States. For example, Gavit (1922, p. 241) found for the period 1913-1914, an interval of 10.6 years between year of arrival and filing of petitions for citizenship by immigrants 21 and older. Keeping in mind this relationship between year of arrival and citizenship status as well as the findings reported earlier in Chapter 3 that year of arrival appeared to be related to the degree of residential segregation, we can pose the question of whether the relationship between segregation and citizenship status is not simply due to their mutual relationship with year of arrival. Consideration of this problem is limited to 1930 since it is only for this year that the necessary data on year of arrival are available. Furthermore, the 1930 citizenship data are not the same for cities above and below 500,000. Unlike the previous material on citizenship, the results reported here are based on data for both sexes.

Table 48 indicates that the correlations (tau) between year of arrival and the per cent of the immigrant group's members who are alien (column 2) or naturalized (column 3) are in most cases fairly high. Thus the more recent a group's median year of arrival, the greater the proportion naturalized. The correlations between segregation and year of arrival, reproduced in column 6 from Chapter 3, are positive in all cases but vary considerably in magnitude. As we noted in Chapter 3, the more recent the median year of arrival of a group the greater its segregation from native whites. The effect of segregation on the per cent of a group alien both before and after controlling for year of arrival (columns 4 and 7, respectively) indicates that in all cases the correlations are lower after year of arrival has been taken into account. For example, the correlation of .50 in Syracuse declined to .16 and Cleveland's correlation dropped from .64 to .22. Nevertheless, even after year of arrival is taken into account the relationships between segregation and per cent alien are still positive, ranging from a neutral .03 (Columbus) to .46 (Boston).

Similar results were found in examining the relationship between segregation and naturalization. This is by no means completely redundant with the foregoing analyses of aliens, since the segment of the foreign-born population having first papers was not included in either category. The correlations indicate that naturalization goes up with lower segregation (column 5) and with longer length of residence (column 3). Once again the partial correlations between segregation and naturalization (column 8) indicate that segregation is consistently related to citizenship status in the direction hypothesized, that is, in this case segre-

TABLE 48.--Correlations and partial correlations (tau) between naturalization status, year of arrival, and segregation from native whites, 1930

City	Tau					Partial tau	
	Median year of arrival and per cent:		Segregation v. NW and per cent:		Median year of arrival and segregation v. NW	Segregation v. NW and per cent: (holding arrival constant):	
	Alien	Naturalized	Alien	Naturalized		Alien	Naturalized
(1)	(2)	(3)	(4)	(5)	(6)	(7)	(8)
Boston	.62	-.67	.47	-.51	.18	.46	-.53
Buffalo	.64	-.64	.29	-.11	.29	.14	.10
Chicago	.73	-.51	.42	-.47	.24	.37	-.42
Cincinnati	.76	-.45	.44	-.24	.42	.17	-.06
Cleveland	.78	-.27	.64	-.62	.69	.22	-.62
Columbus	.71	-.71	.24	-.38	.31	.03	-.24
Philadelphia	.58	-.44	.42	-.27	.47	.20	-.08
Pittsburgh	.44	-.40	.56	-.60	.47	.45	-.51
St. Louis	.49	-.45	.56	-.60	.56	.40	-.47
Syracuse	.86	-.57	.50	-.71	.50	.16	-.60

Note: See Table 4 for abbreviations. Citizenship data for all ages, both sexes, and with "unknown" excluded from computations, except for Columbus, Cincinnati, and Syracuse, where citizenship data are for persons 21 and older, both sexes, and "unknown" not excluded.

gation and naturalization are inversely related. There is however one "deviation," Buffalo, where the zero order tau (-.11) is still only slight after holding year of arrival into account, but does shift direction (.10).

Scottish Citizenship

Of special interest are the Scottish rates for citizenship status. In contrast to the general association between length of residence and segregation from native whites found in 1930, sharp deviations were reported in Chapter 3 for the Scottish, who had relatively low segregation indexes but were rather recent migrants in the six cities in 1930 in which they were included. This striking set of deviations in ranks (columns 3 and 4 of Table 49) led to a consideration of the possible effect of ethnic origins of the native population on the segregation of later immigrants if they merely followed the residential patterns of the early settlers. The ranks of the Scots in terms of their per cent alien (column 5) offers additional information about the factors accounting for their low segregation indexes. Since the general associations found between immigrant year of arrival and per cent alien are presumably independent of the ethnic composition of native whites in each city, we would not expect as sharp a discrepancy between Scottish alien and year-of-arrival ranks as that found between year of arrival and segregation for the Scots. Given the independent influences of both year of arrival and segregation on the proportion of an immigrant group alien, as reported above, and assuming the influence of composition on segregation but not on the propensity to become a citizen, then we would expect to find the Scottish proportion alien to be intermediate between their segregation and year-of-arrival ranks in each city. Such is precisely the case. The reader will observe that the Scottish rank within each city in terms of their per cent alien (Table 49, column 5) is intermediate between their ranks in each city in terms of year of arrival (column 3) and segregation (column 4) with the exception of Buffalo where they had both the most recent median year of arrival and the largest proportion alien of the ten groups studied. Similar results were obtained when the Scottish rank with respect to naturalization (column 6) was examined in

TABLE 49.--Median year of arrival, segregation from native whites, and citizenship status ranks of Scottish immigrants in six cities, 1930

City	Number of FBW groups ranked	Rank of Scots in city			
		Median year of arrival	Segre- gation v. NW	Per cent alien	Per cent naturalized
(1)	(2)	(3)	(4)	(5)	(6)
Boston	10	9	2	5	5
Buffalo	10	10	4	10	10
Cincinnati	11	10	6	8	8
Columbus	11	8	2	6	5
Philadelphia	11	11	3	9	10
Pittsburgh	11	9	3	7	7

Note: See Table 4 for abbreviations.
Median year of arrival ranked from oldest to most recent. Segregation and per cent alien ranked from lowest to highest. Per cent naturalized ranked from highest to lowest.

contrast with their year of arrival and segregation ranks.

Since, in most cases, the range between the Scottish ranks on year of arrival and segregation is greater than the range outside of these ranks, one might be tempted to argue that the intermediate ranks for per cent alien would be largely expected simply on the basis of a random distribution model, that is, that the likelihood is greater of finding the Scottish alien ranks falling between the other two sets of ranks (segregation and year of arrival) than exceeding or falling below both of these sets of ranks. A detailed examination of this problem is made in Table 50. For each of the six cities in which the Scottish immigrants were considered in 1930, the total number of immigrant groups examined is given in column 6. The number of ranks below the 1930 Scottish segregation ranks are shown in column 2 and the number of ranks above the Scottish median year of arrival in 1930 are shown in column 3. In each city there are also the rank positions of Scots to consider. Since their segregation and year of arrival ranks were never the same, this amounts to two ranks in each city. Adding across, the total number of ranks equals the total number of groups in the city (columns 2 through 5 equals column 6). Applying Table 50 to the problem at hand we may note that in Philadelphia, for example, where the Scottish ranked eleventh in median year of arrival and third in segregation out of the eleven groups studied, the random distribution probability of the per cent alien rank being intermediate is 7/11ths but is only 2/11ths for being less than either of the ranks and cannot at all be greater than the median year-of-arrival rank.

TABLE 50.--Number and proportion of rank positions in relation to Scottish ranks in segregation and median year of arrival, 1930

City	Number (and proportion)				
	Below segregation rank	Above median year of arrival rank	Between segregation and year of arrival rank	On ranks	Number of ranks
(1)	(2)	(3)	(4)	(5)	(6)
Boston	1(.10)	1(.10)	6(.60)	2(.20)	10(1.00)
Buffalo	3(.30)	-(.00)	5(.50)	2(.20)	10(1.00)
Cincinnati	5(.45)	1(.09)	3(.27)	2(.18)	11(1.00)
Columbus	1(.09)	3(.27)	5(.45)	2(.18)	11(1.00)
Philadelphia	2(.18)	-(.00)	7(.64)	2(.18)	11(1.00)
Pittsburgh	2(.18)	2(.18)	5(.45)	2(.18)	11(1.00)

It is therefore clear that the fact that the per cent alien ranking for the Scottish is intermediate in Philadelphia is difficult to interpret in itself. That is, there is a high probability of such an occurrence simply on the basis of a null hypothesis that the alien ranking of the Scottish is distributed randomly. However, since we have data for six cities, we can examine the probability of getting intermediate rankings in 5 of the 6 cases using the information given in Table 50 to set up the probability distributions. The results are not as clear-cut as might be desired, but they are still favorable. The probability of getting an intermediate ranking in 5 or more cases is only .09. We may pose the problem from a somewhat different light by noting that the one deviation, Buffalo, still did not involve going outside of the two sets of ranks (segregation and year of arrival). Still the probability is only .08 of finding no cases where the alien rank position of the Scottish is higher than their year of arrival rank or lower than their segregation rank. It goes without saying that the two tests above are not independent of each other.

This analysis of the year-of-arrival relationship with both segregation and naturalization for the Scottish immigrants provides further evidence for our earlier inferences about the effect of the ethnic composition of the native whites on the extent to which immigrant groups segregate residentially. The rank position of the Scottish immigrants with respect to year-of-arrival was far more closely related to Scottish citizenship ranks then to their segregation ranks in each community investigated. Further, the fact that the Scottish citizenship ranks occupy a position intermediate between their length of residence and segregation ranks adds further evidence to the contention that segregation influences the propensity of immigrant groups to become citizens even after differences between the length of residence of the foreign born are taken into account.

Segregation and Intermarriage

The propensity of members of an ethnic group to select mates from the same group has been one of the most highly dramatized and emphasized aspects of ethnic behavior in the United States. The simple examination of the number of exogamous and endogamous marriages for members of a given ethnic group is an inadequate indicator of intermarriage in terms of theories with probability-types of prediction implicit. (See Savorgnan, 1950.) That we can do none of the elegant analyses possible is unfortunate. The necessary data, however, are not available.

A very crude indicator of intermarriage is used, namely, the per cent of the second generation whose parents were of mixed parentage, that is, one parent foreign born and one parent native. The second generation of a given nationality was classified by the Census Bureau into those who had both parents born in a foreign country and those who had one parent foreign and one parent native born. In the event that both parents were foreign-born, but not in the same country, nationality was based on the country of birth of the father. In cases where only one parent was foreign-born, nationality was attributed on the basis of the country of birth of the foreign-born parent. In an earlier study using similar data, it was noted, "It should not be overlooked that in many cases the native parent is a second-generation member of the same stock as the foreign parent, but the census data do not permit us to distinguish such cases from those involving intermarriage in a stricter sense." (Duncan and Lieberson, 1959, p. 370.) It should also be added that we have no information about the number of cases in which there was intermarriage between persons who were born in different foreign countries and that all of the intermarriage material is based on the nativity classifications of off-spring, that is, the second generation. Differential fertility and migration, to name but two factors, tend to reduce the usefulness of such data. Nevertheless, the relationship between segregation from native whites and intermarriage, as measured by the crude indicator used, is a very strong one, as the Spearman rank order correlations in Table 51 indicate. In each city, the proportion of the second generation having "mixed" parents is inversely related to the magnitude of the foreign-born group's segregation from the native white population. There does not appear to be any trend between censuses in the relative magnitude of these correlations.

No effort has been made here to examine the relationship between segregation and intermarriage in terms of a probability problem, that is, to consider the number of expected and actual cases of intermarriage. However the results reported at least are consistent with the assumption that if residential propinquity is a factor in choice of mate, then the more segregated a given foreign-born group is the more likely is a marriage between members of the same group. Thus, in terms of assimilation

TABLE 51.--Correlations (Spearman) between residential segregation and intermarriage, 1910-1930

| City (1) | Segregation FBW v. NW and per cent of NWFMP with both parents FBW | | |
	1910 (2)	1920 (3)	1930 (4)
Boston	.83	.77	.78
Buffalo	.95	.93	.87
Chicago	.82	.61	.88
Cincinnati	.77	.73	.74
Cleveland	.88	.90	.90
Columbus	NA	.78	.79
Philadelphia	.83	.76	.82
Pittsburgh	.88	.94	.92
St. Louis	.73	.77	.85
Syracuse	NA	.90	.93

Note: See Table 4 for abbreviations.
NA: Data not available.

viewed as an absolute descriptive phenomenon, the data on intermarriage clearly point to a negative relationship between segregation and intermarriage. From the point of view of assimilation as a process to be considered under a given set of circumstances, the data reported above are not very informative, since they do not take into account the probabilities of intermarriage based on the composition of the eligible population and, further, do not enable us to isolate a propinquity effect or to determine how strong it is.

Chapter 6

Occupation Composition of Ethnic Groups

One of the most striking and significant aspects of racial and ethnic contact is the differential occupational composition of the groups involved. That groups differ in their participation in the economy of a society or city is rather clear. To document this with cases outside of the United States, we need only consider French Canada where Hughes (1943) reports that persons of British origin are disproportionately concentrated in the managerial and professional niches, while the French Canadians are disproportionately concentrated in the lower levels of the socio-economic hierarchy. In the South African city of Durban, close to 30 per cent of the Europeans are clerical and office workers, while slightly less than 1 per cent of the Africans have such occupations (Kuper et al., 1958, Table VI, p. 56). The concentration of overseas Chinese in commercial pursuits in such countries as Thailand, Malaya, and Indonesia is well-known and, in part, accounts for their current difficulties in these nations.

Turning to the United States, the differences between Negroes and whites in their participation in the national economy is so blatant that no documentation is required. That white ethnic groups differ in their participation in the various economic levels of our society is also rather clear-cut. To use colorful illustrations, consider the fact that in 1950 very nearly 4 per cent of the males born in Italy were occupied as barbers, beauticians, or manicurists while only 0.5 per cent of all white males were so employed. In the case of Irish immigrants, 2.5 per cent of the men were employed as firemen, policemen, sheriffs or marshals while less than 1 per cent of all white males were in these occupations.

Similarly, the Scots were twice as apt to be an accountant or auditor as the total white male population. And, to end these illustrations with a spectacular case of overrepresentation, very nearly 10 per cent of immigrant Greek males in 1950 were occupied as waiters, bartenders, and counter workers. (See Hutchinson, 1956, Appendix Table A-2a, pp. 335-49.)

Since the occupational division of labor is one of the major factors in the differentiation of a society, an examination of the occupational patterns of ethnic groups in several United States cities, their changes between generations, and an attempt at accounting for their differential occupational composition merit considerable interest in this study of ethnic assimilation. The significance of occupational segregation for the assimilation of ethnic groups is rather clear. First, since occupation influences many other aspects of behavior, the concentration of an ethnic group in certain segments of the economy means that the group's life chances with respect to other areas of social life are likewise skewed or distinct from the population as a whole. Secondly, the occupational concentration of an ethnic group means that a group's visibility may be prolonged and maintained for the society at large.

A Model for Viewing the Differential Occupational Composition of Ethnic Groups

Starting with a structural perspective, we may assume that the economy of a city is independent of the ethnic and racial composition of the city's population. That is, the occupational composition of a given city is largely a function of factors other than the racial and ethnic groups present. To be sure, the peculiar needs of each ethnic group as well as the unique skills they may possess have some effect on the economic activities of a given city. For example, some cities in which Germans settled in large number, such as Milwaukee and St. Louis, have become important beer producing centers (Hoover, 1948). And special meat slaughtering requirements for kosher beef has had some effect on the location of meat packers in the east (Alexandersson, 1956). But, on the whole, we may say that the location of the city, the nature of its hinterland, the transportation and market resources at its disposal, and the city's size--to name but a few factors--are of far more significance than the ethnic composition of the city in determining the occupational patterns that exist.

Secondly, since occupations differ in the skills, training, and education required and since ethnic groups differ in such attributes, we may expect to find this factor also leading to some differences in the occupational patterns of ethnic groups.

Thirdly, immigrants from European countries differ in their time of arrival in the United States and since the economy is a changing one with some occupations declining in importance and others rising, we would expect variations in the occupational composition of ethnic groups solely on the basis of differences in when they arrived in the nation. For example, we noted earlier that the differences between immigrant groups in their proportions living in rural areas were related to the numbers coming in various decades.

Finally, in problems involving the inter-generational occupational mobility of ethnic groups, the occupations of parents vitally influence the occupational roles that children fill. Thus differences between first-generation groups are expected to be perpetuated in later generations. The actual extent of the differences being perpetuated would, of course, be a function of the open or closed nature of the society. It is obviously not completely open in the United States, that is, the expected occupational distribution of children of professionals in a given community is quite different from that of the offspring of laborers.

In summary, there are a number of structural reasons for expecting ethnic groups to differ in their occupational composition and in their changes between generations. That is, there are certain qualities or patterns of differential activity characteristic of the society at large--irrespective of the ethnic or racial attributes of the persons involved.

Data and Methods

Considering the significance of occupational composition as well as the clear-cut differences between ethnic groups in their occupational concentration, there is surprisingly little in the way of census data on the occupations of ethnic groups. There is information, to be sure, on the occupations of the total foreign born for specific cities, but not classified by the specific ethnic groups. Indeed, the only year before 1950 in which occupational data for specific ethnic groups were reported in the census for specific cities is for 1900. For the 1950 census, in addition to Hutchinson's (1956) monograph which gives occupational data for specific first and second generation groups in the entire United States, a special report was issued by the Census Bureau giving the occupations, using broad categories, of selected immigrant and second generation groups for the United States as well as for regions and some of the larger Standard Metropolitan Areas (U. S. Bureau of the Census, 1954). The nine metropolitan areas were those that had 500,000 or more persons of foreign-white stock, i.e., persons either born in a foreign country or whose parents were foreign-born. These nine metropolises are Boston, Chicago, Cleveland, Philadelphia, Pittsburgh, Detroit, Los Angeles, New York-Northeastern New Jersey, and San Francisco-Oakland. The reader will recall that residential segregation has been examined in this study for the central cities of the first five of these areas. Thus later in the chapter the significant relationships between residential and occupational segregation are considered for these five cities where both sets of data are available.

The occupational distributions of several immigrant male groups as well as native whites are shown in Table 52 for the Philadelphia Standard Metropolitan Area to serve as an illustration of both the nature of the data used and the method of analysis. First, we may note that only males were considered in this analysis of occupational distributions although data for females were also available. For each male group, the per cent of the total persons who were both employed and reported their occupation was computed. (The small numbers of males who were occupied, but did not report their occupation were excluded from all parts of this chapter.) Thus, for example, of the 9,000 employed males born in Ireland and reporting their occupation (75 additional employed Irish did not report their occupation), roughly 2.8 per cent were professional or technical workers whereas 10.6 per cent

TABLE 52.--Per cent of native-white and foreign-born males employed in major occupation groups, Philadelphia Standard Metropolitan Area, 1950

Major occupation group	England and Wales	Ireland	Germany	Poland	Austria	Russia	Italy	Native white
Professional, technical, and kindred workers	10.8	2.8	7.6	3.7	6.2	7.3	2.3	10.6
Farmers and farm managers	0.8	0.9	2.5	1.3	2.8	0.5	1.5	1.3
Managers, officials, and proprietors, except farm	11.3	8.7	12.6	13.0	19.3	35.2	9.8	11.8
Clerical, sales, and kindred workers	14.6	9.1	7.9	5.8	11.5	15.7	5.1	18.5
Craftsmen, foremen, and kindred workers	29.1	24.0	39.7	24.1	26.6	19.4	29.5	23.7
Operatives and kindred workers	19.2	22.0	19.4	31.3	17.4	15.7	23.7	22.5
Private household workers	1.1	1.0	0.6	0.1	0.1	0.1	0.0	0.1
Service workers, exc. pvt. household	8.1	17.0	7.1	8.6	8.7	3.8	12.0	5.5
Farm laborers, unpaid family workers	. . .	. . .	0.1	0.0	0.3	0.0	0.0	0.1
Farm laborers, exc. unpaid, and farm foremen	1.0	1.2	0.5	0.8	0.1	0.2	0.7	1.1
Laborers, except farm and mine	4.0	13.4	2.1	11.1	7.0	2.0	15.4	4.9
Total (approximate)	100.0	100.0	100.0	100.0	100.0	100.0	100.0	100.0

Note: Excludes employed males not reporting their occupation.

of the employed native-white population were in this occupational category. Thus for each foreign-born group, as well as for the native
whites, the per cent distribution of the group's employed male population was computed as shown in Table 52 for Philadelphia.

The reader should note that the occupational categories are rather
broad, although corresponding fairly well to some of the major socio-
economic classificatory schemes used by sociologists. Secondly, we
may observe that several of the occupational categories contain very
small proportions of the employed population. For example, the highest
per cent of the employed males working as farmers and farm managers
is 2.8 (Austria); private household workers, 1.1 (England and Wales);
and farm laborers--both paid and unpaid-- is 1.2 (Ireland and native
whites). These figures for the male labor force of a metropolitan area
are of course not surprisingly low when we keep in mind that these are
occupations that are primarily rural or, in the case of private household workers, filled largely by women. It is, however, worth noting
since later we will deal with occupational data for which we do not have
information about these occupations. In all cases, these data are based
on 20 per cent samples.

Finally, we should consider how these per cent distributions were
used to compute an index of the degree of similarity in the occupational
distributions of ethnic groups. The index used for residential segregation is also used here to measure the occupational segregation of groups.
Comparing the occupational distribution of the native-white population
with that of persons born in England and Wales (in both cases for the
Philadelphia metropolitan area) we observe a rather striking similarity
in the two groups' distributions. Thus, for example, 10.8 per cent of
England and Wales' employed males were engaged in professional and
allied occupations in contrast to 10.6 per cent of the native-white population. Similarly, 4.0 and 4.9 per cent of the two groups, respectively,
were laborers. By contrast, a much smaller proportion of the Italian
immigrants were professionals (2.3 per cent) and a much larger proportion were employed as laborers (15.4 per cent). A simple summary
measure of the degree of similarity or dissimilarity between the occupational distributions of the groups involved was used. This index of

occupational segregation or dissimilarity between two groups gives the per cent of one group that would have to leave their current occupational category and be placed into other ones in order for the two groups under comparison to have identical occupational distributions. Thus the index of occupational dissimilarity of England and Wales compared with native whites is 9.3 whereas the index between England and Wales compared with Italy is 20.9. For further details on this index, see Chapter 2.

Immigrant, Second Generation, and Negro Occupational Composition

In each of the nine metropolitan areas, general patterns appear with respect to occupational differences between the foreign-born, second-generation, and native-white populations. Since the second-generation groups are part of the total native-white population of each metropolitan area, it is advisable to use the native whites of native parentage, i.e., Americans of third or later generation, in any analysis of changes between first and second generation groups in their occupational dissimilarity with the native-white population (A similar problem was faced and resolved in the same manner when considering first and second generation residential segregation in 1930).

On the average, second-generation members of ethnic groups are closer to the native white of native parentage occupational distribution than are immigrants of the same nationality (compare columns 2 and 3 of Table 53). Secondly, even the first-generation immigrants are far closer than are Negroes to the occupational distribution of this native population segment (columns 2 and 4). Further, the unweighted average index of occupational segregation for the first generation is rather constant from city to city, ranging from a low of 17 in Detroit and Los Angeles to a high of 25 in Boston. Similarly, the second generation average index of occupational dissimilarity ranges only from 10 in San Francisco to 14 in three cities (Boston, Cleveland, and Pittsburgh). The Negro range is also narrow, running from 37 in Detroit to 47 in San Francisco.

Since the groups examined in each city vary, we must consider this matter more closely before attempting further interpretations of

TABLE 53.--Unweighted mean indexes of dissimilarity of occupational composition for native whites of native parentage compared with foreign-white stock and Negroes, males, 1950

Standard metropolitan area (1)	NWNP compared with:		
	FBW (2)	NWFMP (3)	Negro (4)
Boston	25	14	42
Chicago	24	12	42
Cleveland	23	14	44
Detroit	17	11	37
Los Angeles	17	12	41
New York	24	13	39
Philadelphia	20	13	42
Pittsburgh	20	14	40
San Francisco	18	10	47

Note: See Table 4 for abbreviations.
For groups used in columns 2 and 3, see Table 54.

the results. In addition, it is also necessary to consider differences between cities in their occupational composition before making inferences about Negroes. For example, the over-all occupational distribution in Detroit would be far different from that in Boston. Finally, the reader should keep in mind that we are dealing with cross-sectional data and failing, as well, to control for differential migration, fertility, and mortality. That is, there is no assurance that the second generation members of a given group are, even in part, the children of immigrant members of the group in a particular city. Thus, when we talk about a "decline," between first and second generations, it does not necessarily mean an inter-generational familial shift.

Nevertheless, examination of specific ethnic groups indicates that the second generations are closer to native whites of native parentage in their occupational distribution than are first-generation members of the same groups (Table 54). These results offer further evidence of a

TABLE 54.--Indexes of dissimilarity of occupational composition between native whites of native parentage and foreign-white stock, males, 1950

Standard metropolitan area	Generation	England and Wales	Ireland	Norway	Sweden	Germany	Poland	Czechoslovakia	Austria	Russia	Italy
Boston	First	13	31			40	18	23			21	31
	Second	6	8			14	8	16			24	20
Chicago	First	13	25	28	33	20	27	28		21	19	26
	Second	6	10	8	10	8	18	12		7	25	13
Cleveland	First	14	30				20	27	28	23	18	27
	Second	6	9				9	22	18	14	19	15
Detroit	First	14	12				22	18		13	21	19
	Second	8	12				9	11		4	26	6
Los Angeles	First	10	16	19	24	12	16			15	22	18
	Second	8	10	6	9	7	14			14	29	6
New York	First	13	26	29	32	21	22	22		18	24	28
	Second	7	10	10	11	9	9	18		11	23	19
Philadelphia	First	9	21				20	21		18	24	25
	Second	6	8				10	17		6	32	14
Pittsburgh	First	11	20				21	24	25	19	22	21
	Second	7	11				9	16	20	15	27	10
San Francisco	First	9	22				23	13			12	29
	Second	7	11				8	7			18	12

Note: Indexes of dissimilarity not shown for groups in metropolitan areas where occupational distributions were not published by United States Census Bureau.

decline between first and second generations in the unique occupational distributions of ethnic groups. For example, in Philadelphia, all but one of the seven groups under study have higher first-generation than second-

generation indexes of dissimilarity with the occupational distribution
of native whites of native parentage. The decline--keeping in mind that
we are dealing with cross-sectional data-- is predominant in the other
metropolitan areas as well. There is, however, one ethnic group that
comprises a major exception to this general pattern. Aside from New
York, the second-generation Russians are less like the native white of
native parentage occupational distribution than are first-generation
Russians. To be sure, in some metropolitan areas the increase for second-generation Russians over their first generation is, at most, a minor
one. However, the fact that this is the only group showing such a shift,
as well as the persistency of the shift, leaves little doubt about the significance of the finding.

Shifting to an inter-city consideration of ethnic occupational patterns, the average indexes for each group in the metropolitan areas are
reported in columns 3 and 4 of Table 55. Taking the group we are best
acquainted with first, we note that the average Russian immigrant index
in the nine cities is lower than that for second generation Russians (20
compared with 25). For all other groups, the opposite holds. This is to
be expected since columns 3 and 4 of Table 55 are merely summaries of
the patterns observed in the preceding table. In columns 5 and 6 the
same groups are compared with all other employed males rather than
with the native white males of native parentage. In making this new set
of comparisons, we are in effect asking how a given first or second generation group differs from the entire male occupational distribution of
its community. That is, other foreign-born and second-generation groups,
as well as Negroes and Orientals are also included in the comparison. If
we make the rather reasonable assumption that these additional groups
are lower on the occupational scale for the most part than the native whites
of native parentage, then some rather interesting differences may be noted
between the two sets of indexes. With the exception of England and Wales
and Russia, where there is no difference, the foreign-born are closer to
the occupational distribution for the rest of their metropolitan area than
they are to the distribution for the native white of native parentage segment (compare columns 3 and 5). This is not, however, the case for most

TABLE 55.--Unweighted mean indexes of occupational dissimilarity
for foreign-born and second-generation males compared
with native-white males of native parentage and with all
other employed males, average for selected standard
metropolitan areas, 1950

Group (1)	No. of Areas (2)	NWNP v.		All males v.	
		FBW (3)	NWFMP (4)	FBW (5)	NWFMP (6)
England and Wales	9	12	7	12	11
Ireland	9	23	10	18	12
Norway	3	25	8	23	12
Sweden	5	30	10	28	14
Germany	9	19	8	17	10
Poland	8	22	15	16	12
Czechoslovakia	4	26	17	19	13
Austria	7	18	10	14	11
Russia	9	20	25	20	31
Italy	9	25	13	20	9

Note: See Table 4 for abbreviations. Results reported in columns
5 and 6 are adjusted for the proportion the foreign-born or second-generation group is of the total employed male population of the standard
metropolitan area.

of the groups of second-generation males. All five of the "old" ethnic
groups (England and Wales through Germany) as well as the Austrian
and Russian second generations have occupational distributions that are
closer to that of the native whites of native parentage than to the total
male population (compare columns 4 and 6). The Polish, Czech, and
Italian second-generation occupational distributions are, on the average,
more like that of the total city population than that of the higher status
native whites of native parentage group.

What these results suggest, and the averages in Table 56 indicate, is that some foreign- and second-generation groups are closer to the occupational distributions of native whites of native parentage than they are to some other segments of their community's male labor force. The unweighted mean indexes between native whites of native parentage and various foreign-born and second-generation groups are again shown in columns 4 and 7 of Table 56. In all cases, the Negro male occupational distribution in each metropolitan area is less similar to the first- or second-generation groups than is the occupational distribution of the native whites of native parentage (compare columns 2 and 4 for immigrants, and columns 5 and 7 for the second generation). In all metropolitan areas considered, the second-generation groups were on the average closer to third and later generation males than they were to the distribution of other second-generation groups examined in their city (compare columns 7 and 6), but still the Negroes had the most dissimilar occupational distributions (compare columns 5 and 6). The foreign-born groups, by contrast, are in several cities closer to each other in their occupational distributions than they are to that of native whites of native parentage (compare columns 3 and 4). Nevertheless, they are more dissimilar to that of the Negroes than they are among themselves (columns 2 and 3). Finally, we may note the general decline between first and second generations in dissimilarity with later generation whites is accompanied by an increase in dissimilarity with the occupational distribution of Negroes (columns 2 and 5).

Occupational Status

Let us stand back and look at the forest. We have observed that immigrants in 1950 are clearly differentiated from native whites of native parentage in their propensities to fill certain occupational niches. They are even further differentiated from the occupational composition of Negroes. The second-generation groups in these centers are less dissimilar in occupations to the native whites of native parentage but are more dissimilar to Negroes than are the immigrant groups. This shift away from Negroes clearly suggests an upward movement in occupational position for the second-generation groups. That second

TABLE 56.--Unweighted mean indexes of dissimilarity of occupational
composition for first and second generation groups compared with Negroes, other groups of the same generation,
and native whites of native parentage, males, 1950

Standard metropolitan area (1)	FBW v.			NWFMP v.		
	Negro (2)	Other FBW (3)	NWNP (4)	Negro (5)	Other NWFMP (6)	NWNP (7)
Boston	38	30	25	43	20	14
Chicago	36	22	24	42	16	12
Cleveland	33	19	23	40	18	14
Detroit	35	20	17	41	16	11
Los Angeles	44	20	17	47	13	12
New York	35	23	24	40	17	13
Philadelphia	37	23	20	43	20	13
Pittsburgh	34	24	20	41	19	14
San Francisco	40	20	18	50	14	10

Note: See Table 4 for abbreviations.

generation groups move upward is hardly surprising, but there is a
rather important sociological problem to be considered with respect
to these shifts. That is, can these changes be viewed as reflecting ethnic assimilation? If ethnic groups are moving in such a direction, then
we would expect knowledge of the European origins of second-generation Americans to be less significant in predicting their behavior than
would knowledge of the European origins of first-generation Americans.
Presumably, the major immediate social factor influencing the actual
occupation of a given individual in a community is his education, since
we are holding constant both community and sex in this analysis. Thus
the higher the educational level of a given ethnic group, the higher we

should expect the occupational level to be. If ethnic origin was no longer significant, then we would expect a perfect correlation between the educational and occupational level of the groups.

The unsatisfactory nature of the data requires a brief consideration. First, although educational data are available for all foreign-born males and second-generation males by nationality, we will only consider males between the ages of 25 to 44 in each generation. This is done for two reasons. First, it is important to control for differences between groups in their age distribution because of the changing nature of our labor force and frequency of achieving various educational levels. Secondly, and of greater importance, the educational levels of large numbers of older males who have retired or are no longer working would otherwise be included in determining the educational level of the working portion of an ethnic group's labor force.

The rankings given to each occupational category are indicated below:

Professional, technical, and kindred workers	1
Managers, officials, and proprietors, except farm	2
Clerical, sales and kindred workers	3
Craftsmen, foreman, and kindred workers	4
Operatives and kindred workers	5
Service workers, except private household	5.5
Laborers, except farm and mine	6

These rankings are adopted from Edwards' social-economic groupings as used by Duncan and Duncan (1955a). There are several occupational categories used in this study that are not included in the set of rankings above (see Table 52). However only small proportions of each group's labor force are, as we noted earlier, employed in these occupations; and so the measure of mean occupational status used for each group is reasonably accurate--given the fact that the occupational categories themselves are fairly diverse. The measure of average status was obtained by multiplying the proportion of a given group's labor force in an occupational category by the ranking of the category. For example, if all members of a group were professionals, then their mean ranking would be, of course, 1. If half were professional and half laborers, then the mean would be 3.5 (.5 X 1 plus .5 X 6). Differences between groups in their proportions in occupational categories not included in the rankings did not affect the groups' mean rank since these means were computed on the basis of the proportion of each group employed in the ranked occupations shown above.

Turning at last to the results, we may observe in Table 57 that there are a number of surprising deviations from the expected path of higher socio-economic status for second-generation groups. Consider, for example, the first and second generations from England and Wales-- keeping in mind that the lower the index, the higher the status. In every metropolitan area except New York, the first generation had a higher occupational position than did the second generation. Similarly, for the Germans, there are a number of such reversals; and this holds for a number of other groups as well. The Italian second generations, by contrast, are in higher occupational positions than their first-generation counterparts in all nine metropolitan areas. A similar upward movement is observed for the Swedes in the five centers investigated. In short, there is no clear-cut pattern apparent in the results shown in Table 57. Indeed, the unweighted mean index of occupational status is higher for the first generations in several of the cities. For example, the first generation mean index is 3.92 in Pittsburgh whereas the second generation mean is 4.03 in the same city.

It is therefore all the more impressive to discover that the educational level of the various foreign-born and second-generation groups goes a long way in accounting for the differences in occupational levels between the groups of a city. That is, the correlations shown in Table 58 between the median education of the immigrant or second-generation groups in each metropolis and their occupational status are nearly always quite high. Further, in all metropolises, the correlations are even higher for the variations between second-generation groups in their occupational and educational level. For example, the seven foreign-born groups in Detroit have the lowest foreign-born Spearman correlation between educational level and occupational status, .40. However the second-generation males for these seven groups in Detroit have a Spearman correlation of .96 between these two variables. In view of the fact that

TABLE 57.--Indexes of occupational status for first and second generation males, ages 25-44, in nine standard metropolitan areas with 500,000 or more foreign-white stock, 1950

Group	Generation	Standard metropolitan area									Group mean
		Boston	Chicago	Cleveland	Detroit	Los Angeles	New York	Philadelphia	Pittsburgh	San Francisco	
England and Wales	First	3.30	3.26	3.23	3.43	3.05	3.22	3.27	3.75	3.13	3.29
	Second	3.44	3.37	3.49	3.54	3.27	3.22	3.51	3.85	3.17	3.43
Ireland	First	4.44	4.36	4.31	3.80	2.89	4.31	4.26	4.43	4.21	4.11
	Second	3.81	3.67	3.68	3.46	3.42	3.71	3.82	3.89	3.45	3.66
Norway	First		3.97			3.88	3.84				3.90
	Second		3.39			3.52	3.44				3.45
Sweden	First	3.61	3.80			3.57	3.77			3.55	3.66
	Second	3.37	3.32			3.24	3.23			3.25	3.28
Germany	First	3.21	3.56	3.70	3.64	3.16	3.50	3.70	3.62	3.32	3.49
	Second	3.35	3.60	3.63	3.73	3.35	3.45	3.63	3.90	3.44	3.56
Poland	First	3.70	3.94	3.74	3.90	3.18	3.49	3.71	4.10		3.72
	Second	3.85	4.03	4.05	4.07	3.12	3.64	4.14	4.41		3.91

TABLE 57--Continued

Group	Generation	Standard metropolitan area									Group mean
		Boston	Chicago	Cleveland	Detroit	Los Angeles	New York	Philadelphia	Pittsburgh	San Francisco	
Czechoslovakia	First		3.95	3.86			3.77		4.39		3.99
	Second		3.80	3.98			3.95		4.43		4.04
Austria	First		3.57	3.66	3.37	2.92	3.17	3.31	3.78		3.40
	Second		3.66	3.80	3.84	3.16	3.17	3.60	4.34		3.65
Russia	First	3.11	3.01	2.65	3.00	2.80	3.05	2.89	3.05	3.23	2.98
	Second	2.79	2.81	3.00	3.03	2.76	2.78	2.84	3.26	2.91	2.91
Italy	First	4.20	4.04	3.92	4.11	3.80	4.13	4.11	4.22	4.02	4.06
	Second	4.03	3.94	3.90	3.96	3.73	3.96	4.02	4.16	3.83	3.95
City mean	First	3.65	3.75	3.63	3.61	3.25	3.62	3.61	3.92	3.58	
	Second	3.52	3.56	3.69	3.66	3.28	3.45	3.65	4.03	3.34	

TABLE 58.--Kendall and Spearman correlations between median education and occupational ranking of selected groups of
foreign-white stock in 1950, males, 25-44 years of age

Standard metropolitan area	Number of groups	Correlation between median education and occupational ranking			
		Spearman		Kendall	
		FBW	NWFMP	FBW	NWFMP
Boston	7	.62	.68	.71	.86
Chicago	10	.80	.87	.62	.76
Cleveland	8	.81	.98	.64	.93
Detroit	7	.40	.96	.28	.90
Los Angeles	9	.58	.73	.50	.61
New York	10	.84	.94	.67	.89
Philadelphia	7	.67	.97	.48	.90
Pittsburgh	8	.79	.89	.64	.75
San Francisco	6	.66	.90	.47	.73

Note: See Table 4 for abbreviations.

the Spearman is somewhat more sensitive to large deviations than is the
Kendall rank order correlation, the latter was also computed for the
same sets of occupational and educational data. Here too, the same pattern of increasing association between education and occupation for the
second-generation groups was found. Thus this pattern is apparently
not due to any extreme shifts for a single group's first and second generation position. It thus appears that there is an increase in status
crystallization for the second-generation groups. Or, to put the matter
in another way, given the educational levels of a number of groups in a
metropolis, a rather good prediction can be made of their relative occupational ranks without any further information about these groups.
Further, an even better prediction of the occupational rankings of second-generation groups can be made with knowledge of their educational
levels. In short, the relative positions of various foreign-born and

second-generation groups in the occupational hierarchy can be readily understood in terms of the general societal association between education and occupational position.

Carrying this style of analysis a step further, let us consider the variations between cities in the occupational and educational rankings of the ethnic groups. Since data are not published for all of the groups in all nine metropolitan areas, examination is limited to the five groups for which such occupational and educational information is available in all nine areas as well as for the Poles who are omitted only in San Francisco. The results here are nearly as cogent as the within-city analysis. Ignoring Russian immigrants for the moment, it is evident that there is a close association between each group's variations in educational and occupational levels in the nine (or eight) metropolitan areas (Table 59). This then adds all the more weight to the position taken that the occupational variations of ethnic groups may be viewed largely as a function of their educational levels.

TABLE 59.--Correlations (Spearman) between median education and occupational status for selected first and second generation groups of males, ages 25-44, 1950

Group	Between city correlation of occupation and education	
	FBW	NWFMP
England and Wales	.68	.75
Ireland	.70	.88
Germany	.64	.88
Poland	.67	.88
Russia	-.43	.82
Italy	.72	.59

Note: See Table 4 for abbreviations. Occupational data for Polish first and second-generation groups in San Francisco are not published. Thus only eight metropolitan areas used in Polish correlations.

What accounts for the deviation for Russian immigrants wherein a negative association exists between occupational and educational level is uncertain. However, a far more important problem remains unresolved. Namely, although the second-generation groups are closer to the native whites of native parentage in occupational distribution than are the first-generation groups, in a number of cases this shift has been accompanied by a decline in status--at least for the segment between 25-44 years of age. The second generation groups are mostly higher in median education so that education not only fails to account for the drop in status, but, further, would also lead to an expectation of higher socioeconomic status for the second generation groups.

In addition, Nam (1959) has investigated the socio-economic position of first and second generation male groups in the United States in 1950 and, using the same data, has come up with what would appear to be different results. Concerning himself largely with the entire United States, and after standardizing for age and urban-rural residence, he found the second-generation groups in higher median socio-economic status positions than their first-generation groups. The only exception was England and Wales where both generations had identical status positions. To be sure, Nam's ranking procedure for socio-economic position differed from that used here since he used a median whereas a mean was employed in this study and, further, a somewhat different ranking procedure for socio-economic position was utilized.

However, when Nam later reports the generational changes for the Irish, German, Russian, and Italian groups within United States regions and in the New York, Philadelphia, Los Angeles, and San Francisco metropolitan areas, a number of declines in status are found. In five of the six United States regions, the German foreign-born population had higher status, as measured by Nam, than did the group's second generation in these regions. In the sixth region, the Middle Atlantic, the index of socio-economic status was the same for the two generations. Moreover, both the Irish and German second generations declined in Los Angeles, as did the German second generation in San Francisco. (See Nam, 1959, Table 3.) Precisely the same shifts were found for the first and second generations of the four groups in the limited number of metropolitan areas considered by Nam. That is, using only males between 25 and 44 years of age, the only cases of downward status shown in Table 57 for the second generations of these four groups in the metropolitan areas considered by Nam are the Germans and Irish in Los Angeles, and the Germans in San Francisco. Thus, it appears not unlikely that if Nam had computed such socio-economic indexes for other groups and for more metropolitan areas, he too would have turned up with a number of cases of downward mobility.

What accounts for this surprising shift downward for some groups in their occupational status is difficult to determine. There are, as always, several methodological matters which could be responsible. First, the occupational categories are rather broad and therefore important differences between first and second generation groups in their position within a broad occupational category are hidden in this study. Second, incorrect rankings of occupations could mean shifts in occupational status that are not reflected correctly in the index of socio-economic status used. Finally, it may be that highly selective inter-regional and inter-city migration accounts for some of the status declines. The additional relationships with respect to ethnic status positions that are noted below must therefore be viewed as tentative, suggestive, and requiring further investigation.

The reader will recall that the association between status and education for second-generation groups is higher than it is for first-generation members of the same groups. A somewhat different way of examining this association between education and status involves considering the actual occupational distributions of ethnic groups with that which would be expected solely on the basis of their educational attainments, that is, based on the clear-cut relationships between educational level and occupational level. We should hardly expect a group of males with merely a grammer school education to have the same occupational distribution as a group with college degrees, for example. By using census data for the year 1950, it was possible to determine the occupational distribution cross-classified by education for white males between 25 and 44 years of age in the northern and western segments of the United States. Roughly 57 per cent of white males who were college graduates were employed in the professional, technical, and kindred category whereas slightly more than 2 per cent of males without any school years completed were so employed. Incidentally, the fact that 2 per cent were in this category supports the earlier methodological remark with respect to the broad meanings of the occupational categories used. At any rate, using this set of occupational distributions classified by education completed as a kind of standard or basis of expectation, the occupational distributions of first and second generation groups in the Boston metropolitan area were examined in terms of what would be "expected" given their educational distribution and the general relationships between education and occupation in the larger society. Since these groups comprise but a small portion of the northern and western United States male population, no adjustments were made to take into account their weights in the expected distributions used.

The expected occupational distribution for each first and second generation group in Boston was then compared with the actual distribution for the group in that city. The results shown in Table 60 indicate that the occupational distribution for the second generation of each group is closer to what would be expected on the basis of its educational level than is the occupational distributions for the first generation of each group. For example, the index of dissimilarity between the expected and actual occupational distributions of first generation Irish males is 25, whereas it is only 16 between the expected and actual second generation Irish occupational distributions. Such is the case for all seven groups, although the declines for the Polish and Russian groups are essentially nil. Thus it appears that there is less of an "ethnic effect" interfering with occupational selection for second-generation groups than for first-generation groups. Further, in comparing the actual status positions of these groups with that which would be expected on the basis of their educational distributions, it was found that there is a decline for the second-generation members of groups whose first generation had a status position higher than expected on the basis of their educational attainments. For example, the English, Swedish, and Russian first-generation groups exceeded their expected status positions to a greater degree than did their second-generation members, who also

TABLE 60.--Occupational and socio-economic status positions of first and second generation groups compared with positions expected on the basis of the relationship between education and occupation in the northern and western regions of the United States, males 25-44, Boston Standard Metropolitan Area: 1950

Group	Generation	Index of dissimilarity between expected and actual occupational distribution	Status	
			Actual	Expected
England and Wales	First	17.22	3.30	3.48
	Second	10.54	3.44	3.53
Ireland	First	25.10	4.44	4.07
	Second	15.84	3.81	3.58
Sweden	First	22.21	3.61	3.78
	Second	14.14	3.37	3.44
Germany	First	17.60	3.21	3.18
	Second	11.26	3.35	3.40
Poland	First	12.63	3.70	3.75
	Second	12.60	3.85	3.62
Russia	First	23.56	3.11	3.58
	Second	23.40	2.79	3.12
Italy	First	16.26	4.20	4.08
	Second	9.69	4.03	3.87

have higher status positions than expected on the basis of their educational attainments.

Continuing this line of examination with respect to generational shifts in occupational status, the declines were examined in each of five Standard Metropolitan Areas in connection with inter-generational changes in the degree of dissimilarity to the occupational distribution of native whites of native parentage in their metropolitan area. In each case, there was a consistent association between the magnitude of the decline in status and the magnitude of the decline between generations in a group's occupational dissimilarity with native whites of native parentage (Table 61).

TABLE 61.--Correlations (Spearman) between inter-generational declines in socio-economic status and declines in dissimilarity of occupational distributions from native whites of
native parentage, ages 25-44, 1950

Standard metropolitan area	Correlation
Boston	.46
Chicago	.65
Cleveland	.31
Philadelphia	.32
Pittsburgh	.55

Residential and Occupational Segregation

Consideration of the relationships between residential and occupational segregation logically involves some form of interaction. Duncan
and Duncan (1955a) have demonstrated that occupational groups in Chicago vary in the degree of residential segregation from one another. Thus,
members of a given occupational group are least segregated from persons
belonging to occupations of similar socio-economic level and most segregated from persons of the most distant socio-economic levels. Their
findings have been examined and confirmed for several other cities in
the United States by Wilkins (1956).

The association between residential and occupational segregation
is shown in Table 62. Keeping in mind that residential segregation was
computed on the basis of the central cities whereas occupational segregation was computed for the entire metropolitan area, we observe in four
of the five centers a rather high association between residential and occupational segregation of foreign-born groups from the native-white pop-

ulation. In Boston, there is essentially no relationship at all. With respect to Negroes, the magnitude of a foreign-born group's residential segregation cannot be viewed as a function of the group's similarity to the occupational distribution of Negroes. This is to be expected since

TABLE 62.--Correlations (Spearman) between similarity in occupational composition and residential segregation, 1950

| City | Number of groups | Occupational and residential similarities of FBW and: | |
		NW	Negro
Boston	7	-.07	-.43
Chicago	9	.62	.13
Cleveland	8	.53	-.40
Philadelphia	7	.68	.29
Pittsburgh	8	.81	.02

Note: See Table 4 for abbreviations.

Negro-white residential segregation is clearly not primarily a function of economic factors. However the high correlations in four of the five metropolitan areas with respect to native whites calls for further analysis. In Chapter 3 we had concluded, on the basis of housing cost information in Cleveland, that ethnic segregation from native whites was not a function of simple economic differences between groups in their housing costs. Here then, in the case of occupational segregation, are results that would appear to contradict our earlier inference. Although no resolution of the problem is possible without further analysis (involving data that are not available), the fact that occupational and residential segregation are associated in four of the five cities does not necessarily contradict our conclusions about the relationships between housing costs and segregation in Chapter 3 or the general approach to segregation used in Chapters 3 and 4. Although the two variables under consideration are associated, the magnitude of the differential residential patterns that

could be explained by ethnic differences in occupational composition remains a moot point. Thus, in the case of the effect of housing costs on
segregation in Cleveland in 1930, we were able to investigate the existing correlations and determine that the associations accounted for only
a small proportion of the magnitudes of the segregation indexes between
the immigrant groups and the native-white population. An additional
matter requiring further consideration is the fact that occupational
groups differ in their degree of segregation from one another (Wilkins,
1956; Duncan and Duncan, 1955a.) The summary measures of occupational segregation that correlated with residential segregation in four
cities fail to take this matter into account. Thus two immigrant groups
could have the same index of occupational segregation from native
whites, but be expected to differ in their degree of residential segregation from native whites because of their differences in occupational
composition that account for the same index of occupational segregation. These indexes are shown in Table 63 merely to illustrate an additional factor that should be considered in any further analysis of the
correlations shown in Table 62.

Residential Segregation and Occupational
Change Between Generations

If the reader has found an unusually cautious note in the treatment
of occupational segregation and residential segregation, then he is ad-
vised that the subject to be discussed here is even more daring in the
use of data and material. Nevertheless, our lack of information about
occupational mobility between generations in general--to say nothing of
that for specific ethnic groups--is embraced as justification for the procedures used. The occupational distribution of each foreign-born and
second-generation group in the nine metropolitan areas is available for
each of three age categories. These age groups are: 14 to 24, 25 to 44,
and 45 and over. (We have already had occasion to use the groups between 25 and 44 years of age in our consideration of the relationship between education and occupation.) Suppose we assume no migration within the United States for either the first or second generations and, further,

TABLE 63.--Indexes of dissimilarity in residential distribution among major occupation groups, for employed males in the Chicago metropolitan district, 1950, by census tracts

Major occupation group	Major occupation group (see stub)						
	(2)	(3)	(4)	(5)	(6)	(7)	(8)
(1) Professional, technical, and kindred workers	13	15	28	35	44	41	54
(2) Managers, officials, and proprietors, exc. farm workers	...	13	28	33	41	40	52
(3) Sales workers	...	...	27	35	42	38	54
(4) Clerical and kindred workers	...	...	...	16	21	24	38
(5) Craftsmen, foremen, and kindred workers	...	...	...	...	17	35	35
(6) Operatives and kindred workers	...	...	...	...	...	26	25
(7) Service workers, exc. private household	...	...	...	...	...	...	28
(8) Laborers, exc. farm and mine	...	...	...	...	...	...	...

Source: Duncan and Duncan, 1955a, Table 3.

that first-generation males 45 years of age and older are the parents of all second-generation males between 25 and 44 years of age. Males between 14 and 24 are excluded since many are still in school or have not

TABLE 64.--Occupations of sons, distributed by occupation of father, for four cities combined (Chicago, Los Angeles, Philadelphia, San Francisco), 1950

Occupation of son's longest job	Occupation of father's longest job (see stub)									
	(1)	(2)	(3)	(4)	(5)	(6)	(7)	(8)	(9)	(10)
(1) Professional, technical, and kindred workers	29.0	2.7	13.9	16.5	7.3	7.8	...	8.9	5.9	3.7
(2) Farmers and farm managers	...	0.8	...	...	0.2	0.1	...	...	...	...
(3) Managers, officials, and proprietors, except farm	22.5	12.5	31.4	16.3	14.1	7.8	18.3	13.2	6.5	6.5
(4) Clerical, sales, and kindred workers	15.1	6.6	17.6	32.6	14.2	13.9	18.3	13.0	3.9	9.8
(5) Craftsmen, foremen, and kindred workers	14.6	20.7	13.7	13.6	32.4	27.3	18.3	18.8	11.8	26.6
(6) Operatives and kindred workers	9.2	25.8	12.0	12.2	20.5	32.0	4.6	21.7	31.8	33.7
(7) Private household workers	...	0.2	0.2	...	0.2	0.0	...	0.4	...	0.2
(8) Service workers, except private household	6.1	14.5	8.1	6.2	6.4	6.3	22.3	20.3	10.1	9.5

TABLE 64.--Continued

Occupation of son's longest job	Occupation of father's longest job (see stub)									
	(1)	(2)	(3)	(4)	(5)	(6)	(7)	(8)	(9)	(10)
(9) Farm laborers and farm foremen	0.4	0.6	0.1	...	0.2	0.0	...	...	...	...
(10) Laborers, excpet farm and mine	2.9	15.7	3.1	2.6	4.6	4.7	18.3	3.7	29.9	10.1
Total (approximate)	100.0	100.0	100.0	100.0	100.0	100.0	100.0	100.0	100.0	100.0

Note: Son's longest job was longest job in 1950; father's was longest job during lifetime. Fathers or sons not reporting occupation are excluded. Clerical and sales workers are separate categories in original data source, but were combined here to be comparable to occupational data for ethnic groups.

Source: Unpublished data from Occupational Mobility Survey, Table W-9. For details of study, see Palmer, 1954.

selected their adult occupation. Ignoring questions of migration, mortality, and differential fertility, we will examine the relationship between the occupational composition of foreign-born males who are at least 45 years of age and the composition of second-generation males of the same nationality who are between 25 and 44 years of age. We shall call the first group, "immigrant fathers" of the second group. To be sure, we would hardly think of a man of 44 years of age as having a father one year older. But, since these are broad age categories, we can assume that the younger immigrant fathers have sons at the 25 year old level, rather than those second-generation males who are close to 44 years of age.

Using unpublished data from a study conducted by Gladys L. Palmer, we can derive a necessary set of inter-generational mobility rates (shown in Table 64). These data indicate rather clearly that occupational choice of sons is related to their fathers' occupations. To illustrate, 29 per cent of the sons of professional workers are themselves professionals, whereas only 4 per cent of the sons of laborers are professionals. By contrast, 3 per cent of the sons of professionals are laborers, whereas 10 per cent of the sons of laborers are themselves laborers. The point is that father's occupation clearly influences the occupations of sons. Now then, how do our arbitrarily delineated ethnic father and son combinations fit in to this general scheme? By assuming that foreign-born males who are at least 45 years of age are the fathers of all second-generation males of the same nationality who are between 25 and 44 years of age, we can examine the extent to which each ethnic group follows the general occupational inheritence pattern in four large metropolitan areas.

Table 65 indicates the differences between the actual and expected occupational distributions for second-generation males in the five metropolitan areas where residential segregation was also considered. Inspection of these indexes of dissimilarity shows that in some cases a remarkably good prediction could have been made of the occupational distribution of second-generation groups based on the crude and broad assumptions discussed earlier. For example, the index of dissimilarity between actual and expected occupational distribution for Italian second-

TABLE 65.--Indexes of dissimilarity between the actual occupational
distribution and the occupational distribution expected on
the basis of inter-generational mobility patterns, second-
generation males (25 to 44 years of age) in selected large
cities: 1950

Group	Standard metropolitan area				
	Boston	Chicago[a]	Cleveland	Philadelphia[a]	Pittsburgh
England and Wales	5.04	5.78	11.76	11.68	12.68
Ireland	13.64	12.26	8.28	8.98	11.63
Norway	. . .	10.01	. . .	. . .	. . .
Sweden	15.42	13.72	. . .	. . .	. . .
Germany	9.70	8.66	10.34	12.54	14.45
Poland	8.82	13.71	15.54	16.14	20.35
Czecho-slovakia	. . .	9.30	13.42	. . .	20.51
Austria	. . .	8.51	11.98	7.28	19.69
Russia	25.22	23.79	19.04	22.61	14.66
Italy	7.68	8.99	5.75	9.07	10.43

[a]Indexes of dissimilarity adjusted for the group's estimated proportion of the total male population in the four cities for which generational mobility patterns were obtained (see Table 64). These adjustments lead to minor changes and did not affect the groups' rank order
in either Chicago or Philadelphia.

generation males is low in all five areas as is the case for England and
Wales. By contrast, the Russians deviate fairly highly in all cities.

The critical question to ask is what impact does residential segregation of immigrants have on the inter-generational occupational patterns between first- and second-generation groups? The results,
shown in Table 66, indicate that the more highly segregated foreign-
born groups in each of the five communities considered have greater
deviations from the general inter-generational occupational pattern.
That is, if a foreign-born group is relatively similar to the residential

TABLE 66.--Correlation (Spearman) between segregation from native whites and deviation of second-generation males, ages 25-44, from "expected" occupational composition, 1950

City	Number of groups	Correlation
Boston	7	.32
Chicago	9	.67
Cleveland	8	.36
Philadelphia	7	.29
Pittsburgh	8	.50

Note: See text for discussion of method used to compute expected occupational distributions of second-generation males, 25-44.

distribution of the native-white population, then its second-generation members are apt to follow the general occupational pattern that would be expected on the basis of what their parents' occupations are. By contrast, a group that is highly deviant from the general inter-generational occupational pattern is also, as in the case of the Russians, a group whose foreign-born members are relatively highly segregated. Or, to put it another way, the greater the degree of differentiation of a group residentially, the greater their differentiation from other aspects of the general social structure.

Changes in Political Boundaries Between 1910 and 1920 Affecting Comparability of Analyses for the Two Census Years

Denmark: Annexation of Northern Schleswig from Germany.

France: Annexation of Alsace-Lorraine from Germany.

Austria: Annexation of territory from Hungary. Detachments of territory to Czechoslovakia (inferred, on basis of census report on Hungarian boundary changes, as being Bohemia and Moravia), to Poland (Galicia), to Yugoslavia (territory not determined), to Rumania (Bukowina), and to Italy (Trentino region, Gorizia, Istrian peninsula, and Trieste); and detachment of Fiume to form a free state.

Germany: Detachments of territory to France (Alsace-Lorraine), Belgium (Eupen and Malmedy), Poland (West Prussia and Posen), Denmark (Northern Schleswig), and Saar Basin (League of Nations); and detachment of Danzig to form a free city.

Hungary: Detachments of territory to Austria, Czechoslovakia (Ruthenia and Slovakland), Rumania (Transylvania and part of Banat), and Yugoslavia (territory formerly Hungarian not determined).

Rumania: Annexations of territory from Austria (Bukowina), Hungary (Transylvania, part of Banat, and other territories), and Russia (Bessarabia).

Russia: Detachments of territory to Poland (Russian Poland), Rumania (Bessarabia), and detachment of Lithuania.

Greece: Annexations of territory from Bulgaria (Bulgarian Thrace) and Turkey in Europe (Turkish Islands of the Aegean, Turkish Thrace, and Smyrna).

Italy: Annexations of territory from Austria (Trentino region, Gorizia, Istrian peninsula. Trieste).

Note: Important changes affecting only countries not studied in 1910 and 1920, e.g., Poland, are not indicated above.

Source: Department of Commerce, Bureau of the Census, Fourteenth Census of the United States, Vol. II, Population 1920, General Report and Analytical Tables (Washington: Government Printing Office, 1922), p. 687.

Sources and Use of Chicago Data

Many of the data used herein for Chicago were obtained from a previously published study (Duncan and Lieberson, 1959). (For a brief summary of the history and nature of the 75 Chicago Community Areas, see Philip M. Hauser and Evelyn M. Kitagawa, eds., Local Community Fact Book for Chicago (Chicago: Chicago Community Inventory, University of Chicago, 1953), p. xi.) The residential segregation data for 1930 and 1950 in Chicago were obtained from this earlier study as well as occupational data and various indexes of assimilation. The segregation indexes were based on the residential distribution patterns of groups in the 75 Community Areas of Chicago. These spatial units are considerably larger than the tract units used in computing the 1930 and 1950 segregation indexes in the other nine cities for 1930 and 1950. Consequently, as was noted earlier, Chicago's 1930 and 1950 segregation indexes are lower than would have been obtained if distributions by tract had been used. This is important in making inter-city comparisons of segregation for a given ethnic group in 1930 and 1950 since the Chicago indexes are lower than would have been obtained if comparable spatial units had been used. The 1910 and 1920 segregation data for Chicago are based on data computed for this study and are on a ward basis as are the 1910 and 1920 data for the remaining nine cities. The substantive significance of the Chicago findings for this study has been noted earlier in Chapter 1.

First Generation Data for
Syracuse in 1930

Data for the tract distributions of the foreign born by country of birth were not available for Syracuse in 1930. The only complete set of tracted data for the foreign born in 1930 were for a number of the foreign born families in Syracuse by country of birth of the head of household. Consequently these data were used as a substitute and are the source of all discussions and analyses of first generation segregation in Syracuse in 1930. Obviously the residential pattern of foreign born families is not the same as the residential distribution of the total foreign born population in a given city. The omission in the family index of single foreign born adults and the spatial variations in family size for a given group would obviously tend to make these two indexes somewhat different.

Since 1930 residential data for foreign born groups by country of birth were published for certain selected census tracts in Syracuse, it is possible to compare for these census tracts the per cent of each foreign born population and the per cent of total families of each foreign born group that are in these selected tracts. The results are presented below:

Syracuse, Selected Tracts, 1930

Per cent of city's total:

	Foreign born population	Foreign born families
Irish Free State	36.9	36.9
Sweden	29.1	21.6
Germany	42.9	44.1
Poland	82.8	83.2
Czechoslovakia	75.4	76.8

Austria	49.2	48.4
Russia	64.8	63.6
Italy	81.3	79.7

The figures for each group are fairly similar and indicate that the distributions by family are fairly close approximations to the total foreign born population distributions for each foreign born group. The variations between groups in the per cent of their city totals that were included in these selected tracts cannot be attributed to anything of significance since it is not known what criteria were used in the selection of these tracts. Further, one would expect, if a non-random selection method were used, to find groups varying in their proportions included.

Indexes of dissimilarity were computed between the per cent distributions of the foreign born populations in these selected tracts and their comparable distribution of foreign born families for four groups. The indexes of dissimilarity obtained and the groups used are indicated below:

Czechoslovakia	6.52
Italy	9.70
Poland	1.96
Russia	1.88

These indexes for the four groups with the largest proportion of their total population included in data for foreign born persons in selected tracts indicate a fairly high degree of similarity between the two distributions in Syracuse. The relationship between family and individual distributions has been examined herein in, of course, a rather superficial manner. Nevertheless the results seem to justify the use of family data for determining the residential patterns of Syracuse immigrants in 1930.

Changes and Additions in Census
Tracts Between 1930 and 1950

Boston

Tracts combined in 1950 to make comparable with 1930 tracts that
were later subdivided:

1930	1950	1930	1950
B-5	B-5A, B-5B	W-3	W-3A, W-3B
K-4	K-4A, K-4B	W-4	W-4A, W-4B
P-1	P-1A, P-1B, P-1C	W-6	W-6A, W-6B, W-6C, W-6D
T-3	T-3A, T-3B	X-3	X-3A, X-3B
T-4	T-4A, T-4B	X-4	X-4A, X-4B
T-5	T-5A, T-5B	X-5	X-5A, X-5B, X-5C
T-7	T-7A, T-7B	X-6	X-6A, X-6B X-6C
T-8	T-8A, T-8B	Y-3	Y-3A, Y-3B
U-6	U-6A, U-6B		
V-4	V-4A, V-4B	Y-5	Y-5A, Y-5B, Y-5C
W-1	W-1A, W-1B	Z-1	Z-1A, Z-1B, Z-1C

Tracts combined in 1930 and 1950 due to tract boundary revisions
since 1930:

Tracts Combined	Tracts Combined
A-1, A-2, A-3, A-6, B-5A, B-5B	M-3, M-4
C-1, E-2	O-2, P-1A, P-1B, P-1C
I-4, L-5	S-1, S-2
M-1, N-1	W-3A, W-3B, W-4A, W-4B

Buffalo

Tracts combined in 1930 and 1950 due to tract boundary revisions
since 1930:

Tracts Combined

1, 3, 5
4, 11, 19
41, 44

Note: Annexations of park areas with no population to Buffalo in 1935 affected boundaries of tracts 1, 10, and 46 slightly, but not taken into account.

Chicago

Community area - no adjustments made.

Note: Minor changes in Chicago between 1930 and 1950 not taken into account.

Cincinnati

Revisions and annexations between 1940 and 1950 too extensive for adjustments.

Cleveland

Tracts combined in 1930 and 1950 due to tract boundary revisions since 1930:

Tracts Combined

D-2, D-5, D-7
H-9, I-8

Note: Tract Z-1 in 1950 includes only part of the area included in 1930. Tract W-7 in 1950 includes part of tract not previously in the city. Miles Heights village, annexed to Cleveland in 1932 and thereafter comprising tracts U-8, U-9, V-1, V-2, V-3, not included in 1930 computations. Miles Heights village population in 1930 was 2,042.

Columbus

Tracts combined in 1930 and 1950 due to tract boundary revisions since 1930:

Tracts Combined	Tracts Combined
2, 3	41, 51
4, 5	43, 44
7, 8, 9	47, 48
20, 32	49, 50
24, 25	55, 59
29, 36	57, 58
33, 34	

Note: Annexations since 1930 resulted in slight changes in boundaries of tracts 7, 27, and 42. Tracts 4, 5, 25, 51, 57, 58, and 61 included annexed areas in 1950. None of these changes taken into account. East Columbus village and part of Mifflin township annexed in 1932 and 1935 and formed tract 26 in 1950. This tract omitted from 1950 computations.

Philadelphia

Tracts combined in 1930 and 1950 due to tract boundary revisions since 1930:

Tracts Combined	Tracts Combined
22Q, 22S	40A, 40G
34J, 34L	40D, 40-AA
35F, 35H	40-S, 40-T, 40-U, 40-X, 40-Y
35-R, 35-S, 35-T, 35-V, 33-F, 35-HH	41-A, 41-V
35-PP, 35-QQ	41-F, 41-G, 41-R
35-DDD, 35-EEE	41-H, 41-Q
38-A, 38-E, 38-F	42-CC, 42-DD
39-G, 39-H, 39-I, 39-J, 39-K	48-B, 48-C, 48-D, 48-E

Pittsburgh

Tracts combined in 1930 and 1950 due to tract boundary revisions since 1930:

Tracts Combined	Tracts Combined
3-C, 3-E	19-B, 19-C
5-F, 5-G	20-J, 20-K, 20-L
10-E, 10-F	26-A, 26-F
11-A, 11-B, 11-D	26-C, 26-Z (26-Z only in 1950)
13-E, 13-F, 13-Z (13-Z only in 1950)	31-A, 31-B, 31-C (31-C only in 1950)
15-A, 15-C	32-A, 32-Z (32-Z only in 1950)

Note: Tracts 13-Z and 26-Z (areas annexed before 1930 but not reported in 1930 tract publications) and tracts 31-C and 32-Z (areas annexed in 1931) are included in 1950 analysis, although excluded from 1930 analysis. Tract 26-Y, also annexed in 1931, is excluded from 1950 as well as 1930 analysis. 1950, tract 26-A includes part of tract 230 (previously a suburban tract) and tract 32-A includes part of tract 9 (previously a suburban tract). None of these changes taken into account.

St. Louis

Tracts combined in 1930 and 1950 due to tract boundary revisions since 1930:

Tracts Combined

15-G, 24-E
15-B, 16-A, 16-B
26-B, 26-C

Syracuse

Revisions between 1930 and 1940 too extensive for adjustment.

Census Tracts Included in Zones of
Cities, 1930 and 1950

Boston

Zone	Census Tracts
1	G-1, G-2, G-3
2	F-1, F-2, F-3, F-4, F-5, F-6, G-4, H-1, H-2, H-3, H-4, I-1, I-2, I-3, J-1, K-1, K-2
3	B-4, C-1, E-1, E-2, I-4, J-2, J-3, K-3, K-5, L-1, L-4, L-5, M-1, M-2, M-3, M-4, N-1, O-3, O-4
4	A-5, B-1, B-2, B-3, C-2, C-3, D-2, D-3, D-4, J-4, J-5, L-2, L-3, L-6, N-3, N-4, O-1, O-2, P-1, P-2, Q-1, Q-2, R-1
5	A-4, D-1, K-4, N-2, P-3, Q-3, Q-4, Q-5, R-2, R-3, S-1, S-2
6	A-1, A-2, A-3, A-6, B-5, P-4, P-5, P-6, S-3, S-5, S-6, T-2, U-1, U-2, U-3, U-4
7	S-4, T-1, T-3, T-4, T-5, T-6, U-5, V-1, V-2, V-3, Y-2
8	T-7, T-9, U-6, V-4, V-6, X-1
9	T-8, T-10, V-5, W-2, X-2, X-4, Y-1, Y-3
10	W-1, W-3, W-4, X-3, X-5, X-6, Y-4, Y-5
11	W-5
12	B-6, W-6, Z-1, Z-2

Buffalo

Zone	Census Tracts
1	72
2	13, 14, 25, 68, 71
3	12, 15, 31, 67, 69, 70

Zone	Census Tracts
4	26, 32, 66
5	1, 3, 5, 16, 17, 18, 27, 33, 61, 65
6	20, 35, 60, 63, 64
7	2, 4, 11, 19, 21, 23, 24, 28, 29, 34, 52, 53, 62
8	8, 9, 22, 30, 36, 39, 40, 54, 55, 59
9	6, 7, 10, 37, 38, 41, 42, 43, 44, 45, 46, 47, 48, 49, 50, 51, 56, 57, 58

Chicago

Zone	Community Areas
1	8, 28, 32, 33
2	7, 24, 31, 34, 35, 60
3	5, 6, 21, 22, 23, 26, 27, 29, 30, 36, 37, 38, 39, 40, 58, 59, 61
4	3, 4, 14, 16, 19, 20, 25, 41, 42, 57, 62, 63, 67, 68
5	1, 2, 12, 13, 15, 18, 43, 44, 45, 56, 65, 66, 69, 71
6	10, 11, 17, 46, 47, 48, 50, 64, 70, 73
7	9, 49, 51, 52, 72, 74, 75
8	53, 54, 55

Cincinnati

Zone	Census Tracts
1	6, 7
2	5, 9, 10, 11, 12
3	3, 4, 8, 13, 16, 17, 18
4	1, 2, 15, 19, 21, 22, 23, 24, 25
5	14, 20, 26, 27, 31, 33, 35, 91
6	29, 30, 32, 34, 37, 43, 90
7	28, 36, 39, 42, 67, 87, 93, 96
8	38, 41, 66, 69, 72, 86, 89, 92, 94, 95, 103
9	40, 44, 47, 49, 50, 65, 68, 70, 71, 77, 88, 97, 98
10	45, 48, 51, 52, 73, 74, 75, 76, 78, 79, 85, 99, 100, 107
11	46, 53, 54, 59, 63, 64, 80, 101, 102
12	55, 56, 57, 61, 62, 81, 84, 104
13	58, 60, 82, 83, 105, 106

Cleveland

Zone	Census Tracts
1	G-6, G-7, I-1
2	C-3, C-6, C-7, D-1, D-2, D-3, G-1, I-2, I-4
3	C-1, C-2, C-5, C-8, C-9, D-4, D-5, D-7, G-2, G-3, G-8, G-9, I-3, I-5, I-6, J-1
4	B-6, B-8, B-9, C-4, D-6, D-8, G-4, G-5, H-3, H-5, H-7, I-7, J-2, J-3
5	A-2, A-9, B-5, B-7, D-9, E-3, E-6, H-2, H-4, H-8, H-9, I-8, I-9, J-4, J-6
6	A-7, A-8, E-1, E-2, E-4, E-5, H-1, H-6, J-5, J-7, J-8, L-3, L-7, L-9, M-7, M-8, N-2, N-7
7	A-1, A-6, B-4, E-7, F-3, J-9, K-1, K-2, K-5, L-1, L-4, L-8, M-1, M-3, M-9, N-3, N-6, N-9
8	A-3, A-4, A-5, B-2, B-3, E-8, F-1, K-3, K-6, K-7, K-8, L-2, L-5, L-6, M-4, M-5, N-1, N-4, N-8, O-1, O-2, O-3, O-4, R-9, T-1
9	B-1, E-9, F-2, F-4, F-5, F-6, F-7, K-4, K-9, M-2, M-6, N-5, O-5, O-7, O-8, P-4, R-1, R-3, R-6, R-7, S-1, S-2, S-3, S-6, T-2, T-3, T-4, T-5, W-3
10	O-6, O-9, P-1, P-2, P-5, P-6, R-2, R-4, R-5, R-8, S-4, S-5, S-7, S-8, T-6, T-7, T-9, U-1, U-3, W-2, W-5, W-9, X-1, X-4
11	P-3, P-7, P-8, S-9, T-8, U-2, U-4, W-1, W-4, X-2, X-3, X-6
12	P-9, Q-3, U-5, U-6, U-7, U-9, V-2, W-6, X-5
13	Q-1, Q-2, Q-4, Q-5, Q-6, Q-7, Q-8, Q-9, U-8, V-1, V-3, W-7, W-8, Z-1

Columbus[1]

Zone	Census Tracts
1	1B, 2A
2	1C, 2B, 3B, 4A
3	2C, 3A, 3C, 4B, 5A, 5B, 7B, 8B
4	6A, 9B, 10A, 11A
5	1A, 9A, 10B, 12A, 13A, 13B
6	4C, 5C, 6B, 6C, 7A, 12B, 14A, 15A, 16A, 19A
7	1D, 11B, 18A

Zone	Census Tracts
8	8A, 17A, 21A, 22A, 31A
9	7C, 23A, 24A
10	8C, 9C, 20A, 30A, 31B
11	25A, 26A, 27A, 28A, 29A

[1]1930 tract code used.

Philadelphia

Zone	Census Tract
1	3A, 3B, 4A, 4B, 5A, 6A, 7A, 7B, 7C, 8A, 8B, 9A, 10A, 12B, 13B
2	2A, 2B, 2C, 7D, 9B, 10B, 11A, 11B, 12A, 13A, 14A, 14B, 15B, 26B, 30A
3	1A, 1B, 1C, 15A, 15C, 15E, 16A, 17A, 18A, 20D, 26A, 26C, 26D, 30B, 36A, 36B, 47D
4	15D, 18B, 18C, 19C, 20A, 20B, 20C, 27A, 36C, 39A, 39B, 39C, 39D, 47A, 47C, 48A
5	18D, 24D, 24E, 24F, 26E, 27B, 27E, 28E, 29A, 29C, 29D, 31B, 31C, 32A, 32B, 32C, 32D, 36D, 36E, 37D, 37E, 39E, 39F, 47B
6	19A, 19B, 24C, 24G, 25D, 27C, 27D, 28A, 28B, 29B, 31A, 32E, 37C, 37F, 40A, 40G, 48B, 48C, 48D, 48E
7	24B, 25A, 25B, 25C, 26F, 28C, 28D, 32F, 33G, 33H, 33I, 33J, 33K, 37A, 37B, 38H, 38I, 38J, 40B, 40C, 40F, 43D, 43E, 44B, 45H, 45I, 45J, 46A, 46H, 46I
8	22KK, 24A, 33B, 33C, 33D, 33E, 33F, 34A, 34F, 34G, 34H, 34P, 34Q, 38A, 38B, 38E, 38F, 38G, 38K, 39G, 39H, 39I, 39J, 39K, 40D, 40E, 40H, 40I, 40J, 40L, 40M, 40AA, 42FF, 42KK, 43A, 43B, 43C, 44A, 44C, 45D, 45E, 45F, 45G, 45K, 46B, 46C, 46D, 46E, 46F, 46G, 48F
9	21A, 21V, 22CC, 22DD, 22HH, 22II, 22JJ, 23E, 23F, 23G, 23H, 23I, 23J, 23K, 33A, 34B, 34C, 34D, 34E, 34I, 34J, 34L, 34M, 35DDD, 35EEE, 38C, 38D, 40K, 40N, 40O, 40P, 40Q, 40R, 40BB, 42AA, 42BB, 42CC, 42DD, 42EE, 42GG, 42HH, 42II, 42JJ, 42Q, 42X, 42Y, 42Z, 45A, 45B, 45C, 46J
10	21B, 21C, 21Q, 21R, 21S, 21T, 21U, 22A, 22W, 22X, 22Z, 22AA, 22BB, 22EE, 22FF, 22GG, 23A, 23B, 23C, 23D, 34K, 34N, 34O, 35WW, 35XX, 35YY, 35ZZ, 35AAA, 35BBB, 35CCC, 40S, 40T, 40U, 40V, 40X, 40Y, 41K, 41L, 41M,

Zone	Census Tract
	41O, 42A, 42B, 42O, 42P, 42R, 42S, 42T, 42U, 42V, 42W
11	21K, 21L, 21M, 21N, 21O, 21P, 22B, 22C, 22D, 22E, 22Q, 22R, 22S, 22T, 22U, 22V, 22Y, 35NN, 35OO, 35PP, 35QQ, 35RR, 35SS, 35TT, 35UU, 35VV, 40W, 40Z, 41I, 41J, 41N, 41P, 42C, 42D, 42E, 42F, 42K, 42L, 42M, 42N
12	21D, 21E, 21F, 21G, 21H, 21I, 21J, 22F, 22G, 22H, 22L, 22M, 22N, 22O, 22P, 35R, 35S, 35T, 35V, 35Z, 35AA, 35BB, 35CC, 35DD, 35EE, 35FF, 35GG, 35HH, 35II, 35JJ, 35KK, 35LL, 35MM, 41E, 41F, 41G, 41H, 41Q, 41R, 41S, 42G, 42H, 42I, 42J
13	22I, 22J, 22K, 35U, 35W, 35X, 35Y, 41D, 41T
14	35L, 35M, 35N, 35O, 35P, 35Q, 41A, 41B, 41C, 41U, 41V
15	35A, 35B, 35C, 35D, 35E, 35F, 35G, 35H, 35I, 35J, 35K

Pittsburgh

Zone	Census Tract
1	1A, 2A, 2B, 3A, 3B, 3C, 3E
2	1B, 2C, 2E, 3D, 17A, 19B, 19C, 22E, 22F, 22G, 23B, 23C
3	2D, 4A, 4B, 5A, 5C, 5D, 5F, 5G, 17B, 17C, 18A, 18B, 18C, 19D, 22A, 22B, 22C, 22D, 23A, 24A, 24B, 25D
4	4C, 4G, 5B, 5E, 5H, 6A, 6B, 16A, 16B, 18D, 19A, 19E, 21D, 21E, 21F, 24C, 25A, 25B, 25C, 26H, 30A
5	4D, 4F, 4H, 4I, 5I, 5J, 6C, 6D, 6E, 16C, 18E, 19F, 20G, 20H, 20I, 20J, 20K, 20L, 21A, 21B, 21C, 26G, 26I, 26J, 26K, 27G
6	4E, 7A, 8B, 8C, 9A, 9C, 19G, 20F, 26E, 27D, 27E, 27F, 28F, 29A, 29B
7	7B, 7C, 8A, 8D, 8E, 8F, 9B, 14A, 14G, 15A, 15B, 15C, 15D, 19H, 19I, 20E, 26A, 26C, 26D, 26F, 26Z, 27C, 28B, 28C, 32C
8	7D, 7E, 7F, 8G, 8H, 10A, 10E, 10F, 11H, 14B, 20A, 20B, 20C, 20D, 26B, 27A, 27B, 28D, 29C, 32A, 32B, 32Z
9	7G, 7H, 10B, 10C, 10D, 11A, 11B, 11C, 11D, 11F, 11G, 11I, 11J, 12D, 12E, 12F, 14C, 14D, 14F, 14H, 14I, 15E, 28A, 28E
10	11E, 12A, 12B, 12C, 12G, 12H, 13A, 13B, 13C, 13D, 13E, 13F, 13Z, 14E, 14J, 14K, 31A, 31B, 31C

St. Louis

Zone	Census Tract
1	22C, 25A, 25C, 25D

Zone	Census Tract
2	21C, 21D, 22B, 22D, 25B
3	20C, 21A, 21B, 22A, 23B, 23D, 23E, 26A, 26B, 26C
4	11E, 17C, 18D, 18E, 20A, 20B, 23A, 23C, 24D, 26D, 26E
5	9E, 10D, 10E, 11A, 11D, 16E, 17B, 17D, 18C, 19C, 24B, 24C
6	9A, 9C, 9D, 10A, 10B, 10C, 11B, 11C, 15B, 15G, 16A, 16B, 16C, 16D, 17A, 18A, 18B, 19A, 19B, 24A, 24E
7	4D, 6G, 7G, 9B, 12C, 12D, 13C
8	4C, 5E, 6D, 6E, 6F, 7F, 8F, 12A, 12B, 13A, 13B, 13D, 15C, 15E, 15F
9	1B, 1C, 1D, 1G, 2D, 2E, 3D, 3E, 3F, 3G, 4A, 4B, 5A, 5B, 5C, 5D, 6A, 6B, 6C, 7A, 7B, 7D, 7E, 8A, 8E, 14A, 14B, 14C, 15A, 15D
10	1A, 1E, 1F, 2A, 2B, 2C, 3A, 3B, 3C, 7C, 8B, 8C, 8D

Syracuse

Zone	Census Tract
1	30, 31, 32
2	12, 13, 16, 22, 23, 24, 33, 40, 41, 42
3	5, 6, 11, 14, 15, 21, 25, 29, 34, 39, 43, 44, 52, 53
4	2, 7, 8, 9, 17, 27, 28, 35, 37, 38, 45, 49, 50, 51, 54, 55, 58, 59
5	1, 3, 4, 18, 20, 36, 46, 48, 56, 57
6	10, 19, 26, 47
7	61
8	60

Note: Tracts 13 and 37 are for 1950 only. See Appendix D.

Selected Characteristics of Ethnic Groups in Each City, 1910 to 1950

Item Number	Characteristic
(1)	Foreign born residential segregation from native whites, by wards, 1910.
(2)	Foreign born residential segregation from native whites, by wards, 1920.
(3)	Foreign born residential segregation from native whites, by census tracts, 1930c/.
(4)	Foreign born residential segregation from native whites, by census tracts, 1950c/.
(5)	Foreign born residential segregation from native whites of native parentage, by census tracts, 1930c/.
(6)	Native whites of foreign or mixed parentage (second generation) residential segregation from native whites of native parentage, by census tracts, 1930c/.
(7)	Foreign born residential segregation from Negroes, by wards, 1910.
(8)	Foreign born residential segregation from Negroes, by wards, 1920.
(9)	Foreign born residential segregation from Negroes, by census tracts, 1930c/, d/.
(10)	Foreign born residential segregation from Negroes, by census tracts, 1950c/.
(11)	Native whites of foreign or mixed parentage (second generation) residential segregation from Negroes, by census tracts, 1930c/, d/.
(12)	Per cent of the foreign born population, ten years of age and older, who are unable to speak English, 1930.
(13)	Per cent of the foreign born population, ten years of age and older who are illiterate, 1930.
(14)	Per cent of the foreign born population in 1930 who arrived in the United States in 1900 or earlier.

Item Number	Characteristic
(15)	Native whites of mixed parentage as a per cent of native whites of foreign or mixed parentage (second generation), 1930.
(16)	Per cent of foreign born families who are home owners, 1930.
(17)	Median value of nonfarm homes of foreign born families in dollars, 1930.
(18)	Median rent of nonfarm homes of foreign born families in dollars, 1930.
(19)	Per cent of foreign born males 21 years of age and older who are aliens, 1910.
(20)	Per cent of foreign born males 21 years of age and older who are aliens, 1920.
(21)	Per cent of foreign born males 21 years of age and older who are aliens, 1930.
(22)	Per cent of foreign born males in the Standard Metropolitan Area who are aliens, 1950.
(23)	Occupational dissimilarity between foreign born males and native white males in the Standard Metropolitan Area, 1950.
(24)	Occupational dissimilarity between foreign born males and native white males of native parentage in the Standard Metropolitan Area, 1950.
(25)	Occupational dissimilarity between native white males of foreign or mixed parentage (second generation) and native white males of native parentage in the Standard Metropolitan Area, 1950.

Notes

a/ Segregation indexes based only on population born in England in 1910 and 1920.

b/ Irish Free State in 1930 and 1950; Ireland in 1910 and 1920.

c/ Segregation measures in Chicago in 1930 and 1950 based on "Community Areas" rather than census tracts.

d/ Segregation from total non-white population in Cincinnati rather than Negro population. However, almost all non-whites in the city were Negroes in 1930.

e/ Great Britain and Northern Ireland in 1930 and 1950.

f/ Segregation indexes of foreign born groups in Syracuse in 1930 based on distributions of foreign born heads of families and heads of families of other nativity segments of the population.

g/ Not available. Presumably nearly 100 per cent English speaking.

h/ Wales not available.

i/ More than $10,000.

j/ Not available.

k/ Applies only to those unable to speak English.

BOSTON

Item	England and Wales[a]	Scotland	Ireland[b]	Norway	Sweden	Germany	Poland	Austria	Russia	Lithuania	Greece	Italy
(1)	10.7	14.4	19.0	26.3	22.5	30.5	.	37.4	47.9	.	62.0	65.8
(2)	11.7	20.1	21.5	30.4	23.9	31.9	.	29.1	41.8	.	55.9	56.4
(3)	14.7	23.8	25.5	.	32.0	34.8	50.4	.	64.9	53.0	51.1	53.5
(4)	18.5	22.9	24.4	.	30.5	30.7	45.0	.	64.5	49.2	41.8	47.5
(5)	14.2	18.8	23.3	.	26.4	34.9	57.8	.	71.2	59.6	50.3	61.1
(6)	10.6	14.8	22.6	.	26.2	26.8	55.2	.	69.8	60.2	47.4	60.3
(7)	56.5	59.0	60.8	70.5	57.4	68.2	.	67.7	69.1	.	61.0	80.4
(8)	58.3	63.3	65.2	71.4	64.8	69.9	79.6	65.5	69.4	89.0	49.5	80.8
(9)	75.7	79.0	80.1	.	77.6	80.6	80.4	.	79.8	86.8	73.2	84.5
(10)	78.0	82.4	82.0	.	80.6	78.8	81.8	.	82.8	90.2	77.0	86.5
(11)	77.4	78.5	81.4	.	82.0	79.6	.	.	80.1	81.0	77.1	86.1
(12)	[g/]0.4[h]	[g/]0.3	[g/]1.4	.	0.7	1.4	6.7	.	4.9	8.1	8.7	21.0
(13)	44.9[h]	28.1	48.1	.	1.1	1.5	15.3	.	10.8	19.8	12.7	28.8
(14)	47.0	38.4	22.5	.	44.4	58.9	8.2	.	24.9	16.3	6.6	17.2
(15)	24.6[h]	23.9	38.2	.	19.3	29.0	8.7	.	12.0	7.0	10.5	11.7
(16)	.	.	.	.	39.6	43.9	30.8	.	24.2	43.8	17.8	31.0
(17)	6,632[h]	6,966	6,809	20.0	7,397	7,422	8,776	43.5	[i/]	8,213	8,278	6,382
(18)	39.37[h]	36.71	29.54	24.1	38.85	37.67	34.82	29.7	44.42	26.82	34.08	24.43
(19)	32.8	36.7	21.8	.	30.1	15.5	.	.	48.7	.	76.3	75.3
(20)	20.7	18.3	15.2	.	18.8	12.2	.	.	34.1	.	58.0	61.3
(21)	23.2[h]	24.3	21.3	.	19.7	15.7	34.6	.	24.3	39.2	36.8	45.8
(22)	14.2	[i/]	9.5	.	7.0	14.8	21.6	.	9.1	[i/]	[i/]	9.8
(23)	13.0	[i/]	27.6	.	38.9	18.9	19.9	.	18.7	[i/]	[i/]	27.4
(24)	13.3	[i/]	31.2	.	39.9	17.5	23.4	.	21.0	[i/]	[i/]	31.0
(25)	5.7	[i/]	8.3	.	13.9	8.2	16.0	.	24.3	[i/]	[i/]	19.8

See p. 206 for item identification and notes.

BUFFALO

Item	England and Wales a/	Scotland	Ireland b/	Sweden	France	Germany	Poland	Austria	Hungary	Russia	Italy
(1)	24.9	27.6	36.2	29.9	18.5	33.5	.	53.9	64.9	50.7	71.7
(2)	24.2	26.6	35.1	28.3	25.9	27.1	.	37.4	60.9	52.7	69.9
(3)	25.5	32.3	35.9	.	25.2	30.9	61.2	32.9	63.7	55.9	64.8
(4)	26.4	25.9	36.2	.	23.5	30.1	53.8	25.8	57.9	54.2	48.6
(5)	20.7	27.4	33.2	.	24.7	32.1	70.5	36.8	65.4	55.1	68.5
(6)	14.2	18.2	28.9	.	18.4	24.0	72.1	31.9	66.1	50.8	66.8
(7)	61.2	63.3	65.2	64.6	57.8	76.8	.	85.9	83.5	81.5	81.2
(8)	72.2	75.2	74.1	75.5	68.1	72.6	.	73.9	77.2	48.9	78.3
(9)	81.1	85.0	77.5	.	75.3	79.2	86.4	71.9	86.3	53.7	77.7
(10)	81.5	84.0	81.2	.	83.9	82.0	83.6	77.7	89.0	83.6	80.9
(11)	82.0	82.4	80.5	.	77.5	79.5	88.7	74.7	87.3	63.8	77.2
(12)	g/	g/	g/	.	1.1	2.8	17.6	4.1	5.6	3.3	16.9
(13)	0.2h/	0.2	0.7	.	1.1	1.7	12.3	5.3	5.4	5.5	29.7
(14)	32.8h/	16.6	49.4	.	60.1	59.6	30.4	20.8	8.7	19.7	21.7
(15)	52.0	39.6	32.7	.	41.8	32.5	19.3	26.2	10.4	15.1	17.4
(16)	36.9h/	29.9	56.2	.	66.8	63.3	58.4	55.5	56.1	47.2	44.8
(17)	7,126h/	7,106	6,715	.	6,438	6,418	5,842	6,402	6,479	i/	7,109
(18)	38.06h/	37.30	33.26	.	34.71	30.01	22.39	31.84	28.84	43.37	24.97
(19)	23.0	26.5	10.3	18.5	12.6	12.6	.	74.4	81.0	66.5	49.7
(20)	13.4	13.3	6.4	11.5	6.3	5.9	.	29.4	41.7	32.6	30.2
(21)	17.6h/	20.4	12.5	.	9.5	9.3	19.9	13.5	14.3	11.8	14.9
(22-25) j/	.	.	.	.	.	.	.	.	.	.	.

See p. 206 for item identification and notes.

CHICAGO

Item	England & Wales	Ireland	Norway	Sweden	Denmark	Germany	Poland	Czechoslovakia	Austria	Hungary	Russia	Lithuania	Italy
(1)	18.4	24.6	56.0	34.4	37.1	25.2			50.1	40.6	51.7		67.8
(2)	16.5	27.3	50.6	31.4	32.5	20.3			25.2	33.8	48.3		57.0
(3)c	19.1	31.8		34.0		26.0	50.8	51.9	25.0		49.8	57.0	48.3
(4)c	18.9	31.8		33.2		27.2	45.2	48.8	18.1		44.0	51.5	40.5
(5)c	12.5	26.3		28.1		28.0	62.5	60.5	32.9		55.7	63.9	53.7
(6)c	9.4	22.4		24.0		19.6	63.7	58.9	28.6		46.9	61.4	51.4
(7)	63.0	56.9	81.2	71.4	67.4	76.9			88.0	77.2	87.9		77.1
(8)c	71.0	67.2	86.3	80.3	78.2	80.1			77.0	77.5	86.1		78.3
(9)c	83.6	84.3		90.1		88.6	93.2	92.7	88.4		89.8	90.9	79.2
(10)c	77.8	81.4		85.5		85.4	90.8	89.2	82.5		87.1	84.7	69.6
(11)c	84.4	84.7		90.0		88.2	94.1	92.9	89.5		90.1	91.4	79.2
(12)	g/ 0.3	g/ 0.6		1.3		2.8	14.0	11.4	3.7		4.6	10.9	15.2
(13)	38.8	44.2		1.3		3.2	17.3	10.2	6.1		10.6	22.7	25.8
(14)	52.6	30.0		41.2		54.3	19.6	28.2	18.7		17.3	14.1	17.3
(15)	31.8	50.1		20.8		30.9	13.5	17.0	21.0		13.2	8.5	16.4
(16)				44.0		49.3	49.3	54.4	42.6		22.3	45.2	40.0
(17)	8,290	8,155		8,277		7,596	7,330	7,094	7,429	69.7	i/ 65.20	7,703	7,305
(18)	60.85	49.72		54.46		43.49	26.76	26.00	41.21	25.4	58.1	31.22	28.46
(19)	20.5	12.0	20.0	16.2	17.7	12.6			60.2		29.3		62.1
(20)	11.1	19.2	8.7	8.1	8.2	5.8	17.7	13.1	24.8		16.2	22.9	31.2
(21)	15.3	10.1		16.0		11.7			13.6		6.4		23.8
(22)	10.7	9.2		6.6		8.7	12.6	6.7	6.6		18.7	1/	7.0
(23)	11.7	22.8		32.3		18.3	24.3	25.2	19.1		18.9	1/	23.4
(24)	12.9	25.3		33.3		19.6	26.7	27.6	20.6		25.2	1/	25.9
(25)	6.4	10.3		10.3		7.5	18.5	12.1	6.6			1/	12.7

See p. 206 for item identification and notes.

CINCINNATI

Item	England & Wales a/	Scotland	Ireland b/	France	Germany	Poland	Austria	Hungary	Russia	Rumania	Italy
(1)	21.1	26.8	28.2	18.0	17.9	.	32.1	56.5	65.4	63.1	56.0
(2)	18.6	29.2	26.4	15.5	17.8	.	29.0	41.9	53.7	53.6	52.0
(3)	24.3	40.7	33.2	23.2	20.5	65.7	37.5	42.1	70.1	47.3	46.6
(4)	22.5	37.4	30.4	29.8	23.4	67.8	35.4	31.8	77.3	47.1	36.0
(5)	25.0	40.1	33.6	25.3	23.5	67.4	40.1	44.4	72.1	49.6	46.6
(6)	19.6	26.2	26.3	18.2	18.3	55.9	42.2	43.3	70.7	52.5	40.1
(7)	34.4	36.9	32.3	47.8	57.2	.	52.8	73.0	44.6	44.0	33.9
(8) d/	51.0	56.5	43.2	63.1	65.2	.	63.2	69.6	47.5	64.8	44.4
(9) d/	74.1	82.6	72.1	78.0	77.7	77.6	78.4	81.2	81.4	78.9	74.4
(10) d/	81.8	86.4	82.3	86.2	83.8	88.6	84.3	86.3	90.1	84.0	84.4
(11) d/	74.8	75.5	72.9	77.7	78.0	76.8	78.2	80.6	83.7	79.3	73.4
(12)	g/	g/	g/	0.6	3.1	3.3	4.9	9.5	3.9	6.4	11.1
(13) i/	.	.	.	.	.	.	.	.	.	.	.
(14)	52.7h/	35.0	67.1	60.7	64.1	32.2	27.3	8.5	25.8	8.3	18.7
(15)	60.5	53.3	34.9	48.6	36.5	21.0	23.8	11.5	17.5	14.4	23.0
(16)	41.0	41.7	51.8	50.0	57.2	50.5	48.3	48.3	52.3	45.9	46.7
(17)	7,917h/	8,112	6,710	6,732	6,774	i/	8,324	7,364	i/	7,712	7,148
(18)	33.54h/	41.34	23.51	30.77	24.09	43.69	27.31	20.88	49.22	24.23	23.86
(19)	15.0	23.4	5.9	13.1	7.4	.	41.0	86.2	32.4	i/	57.7
(20)	13.8	8.5	5.8	7.4	4.9	.	27.4	44.5	18.9	50.3	43.3
(21) h/	9.9h/	15.3	5.7	7.6	9.1	9.1	11.8	16.5	8.3	16.9	26.1
(22-25) j/	.	.	.	5.6	.	.	.	.	.	.	.

See p. 206 for item identification and notes.

CLEVELAND

Item	England & Wales	Scotland	Ireland/[b]	Sweden	Switzerland	Germany	Poland	Czechoslovakia	Austria	Hungary	Yugoslavia	Russia	Italy
(1)	15.7	21.9	27.8	39.3	18.6	21.7			37.9	44.2		51.8	74.9
(2)	17.6	23.1	23.1	35.0	18.1	18.9			29.8	46.3		44.6	51.6
(3)	26.6		35.1			24.6	52.7	46.4	29.5	51.7	62.5	62.1	57.6
(4)	24.1		35.9			20.9	48.5	41.1	26.9	45.0	56.3	52.7	49.2
(5)	19.5		29.9			25.5	63.0	57.0	37.1	55.9	66.1	66.3	63.4
(6)	12.8	61.8	24.8	65.2	65.4	18.7	64.7	57.2	35.8	57.3	69.2	62.2	62.4
(7)	59.7	72.1	62.6	71.9	74.1	74.0			72.7	67.9		62.1	65.6
(8)	68.1		72.3			77.8			72.1	76.1		46.2	50.2
(9)	86.1		88.0			88.2	89.7	88.5	84.0	86.8	91.7	85.8	77.7
(10)	86.1		88.3			87.2	87.9	88.8	87.6	86.7	93.3	78.4	84.4
(11)	86.9		87.8			88.2	91.1	88.9	83.8	86.6	92.0	86.2	76.5
(12)	[g]0.5		[g]2.5			3.3	17.3	11.1	5.2	11.0	10.1	6.5	16.2
(13)	37.4		42.1			4.1	21.3	11.1	10.8	10.3	10.9	11.4	26.8
(14)	48.7		30.2			59.6	15.4	28.3	23.6	14.5	9.0	14.7	11.9
(15)	38.1		51.8			28.8	13.4	17.0	19.0	12.4	8.8	12.2	13.3
(16)						61.6	53.9	65.2	51.3	48.8	49.2	36.5	41.8
(17)	7,095		7,038			6,696	6,576	6,273	7,077	6,991	6,316	9,303	6,977
(18)	41.04	29.9	36.05	24.2	15.7	34.91	25.34	26.00	35.56	29.27	25.22	41.46	31.20
(19)	21.4	13.0	12.2	13.0	8.4	16.3			59.9	68.4		62.3	68.3
(20)	10.8		6.9			6.4	25.2	17.5	27.0	31.9	23.4	34.1	43.6
(21)	15.7		13.2			11.7	14.8	8.8	18.5	23.1		20.5	31.6
(22)	9.4		9.4			9.6	21.9	23.0	11.9	[j]	[j]	9.8	10.5
(23)	12.8		27.8			18.1	27.2	28.3	17.8	[j]	[j]	18.5	23.4
(24)	14.2		30.1			20.2	22.1	18.5	23.1	[j]	[j]	17.9	27.2
(25)	6.5		9.4			8.9			14.1	[j]	[j]	19.1	15.0

See p. 206 for item identification and notes.

COLUMBUS

Item	England and Wales	Scotland	Ireland/	Switzerland	Germany	Poland	Austria	Hungary	Russia	Rumania	Greece	Italy
(1)	13.8	16.2	29.6	28.8	39.6	.	41.7	64.2	64.0	.	57.6	35.8
(2)	10.8	18.3	31.1	37.3	37.2	.	34.8	54.8	59.4	.	58.2	45.7
(3)	13.1	23.4	36.8	.	40.2	61.6	49.8	49.3	66.5	65.0	52.3	56.0
(4)	14.4	21.5	28.5	.	32.7	55.8	37.1	48.1	62.6	45.8	28.6	45.8
(5)	12.3	22.8	37.1	.	41.9	63.0	51.6	50.7	68.3	66.6	52.7	56.8
(6)	11.5	13.8	20.5	40.1	25.0	51.4	40.1	51.3	63.1	64.8	41.2	53.3
(7)	28.2	25.9	28.5	57.9	49.7	.	47.1	73.5	59.2	.	58.4	30.4
(8)	38.6	38.6	28.4	.	58.9	.	44.6	57.7	65.8	.	41.8	34.9
(9)	63.9	63.8	55.5	.	74.1	69.8	71.1	72.6	76.3	82.7	51.5	55.6
(10)	72.7	75.6	71.0	.	79.7	75.1	77.2	78.2	82.7	83.0	64.3	71.0
(11)	64.2	62.5	56.3	.	69.9	62.8	68.3	70.4	74.4	83.1	58.5	55.9
(12)	g/	g/	g/	.	2.4	5.2	7.8	12.3	4.8	8.4	5.3	16.2
(13)i/	.	.	.	.	.	.	.	.	.	.	.	.
(14)	49.0h/	30.0	62.7	.	60.4	19.1	22.6	16.3	20.2	5.4	4.1	12.7
(15)	60.8	56.4	40.2	.	41.4	18.3	31.9	13.8	16.2	13.9	28.7	19.4
(16)j/	.	.	.	.	.	.	.	.	.	.	.	.
(17)j/	.	.	.	.	.	.	.	.	.	.	.	.
(18)j/	.	.	.	.	.	.	.	.	.	.	.	.
(19)	11.0	24.0	8.1	5.9	5.7	.	71.8	85.5	46.7	.	88.2	73.8
(20)	8.5	11.9	9.1	4.9	4.3	.	45.7	60.9	25.8	.	74.9	53.2
(21)	13.9h/	18.2	13.3	.	8.5	20.8	30.2	26.5	17.6	21.4	36.3	42.3
(22-25)j/	.	.	.	.	.	.	.	.	.	.	.	.

See p. 206 for item identification and notes.

PHILADELPHIA

Item	England and Wales	Scotland	Ireland b/	France	Germany	Poland	Austria	Hungary	Russia	Lithuania	Rumania	Italy
(1)	21.4	20.4	19.6	21.8	24.9	.	43.0	60.0	57.7	.	67.0	61.0
(2)	20.4	19.7	19.9	18.1	27.4	.	32.9	51.6	50.2	.	50.6	53.2
(3)	24.8	31.2	29.3	.	31.9	55.6	37.4	49.2	57.1	57.3	53.2	60.7
(4)	22.1	29.8	29.8	.	31.7	48.4	34.5	43.6	55.7	47.0	50.3	56.3
(5)	22.4	27.5	27.2	.	31.8	62.3	43.1	52.6	63.6	62.9	59.2	67.4
(6)	17.4	18.8	20.2	45.0	23.6	64.1	39.8	49.2	58.6	62.7	57.2	66.3
(7)	54.4	52.1	36.3	47.3	57.5	.	58.8	68.5	68.5	.	69.3	66.0
(8)	58.1	55.6	41.5	.	60.3	.	55.4	76.3	57.4	.	60.7	64.8
(9)	72.1	74.0	61.8	.	72.0	75.9	70.4	81.7	71.0	72.3	73.6	72.6
(10)	79.0	80.3	71.7	.	79.3	80.0	76.2	77.2	77.8	77.7	79.8	78.9
(11)	72.3	72.1	64.1	.	72.1	78.2	71.2		70.2	72.4	71.9	72.5
(12)	g/	g/	g/	.	3.0	10.9	3.5	3.6	4.9	9.9	5.0	16.7
(13)	0.4	0.3	1.2	.	2.0	15.2	7.0	4.4	9.2	17.8	8.0	25.4
(14)	49.0	26.9	49.5	.	52.6	17.1	27.8	16.1	19.5	16.6	19.1	19.2
(15)	52.9	48.2	30.4	.	30.8	10.4	16.9	12.6	11.8	7.9	13.4	16.6
(16)	60.8	51.7	70.0	.	69.4	64.6	63.3	65.8	58.6	65.7	55.8	68.8
(17)	5,360	5,247	4,843	.	5,280	4,667	5,441	4,933	6,406	5,140	6,024	4,704
(18)	38.08	37.62	35.52	30.6	36.21	24.77	33.79	28.52	41.41	28.24	34.79	28.10
(19)	27.6	29.0	22.1	18.4	19.7	.	66.6	68.8	60.0	.	39.5	75.1
(20)	16.1	14.6	14.2	.	11.0	29.7	34.0	39.6	34.8	31.8	22.2	47.7
(21)	14.2	19.6	14.1	.	14.4	16.8	16.0	13.8	13.7	.	11.2	25.5
(22)	8.2	/	7.8	.	10.4	19.8	12.4	/	5.8	/	/	7.6
(23)	9.3	/	21.4	.	20.0	21.2	17.4	/	23.5	/	/	24.3
(24)	9.4	/	21.4	.	20.5	17.3	17.9	/	24.3	/	/	24.7
(25)	6.1	/	8.4	.	9.7	.	6.3	/	32.5	/	/	13.9

See p. 206 for item identification and notes.

PITTSBURGH

Item	England & Wales	Scotland	Ireland/	Sweden	Germany	Poland	Czechoslo-vakia	Austria	Hungary	Yugoslavia	Russia	Lithuania	Rumania	Italy
(1)	17.7	18.2	17.5	39.4	24.7	.	.	41.0	36.6	.	56.2	.	79.6	41.7
(2)	16.4	16.8	16.8	33.7	20.8	.	.	36.2	40.8	.	54.6	.	69.5	38.4
(3)	18.2	26.4	31.0	.	24.6	54.1	49.6	33.3	.	67.6	61.1	59.0	.	44.1
(4)	18.4	27.4	29.8	.	20.8	47.8	43.8	31.3	.	56.2	59.0	50.3	.	38.0
(5)	17.6	23.4	32.0	.	26.1	61.8	54.2	38.1	.	70.3	64.4	63.5	.	46.4
(6)	16.1	17.9	24.7	57.9	22.5	62.5	53.8	35.3	66.7	70.4	60.6	59.3	49.0	44.5
(7)	49.2	47.4	44.2	53.6	53.3	.	.	63.6	65.6	.	47.7	.	36.2	50.1
(8)	48.2	46.9	44.0	.	52.7	68.1	76.1	60.1	.	82.3	37.2	71.3	.	42.3
(9)	64.0	63.2	59.2	.	68.6	78.9	79.9	65.3	.	81.7	56.1	78.7	.	54.0
(10)	70.8	69.0	66.4	.	75.4	73.9	76.7	76.2	.	83.8	78.8	73.4	.	59.9
(11)	65.8	62.6	60.1	.	68.3	.	.	69.2	.	.	59.6	.	.	55.0
(12)	g/ 1.4	g/ 0.4	g/ 2.7	.	2.4	10.6	8.3	4.7	.	9.8	3.6	8.3	.	11.1
(13)	.	.	.	.	2.5	18.9	10.8	7.4	.	21.5	8.5	19.1	.	22.0
(14)	62.4	38.8	52.5	.	65.8	25.1	23.8	25.4	.	13.9	23.5	22.5	.	19.8
(15)	54.6	49.2	30.2	.	35.3	15.5	13.6	18.5	.	11.5	14.4	10.7	.	19.0
(16)	50.6	46.2	55.0	.	65.4	49.7	56.0	54.8	.	39.4	48.2	52.9	.	50.7
(17)	6,650	7,058	6,468	.	5,896	5,927	5,281	6,193	.	4,924	i/	6,540	.	6,155
(18)	40.64	40.55	36.56	.	30.36	23.13	22.57	28.42	.	22.85	47.98	26.08	.	34.04
(19)	15.9	23.6	14.3	23.4	12.6	.	.	79.3	74.4	.	63.7	.	40.7	65.0
(20)	8.1	15.0	8.7	15.3	6.9	24.3	24.7	48.3	47.6	35.3	38.8	18.0	26.8	62.2
(21)	11.2	16.3	10.8	.	8.8	13.6	8.8	20.9	.	.	15.0	.	.	18.0
(22)	7.6	.	6.2	.	7.1	24.9	24.0	13.4	.	.	11.7	.	.	6.9
(23)	10.9	1/	21.4	.	19.7	24.1	24.9	18.5	.	1/	21.8	1/	.	20.1
(24)	10.6	1/	20.5	.	20.7	16.5	19.7	19.4	.	1/	22.1	1/	.	20.7
(25)	7.4	1/	11.4	.	8.7	.	.	15.0	.	1/	27.4	1/	.	9.9

See p. 206 for item identification and notes.

ST. LOUIS

Item	England & Wales a/	Scotland	Ireland b/	France	Switzerland	Germany	Poland	Czechoslo-vakia	Austria	Hungary	Yugoslavia	Russia	Italy
(1)	19.4	28.8	22.7	15.1	23.8	18.3	·	·	41.3	51.9	·	66.4	69.4
(2)	18.3	28.6	24.8	15.2	25.1	18.5	·	·	29.2	46.0	·	50.1	60.8
(3)	25.0	·	34.4	22.6	·	22.3	50.5	52.7	35.8	37.0	57.5	63.7	54.0
(4)	26.6	·	38.6	24.1	·	21.1	45.4	47.2	25.6	33.9	39.4	65.8	46.3
(5)	24.7	·	34.4	22.6	·	23.7	51.8	53.5	36.6	37.6	57.3	64.7	55.2
(6)	17.9	·	25.5	13.2	·	20.2	51.8	50.9	32.1	35.0	57.4	61.9	51.8
(7)	46.8	48.5	42.2	50.1	59.1	62.1	·	·	62.1	68.3	·	61.4	61.7
(8)	55.6	60.5	52.0	61.3	66.6	71.0	·	·	68.9	78.5	·	53.5	65.3
(9)	81.8	·	80.9	80.9	·	86.4	72.7	89.8	87.1	88.8	80.9	78.8	73.4
(10)	85.4	·	84.3	86.2	·	89.6	84.6	93.4	90.6	91.0	86.2	90.5	82.5
(11)	83.5	·	80.7	84.1	·	86.6	75.2	91.2	87.7	88.4	83.3	81.6	73.0
(12)	g/0.5h/	·	g/1.3	1.7	·	1.9	9.8	5.5	3.6	5.4	9.1	4.4	17.2
(13)	57.9h/	·	64.7	1.7	·	1.8	15.2	3.7	4.9	5.5	10.1	13.1	25.9
(14)	40.0h/	·	35.2	62.2	·	66.6	22.9	37.6	20.0	8.7	7.4	19.7	15.6
(15)	·	·	57.3	49.1	·	39.0	16.4	27.4	27.3	16.2	11.8	13.9	18.2
(16)	·	·	·	50.3	·	58.6	42.2	62.0	53.1	56.9	44.3	34.9	48.1
(17)	6,563h/	·	6,189	5,763	·	6,215	6,496	6,393	5,723	6,151	5,011	8,770	4,581
(18)	41.26h/	·	36.73	35.18	·	30.81	24.69	23.30	26.14	25.68	21.50	42.08	24.07
(19)	20.3	·	6.1	15.6	·	9.3	·	·	47.2	60.4	·	44.5	74.4
(20)	12.7	24.4	4.9	9.0	12.7	5.6	·	·	20.6	23.1	·	27.0	46.6
(21)	17.8	14.0	11.3	11.4	10.7	10.5	28.9	12.9	16.9	20.3	27.0	22.4	43.6
(22–25)j/	·	·	·	·	·	·	·	·	·	·	·	·	·

See p. 206 for item identification and notes.

SYRACUSE

Item	England & Wales a,e/	Scotland	Ireland b/	Sweden	France	Switzerland	Germany	Poland	Czechoslo-vakia	Austria	Russia	Italy
(1)	17.3	20.2	30.6	28.9	25.5	35.1	41.0	·	·	49.8	61.2	55.8
(2)	14.8	14.3	28.6	24.5	17.7	24.7	40.8	·	·	33.8	65.8	53.0
(3)f/	14.5	·	38.4	36.0	·	·	43.8	67.1	62.5	40.9	63.7	61.5
(4)	16.8	·	28.9	33.7	·	·	29.3	55.5	45.1	35.4	59.6	49.1
(5)f/	14.2	·	40.2	36.1	·	·	49.0	68.5	64.4	43.8	63.0	65.6
(6)	9.8	60.5	23.1	30.5	·	·	33.2	65.5	64.2	38.4	60.4	60.8
(7)	61.5	64.4	73.4	67.0	61.5	78.2	80.5	·	·	76.4	52.4	84.2
(8)	59.7	·	75.7	68.6	68.7	76.0	82.4	·	·	63.3	35.7	84.5
(9)f/	87.9	·	91.6	84.5	·	·	93.3	79.3	93.4	77.6	51.1	93.9
(10)	85.6	·	89.9	87.7	·	·	89.2	84.8	87.0	81.2	59.1	93.1
(11)	83.0	·	85.9	82.7	·	·	88.6	83.3	93.8	77.4	51.8	92.6
(12)	g/	·	g/	i/	·	·	1.8	12.5	9.5	2.4	4.1	16.3
(13)k/	44.2h/	·	54.7	i/	·	·	0.4	7.2	4.7	1.3	2.0	10.9
(14)	54.8	·	32.7	35.2	·	·	63.8	15.2	25.1	30.7	23.1	14.1
(15)	48.1h/	·	65.1	58.0	·	·	32.3	10.1	16.3	21.8	16.0	14.9
(16)	·	·	·	i/	·	·	67.4	56.2	54.3	60.3	52.4	52.3
(17)	8,310h/	·	7,500	i/	·	·	7,030	7,156	6,428	8,068	i/	8,113
(18)	40.00h/	26.4	36.36	18.0	14.6	3.3	33.61	25.79	25.62	29.50	37.20	26.36
(19)	17.1	13.2	11.4	21.7	12.8	12.4	7.0	·	·	75.8	59.6	70.6
(20)	13.6	·	8.7	i/	·	·	5.9	·	·	56.2	40.7	58.1
(21)	13.5h/	·	8.9	·	·	·	9.5	42.1	25.9	20.7	22.6	36.5
(22-25)j/	·	·	·	·	·	·	·	·	·	·	·	·

See p. 206 for item identification and notes.

Selected Bibliography

Alexandersson, Gunnar. 1956. The Industrial Structure of American Cities. Lincoln: University of Nebraska Press.

Ball, Harry V., and Yamamura, Douglas S. 1960. "Ethnic Discrimination and the Marketplace: A Study of Landlords' Preferences in a Polyethnic Community," American Sociological Review, 25: 687-94.

Barron, Milton L. (ed.) 1957. American Minorities. New York: Alfred A. Knopf.

Blumer, Herbert. 1958. "Recent Research on Racial Relations: United States of America," International Social Science Bulletin, Vol. 10.

Bunle, Henri. 1950. "The Cultural Assimilation of Immigrants," in Cultural Assimilation of Immigrants, supplement to Population Studies, Vol. 3.

Burgess, Ernest W. 1928. "Residential Segregation in American Cities," Annals of the American Academy of Political and Social Science, 140: 105-15.

Carpenter, Niles. 1927. Immigrants and Their Children, 1920. Washington: Government Printing Office.

Collison, Peter, and Mogey, John. 1959. "Residence and Social Class in Oxford," American Journal of Sociology, 64: 599-605.

Crawford, Ruth. 1916. The Immigrant in St. Louis. Studies in Social Economics, The St. Louis School of Social Economy, Vol. 1, No. 2.

Cressey, Paul F. 1938. "Population Succession in Chicago: 1898-1930," American Journal of Sociology, 44: 59-69.

Crowell, John F. 1898. The Logical Process of Social Development. New York: Henry Holt and Co.

Drake, St. Clair, and Cayton, Horace R. 1945. Black Metropolis. New York: Harcourt, Brace and Co.

Duncan, Otis Dudley. 1957. "Population Distribution and Community Structure," Cold Spring Harbor Symposia on Quantitative Biology, 22: 357-71.

219

_____, and Davis, Beverly Ann. 1953. Contributions to the Theory of Segregation Indexes. Urban Analysis Report No. 14. Chicago: Chicago Community Inventory, University of Chicago.

_____, and Duncan, Beverly. 1955a. "Residential Distribution and Occupational Stratification," American Journal of Sociology, 60: 493-503.

_____, and _____. 1955b. "A Methodological Analysis of Segregation Indexes," American Sociological Review, 20: 210-17.

_____, and _____. 1957. The Negro Population of Chicago. Chicago: University of Chicago Press.

_____, and Lieberson, Stanley. 1959. "Ethnic Segregation and Assimilation," American Journal of Sociology, 64: 364-74.

Freedman, Maurice. 1955. "The Chinese in Southeast Asia," in Andrew W. Lind, ed. Race Relations in World Perspective. Honolulu: University of Hawaii Press.

Ford, Richard G. 1950. "Population Succession in Chicago," American Journal of Sociology, 56: 156-60.

Fordyce, Wellington G. 1937. "Nationality Groups in Cleveland Politics," The Ohio State Archaeological and Historical Quarterly, Vol. 46.

Gavit, John Palmer. 1922. Americans by Choice. New York and London: Harper and Brothers.

Green, Howard Whipple, and Truesdell, Leon E. 1937. Census Tracts in American Cities (Census Tract Manual). Revised Edition. Washington: U. S. Department of Commerce, Bureau of the Census.

Handlin, Oscar. 1957. Race and Nationality in American Life. Garden City, New York: Doubleday Anchor Books, Doubleday and Co.

_____. Boston's Immigrants. 1959. Revised and enlarged edition. Cambridge, Mass.: The Belknap Press of Harvard University Press.

Hawley, Amos H. 1944. "Dispersion versus Segregation: Apropos of a Solution of Race Problems," Papers of the Michigan Academy of Science, Arts, and Letters, 30: 667-74.

Hoover, Edgar M. 1948. The Location of Economic Activity. New York: McGraw-Hill.

Hughes, Everett C. 1943. French Canada in Transition. Chicago: University of Chicago.

Hurd, W. Burton. 1942. "Racial Origins and Nativity of the Canadian People," in Dominion Bureau of Statistics. Seventh Census of Canada, 1931. Vol. 13, Monographs. Ottawa: Edmond Cloutier.

Hutchinson, E. P. 1956. Immigrants and Their Children, 1850-1950. New York: John Wiley and Sons, Inc.

International Union for the Scientific Study of Population. 1950. "Cultural Assimilation of Immigrants," Population Studies, Supplement, March.

Kendall, Maurice G. 1955. Rank Correlation Methods. 2nd ed. revised. London: Charles Griffin and Company Limited.

Kephart, William M. 1954. "Negro Visibility," American Sociological Review, 19: 462-67.

Kiser, Clyde V. 1956. "Cultural Pluralism," in Joseph J. Spengler and Otis Dudley Duncan, eds. Demographic Analysis. Glencoe, Ill.: The Free Press.

Kuper, Leo, Watts, Hilstan, and Davies, Ronald. 1958. Durban: A Study in Racial Ecology. London: Jonathan Cape.

Lieberson, Stanley. 1958a. "Ethnic Groups and Medicine." Unpublished Master's dissertation, Department of Sociology, University of Chicago.

_____. 1958b. "Ethnic Groups and the Practice of Medicine," American Sociological Review, 23: 542-49.

Moran, P. A. P. 1951. "Partial and Multiple Rank Correlation," Biometrika, 38: 26-32.

Nam, Charles B. 1959. "Nationality Groups and Social Stratification in America," Social Forces, 37: 328-33.

Palmer, Gladys L. 1954. Labor Mobility in Six Cities. New York: Social Science Research Council.

Park, Robert E. 1950. Race and Culture. Glencoe, Ill.: The Free Press.

_____, 1952. Human Communities. Glencoe, Ill.: The Free Press.

Robinson, Arthur H. 1956. "The Necessity of Weighting Values in Correlation Analysis of Areal Data," Annals of the Association of American Geographers, 46: 233-36.

Savorgnan, France. 1950. "Matrimonial Selection and the Amalgamation of Heterogeneous Groups," in Cultural Assimilation of Immigrants, supplement to Population Studies, Vol. 3.

Schnore, Leo F. 1956. "The Functions of Metropolitan Suburbs," American Journal of Sociology, 61: 453-58.

Simmel, Georg. 1921. "Social Interaction as the Definition of the Group in Time and Space," in Robert E. Park and Ernest W. Burgess. Introduction to the Science of Sociology. Chicago: University of Chicago Press.

Thomas, Brinley. 1954. Migration and Economic Growth. Cambridge: Cambridge University Press.

U. S. Bureau of the Census. 1952. U. S. Census of Population: 1950. Vol. 3, Census Tract Statistics, Chapter 10. Washington: Government Printing Office.

_____. 1954. U. S. Census of Population: 1950. Vol. 3, Special Reports, Part 3, Chapter A, Nativity and Parentage. Washington: Government Printing Office.

_____. 1958. U. S. Census of Business: 1954. "Central Business District Statistics," Bulletin CBC-96-Summary Report. Washington: Government Printing Office.

U. S. Department of Commerce, Bureau of the Census. 1933. Fifteenth Census of the United States: 1930. Vol. 2. Washington: Government Printing Office.

U. S. Department of Labor, Bureau of Immigration. 1919. Annual Report of the Commissioner General of Immigration to the Secretary of Labor, 1919. Washington: Government Printing Office.

Wilkins, Arthur H. 1956. "The Residential Distribution of Occupation Groups in Eight Middle-Sized Cities of the United States in 1950." Unpublished Ph. D. dissertation, Department of Sociology, University of Chicago.

Wirth, Louis. 1928. The Ghetto. Chicago: University of Chicago Press.

Younge, Eva R. 1944. "Population Movements and the Assimilation of Alien Groups in Canada," Canadian Journal of Economics and Political Science, 10: 372-80.

Zubryzcki, Jerzy. 1959. "Ethnic Segregation in Australian Cities," International Population Conference, Vienna 1959. Vienna: International Union for the Scientific Study of Population.

Index

Ability to speak English, 206-18
    as measure of assimilation, 8-9
    and residential segregation,
        133-39
    see also Year of arrival
Accountant or auditor, 160
Africans vs. Europeans, 159
Age, 50, 63, 96, 134, 139, 146, 172,
    184-85, 188
Alexandersson, Gunnar, 160
Aliens; see Naturalization
Amalgamation, biological, 9-10
American Council of Learned So-
    cieties, 74
Army recruits, 70-71
Asia; see Orientals
Assimilation, 1-2, 157-58
    causes of, different, 92
    definitions of, 7-13, 133
    effect of residential segrega-
        tion on, 44
    individual and aggregate, con-
        trasted, 8-9
    and occupational segregation,
        160
    residential segregation as a
        measure of, 44
    see also specific aspect of as-
        similation
Australia, 145
Austria, 25-26, 29, 65, 71, 80-83,
    88-90, 127-128, 137-138, 164,
    169, 175, 189, 191, 194, 209-218
    -Hungary, 21

Ball, Harry V., 4
Barbers, 9
    and kindred occupations, 159
Barron, Milton L., 8
Beer producing centers, 160
Belgium, 62, 71, 145
Blumer, Herbert, 7
Bohemia, 62, 72
Bosnia, 72
Boston, 13, 24, 28-29, 31, 46-47,
    49, 51, 53-54, 57-59, 61, 66, 69,
    73, 75-82, 84, 94-95, 97, 100-1,

104-8, 110-11, 114, 116, 122, 124-
    28, 130, 136-38, 148, 150-52, 154-
    55, 158, 162, 165-67, 171, 174-76,
    180-83, 189-90, 196, 200, 209
Breese, Gerald William, v
Buffalo, 13, 24, 28-29, 31, 46-47, 49,
    51, 53-54, 57-58, 61, 66, 69-70,
    73, 75-76, 81-82, 84, 94-95, 100-1,
    104-8, 111, 114, 116, 122-30, 135-
    38, 148, 150, 152-56, 158, 196-97,
    200-1, 210
Bunle, Henri, 8
Burgess, Ernest W., 15, 101-3, 109,
    121

Canada, 23, 88-89, 145, 159
Carpenter, Niles, 61-62
Cayton, Horace R., 121
Census data, 13, 26, 102, 163-64,
    191-92, 194-95
    adjustments of, 82, 142-43, 196-
        99
    for Canadian emigrants, 23
    for English speaking countries,
        139
    for ethnic groups, 19-22, 25, 137,
        139
    inferences based on cross-sec-
        tional, 166
    for inferring intermarriage, 156-
        57
    Native white sub-classes in, 74
    on naturalization, 141, 147, 151
    not available for studying occupa-
        tional and residential segrega-
        tion, 183-84
    occupational categories in, 164,
        179
    for occupations of ethnic groups,
        161-62, 167, 172
    socio-economic status indexes
        based on, 49-50, 172
    for Standard Metropolitan Areas
        and central cities, 97, 182
    for year of arrival, 48
    see also Census tracts; Europe,
        political boundaries in; Wards

223

Davis, Beverly; see Duncan, Beverly Davis
Decentralization; see Centralization
Denmark, 28, 71, 145, 191, 211
Density of group, 134
Detroit, 99, 162, 165-67, 171, 173-76
Dispersion; see Centralization; Residential segregation
Displacement, 91
Distance
from central business district; see Centralization social and spatial, 4
Douglas, Paul H., 52
Drake, St. Clair, 121
Duncan, Beverly Davis, v, 14, 30, 33, 40-41, 57, 93, 121, 172, 182, 184-85
Duncan, Otis Dudley, v, vii, 6, 9, 14, 30, 33, 40-42, 46, 57, 93, 98-99, 102-3, 121, 157, 172, 182, 184-85, 193
Dundon, Joseph V., vii
Durban, Union of South Africa, 159

Education, 48-51, 68-70
Edwards, Alba M., 172
Eire; see Irish Free State
England, 29-30, 62, 71-72, 78-79, 86, 139, 145, 207
language; see Ability to speak English
and Wales, 25-28, 60, 80-83, 164-65, 168-69, 173-74, 177-78, 180-81, 189, 209-18
see also Great Britain and Northern Ireland
Ethnic
colonies, 1, 6, 77, 79, 101-2
"effect", 180
groups, 2-3, 18, 20, 27-30
origins of native white population and immigrant segregation, 15, 72-79, 81, 83, 92, 153
centralization, 105-6
old-new differences, 62

see also Immigrants; specific behavioral attribute; specific nationality group
Europe
Central, 62, 64-65
Eastern, 21, 52, 61-62, 64, 70, 81, 107
illiteracy by countries in, 70-71
Northern, 52, 61-65, 75, 79, 107
political boundaries of, 13-14, 20-22, 26, 57, 191-92
Southern, 21, 52, 61-62, 64, 70, 81, 107
Western, 52, 61-65, 75, 79, 107
see also Immigrants, old-new differences; specific country
Europeans compared with Africans, 159

Family distributions and individual distributions, 194-95
Farm laborers, 163-64, 187
Farmers and farm managers, 163-64, 186
Finland, 71
Firemen, policemen, and kindred occupations, 159
First generation; see Foreign born; Immigrants
First papers; see Naturalization
Flemish, 72
Ford Foundation, v
Ford, Richard G., 6, 102
Fordyce, Wellington G., 140
Foreign born, 1, 19-20, 23-29, 31, 194-95; see also Immigrants; specific behavioral attribute; specific nationality group
Foreign white stock, defined, 162
Foremen; see Craftsmen, foremen and kindred occupations
France, 28, 62, 71-72, 145, 191, 210, 212, 215, 217-18
Freedman, Maurice, 10
Freedman, Ronald, v
French Canadians; see Canada

Gavit, John Palmer, 62, 80, 146, 150

Germany, 21, 26-28, 59-60, 62-65, 71-72, 77-83, 88-90, 102, 104-5, 127-28, 137, 139, 145, 160, 169, 173-74, 177-79, 181, 189, 191, 194, 209-18
  language, 137-38
Gerrymandering, 31, 33
Ghettoes; see Ethnic colonies; Residential segregation
Great Britain and Northern Ireland, 29, 72, 82, 86, 88-90, 207, 218; see also England; Ireland; Northern Ireland; Scotland; Wales
Greece, 29, 71-72, 88-90, 102, 127-30, 160, 191-92, 209, 214
Green, Howard Whipple, 24
Grundy, John F., vii

Handlin, Oscar, 62, 77
Hashmi, Sultan, vii
Hauser, Philip M., vii, 193
Hawley, Amos H., 3, 6
Herzegovinia, 72
Hodge, R. William, vii
Holland; see Netherlands
Home ownership
  compared with renting, 93, 96, 100-1
  differences between groups in degree of, 15, 86-87, 98-100, 207, 209-18
  effect of, on residential segregation, 15, 86-91, 98-100
  and housing, 99-101
Home values, 86, 94, 207, 209-18
  and rental values, 93-95
  and residential segregation, 87, 97-98
  see also Housing expenditures
Honolulu, 143
Hoover, Edgar M., 160
Housing
  ability to compete for, 51, 93
  Negro, 3-4, 93
  and socio-economic gradient, 103
  supply of, 4

Housing expenditures
  centralization, suburbanization, and, 118-20
  residential segregation and, 15, 83, 86-98, 183-84
  see also Home values; Rental values
Hughes, Everett C., 159
Human ecology, race and ethnic groups and, 3-7, 18, 101
Hungary, 25-26, 29, 65, 71, 88-90, 127-28, 138, 191, 210-17
  see also Austria-Hungary
Hurd, W. Burton, 139
Hutchinson, E. P., 160, 162

Illiteracy; see Literacy
Immigrants
  compared with Negroes, 2, 80, 88-91, 120-32
  new, 2, 28-29, 120, 145
  occupational differences between, 159-61
  old, 28, 75-78, 139, 145
  old-new distinction defined, 60-63, 65, 79, 107
  skills of, 160-61
  see also Ethnic groups; specific behavioral attribute; specific nationality group
Immigrants, Old-New differences
  in agriculture, 63-65
  in centralization, 106-7, 109, 113
  in literacy, 68-73
  in naturalization, 16-17, 144-46
  in residential segregation, 15, 65-68, 74-76, 79, 81-85, 124, from Negroes, 124, 126-27, 132
  in skills and training, 52, 68-70
  in socio-economic position, 68-73
  in suburbanization, 113-15
  in year of arrival, 16, 52, 60-63, 65, 68-70, 145
  see also Immigrants
Immigration Commission of 1907, 62
Indonesia, 159
Inter-city comparisons of correlations between education

226

230